Social Security Contributions

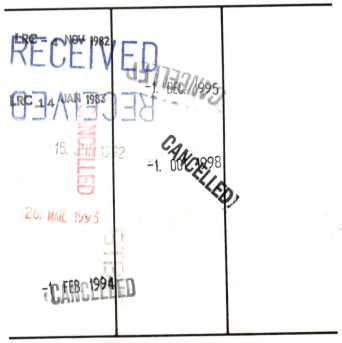

Social Security Contributions

Neil D. Booth FCA

London
Butterworths
1982

England   Butterworth & Co (Publishers) Ltd
London   88 Kingsway, WC2B 6AB

Australia   Butterworths Pty Ltd
Sydney   271-273 Lane Cove Road, North Ryde, NSW 2113
Also at Melbourne, Brisbane, Adelaide and Perth

Canada   Butterworth & Co (Canada) Ltd
2265 Midland Avenue, Scarborough, M1P 4S1

Butterworth & Co (Western Canada)
409 Granville Street, Ste 856, Vancouver BC, V6C 1T2

New Zealand   Butterworths of New Zealand Ltd
Wellington   33-35 Cumberland Place

South Africa   Butterworth & Co (South Africa) (Pty) Ltd
Durban   152-154 Gale Street

USA   Mason Publishing Co
Finch Building, 366 Wacouta Street,
St Paul, Minnesota 55101

Butterworth (Legal Publishers) Inc
160 Roy Street, Ste 300, Seattle, Washington 98109

Butterworth (Legal Publishers) Inc
381 Elliot Street, Newton, Upper Falls,
Massachusetts 02164

© Butterworth & Co (Publishers) Ltd 1982

ISBN 0 406 12899 5 ✓

Phototypeset by Cotswold Typesetting Ltd, Gloucester
Printed and bound by Mansell Ltd, Witham, Essex

Booth: Social Security Contributions—Addendum

THE BUDGET PROPOSALS 1982

In his Budget speech on 9 March 1982 the Chancellor of the Exchequer made the following announcement:

'I . . . propose to cut the rate of the National Insurance surcharge from 3.5% to 2.5% . . . The cut will operate from 2 August which is the earliest practicable date . . . I shall therefore propose an extra 0.5% reduction between August 1982 and April 1983. The effect of this will be to ensure that business as a whole will enjoy in the last two-thirds of 1982-83 the equivalent of a whole year's reduction of 1% in the surcharge.'

These proposals will—if adopted—modify some of the comparisons drawn in the preface and necessitate the updating of paragraph **5.19** and Appendix 7. Certain of the worked examples will also require amendment, specifically those in the following paragraphs:
1.01, 2.04, 5.11, 5.15, 5.18, 5.20, 7.35, 8.03, 8.08, 8.09, 8.10, 8.12 and 8.13.

BUTTERWORTH LAW PUBLISHERS LTD
10 March 1982

Preface

'Insurance—temporary expedient. At no distant date—unnecessary' (David Lloyd George. Speech note made prior to the introduction of the National Insurance Act 1911).

Those words, listened to again today when 'insurance' is financing social security benefit payments of around £350 million per week, have a distinctly hollow ring to them; and all the more so when one considers that 'insurance' ranks before value added tax and corporation tax in the public income and expenditure account and is second only to income tax (which presently outstrips it by a mere 28%). Indeed, the only way in which social security contributions could now become 'unnecessary' would be if the basic rate of income tax were to be raised from 30% to something over 50% and its higher rates were to be increased pro rata! Any attempt to implement such increases would, of course, provoke a public outcry of deafening proportions, yet (accepting for a moment the doubtful truth of the contention that employers pass their contribution burden on to the consumer in the cost of goods and services) the public is, by one means or another, being taxed at just those levels anyway—it is simply not aware of the fact. The majority of employers, however, find themselves unable to pass on their contribution liabilities in their entirety and simply suffer them (to the extent that they cannot be passed on) as yet another charge on diminishing profits. To that extent, therefore, contributions are redistributive because an employer cannot, per se, become a beneficiary under the social security scheme. A large slice of the income he generates (currently equivalent to 13.7% of his payroll) is being compulsorily transferred to assisted members of society and, when one considers that employers' contributions (including surcharge) account for over half of social security income, this can be seen to be redistribution on a massive scale. This book does not set out to pass moral judgment on whether such redistribution is a good or a bad thing. It has, however, been written out of a conviction that a certain amount of subterfuge involving social security contributions has been practiced by successive governments of all colours, and that the majority of employers, employees and their advisers are unaware of what is taking place or of their ability to do something about it. The maximum contribution which could be extracted from an employee in 1980-81 was £579; in 1982-83 it is £1,001: an increase of almost 73%. The maximum payable by an employer in respect of an employee in 1980-81 was £1,175; in 1982-83 it is £1,567: an increase of over 33%. These are enormous increases by any standard, yet there is widespread ignorance of the law which imposes them and which governs the assessment and collection of contributions. This is no doubt attributable, in part, to the fact that social security law is unbelievably complex and fragmentary and receives amendment in almost every session of Parliament. It is also partially attributable to the fact that few people believe that social security law is sufficiently wide to permit planning for contribution in the way that the Taxes Acts permit planning for tax. In intention at any rate, this book will assist both groups. It aims to give a comprehensive exposition of current social security contribution law and to illustrate its practical application; particularly in the area of contribution planning.

My thanks go to Raymond Boughen and my other partners in Rawlinsons for their sustained interest and enthusiasm, to Peter Kennedy and Gillian Kennedy for their painstaking assistance in the checking of proofs, and to the taxbooks department of Butterworths for their invaluable help and advice.

Of necessity, the task of writing this book, once begun, had to be completed quickly—social security law is chameleonic!—yet without the encouragement and whole-hearted support of my wife, Yvonne, this would not have been possible. For that reason it is to her—in reality the book's 'secondary contributor'—that I now have the pleasure of dedicating it.

Neil D. Booth
Rawlinson's, Bradford
February 1982

Contents

Abbreviations

CAA	Capital Allowances Act 1968
CEA	Contracts of Employment Act 1972
DHSS	Department of Health and Social Security
EPA	Employment Protection Act 1975
EP(C)A	Employment Protection (Consolidation) Act 1978
FA	Finance Act 1972
	Finance Act 1978
ICTA	Income and Corporation Taxes Act 1970
NISA	National Insurance Surcharge Act 1976
SSA	Social Security Act 1975
	Social Security Act 1979
	Social Security Act 1980
SS(C)A	Social Security (Contributions) Act 1981
	Social Security (Contributions) Act 1982
SSPA	Social Security Pensions Act 1975

Table of statutes

Table of statutory instruments

List of cases

Chapter 1

Introduction

1.01 The nature of contributions

Social security contributions are effectively a tax on earnings. That conviction has determined the underlying structure of this work and is the justification (if justification be needed) for employing throughout the book the familiar metaphor of the net and its catch. 'Contribution' is, of course, a far less emotive word than 'tax' for it connotes not something coercively expropriated but something willingly supplied. It is, therefore, a singularly inappropriate term (despite a sound historical reason for its use) to apply to an outlay with so little of the voluntary about it; while the addition of the word 'insurance' in the alternative description of the levy—national insurance contributions—is more misleading still, there being little of conventional insurance about the outlay either.

The Department of Health and Social Security (DHSS) has admitted in a recent discussion document that the scheme is 'unlike commercial insurance schemes' (*The Self Employed and National Insurance*, 1980) and confesses two differences: that the state scheme is what it terms a 'pay-as-you-go' scheme in which receipts from current contributors finance payments to current beneficiaries (in contrast to commercial schemes in which premiums are paid in advance and held in reserve); and that, in the state scheme, risk is pooled and the rate of contribution and benefit-entitlement determined merely by reference to a person's earnings category and not (as in commercial schemes) by reference to his personal circumstances, claim-history and risk-rating.

There are, however, other unconfessed differences. The state scheme is compulsory; there is no direct financial relationship between contributions and benefit-entitlement; even minimum benefit entitlement is unascertainable at the premium payment point; and the main contributor to the scheme (the 'secondary contributor') cannot, per se, become a beneficiary under the scheme. The state scheme does, in fact, differ in so many respects from a conventional insurance scheme and disregards so many conventional insurance principles that the briefest of examinations exposes it for what it is: a thinly-disguised arrangement for the redistribution of earnings by direct taxation, and not truly an insurance scheme at all. Even the DHSS agrees that 'a good deal of redistribution' is involved, with 'the better-off paying a bigger share of benefits for the worse-off' (*The Self Employed and National Insurance*, 1980) but an illustration is, perhaps, needed to make the full extent of this plain.

1

EXAMPLE 1(A)

Alec and Brian are both employed by C Ltd: Brian as the sales manager and Alec as a filing clerk. Though both are of exactly the same age and both are contracted-out of the state pension scheme, their earnings and the contributions paid on those earnings in the year ended 5 April 1983 will be as follows:

	£
Alec: Gross pay £1,533.96	
Primary Class 1: 8.75% on £1,533.96	<u>134.22</u>
Brian: Gross pay £11,439.96	
Primary Class 1: 8.75% on £1,533.96	134.22
Primary Class 1: 6.25% on £9,906.00	619.12
	753.34
C Ltd	
Secondary Class 1 on Alec's earnings:	
13.7% on £1,533.96	210.15
Secondary Class 1 on Brian's earnings:	
13.7% on £1,533.96	210.15
9.2% on £9,906,00	911.35
	1,331.65
Total contributions	2,219.21

It is not suggested that these total contributions do not indirectly secure benefits, nor that they are not necessary to secure benefits. What is asserted is that only £268.44 (ie 2 × £134.22, the minimum contribution necessary in 1982–83 to secure benefits) is directly related to benefits in the way that a premium under an insurance scheme is so related. In the event of sickness, unemployment, invalidity, retirement or any other earnings-disruptive circumstance covered by the scheme befalling Alec or Brian during the year beginning 1 January 1984 (the benefit year to which the 1982–83 tax and contribution year relates), the benefits received will be exactly the same, regardless of the disproportionate amounts of contributions paid. In this example, Alec has contributed only 6.05% of the total contributions, yet Brian (who can benefit to no greater extent than Alec) has contributed 33.95%, and C Ltd (which cannot benefit at all) has contributed 60.00%! In short, 87.9% (ie (£619.12 + £1,331.65) × 100/£2,219.21) of all contributions paid in the situation described are a direct redistributive tax on earnings and not (in any accepted sense of the word) a premium.

This example fully supports a comment made recently by a historian of the welfare state:

'Social insurance run by the state was never really comparable with insurance as such and represented what economists call transfer payments, redistributing wealth vertically and horizontally. Though insurance has been undermined actuarially, it survives as legal fiction because for the state it represents a hidden form of taxation and for the individual it preserves the notion of a legitimately earned entitlement to benefit ... The contract between individual and state sanctifies the public largesse' (Derek Fraser, The Evolution of the British Welfare State, The Macmillan Press Limited).

To understand how and why such a secondary, camouflaged scheme of taxation evolved and continues to survive in this country, it is necessary to take a brief (and albeit simplistic) look at some 450 years of history!

THE HISTORY OF THE CONTRIBUTORY SCHEME

1.02   1536 and all that!

The authorisation, in 1536, of parish collections for the 'impotent and poore' was, it may be argued, the first direct acknowledgement by the state of society's responsibility to provide security for its destitute and needy. It was certainly from that Tudor seed that Elizabethan poor law took root; and, central to that poor law, was the still familiar identification of those three distinct groups within society for whom relief is always necessary: the sick, the aged and the unemployed. The relief prescribed under the '43rd of Elizabeth' was not at all sophisticated: cash and kind for the 'impotent', work for the willing unemployed and 'correction' for the idle; and the funds to finance such relief were obtained by the levying of poor rates on property by the overseers who administered the relief, enforced as necessary by magistrates and supervised by the Privy Council.

There are obvious, superficial parallels between this scheme and the one we have today, yet it would be a mistake to see our present scheme as a progressive development of that Elizabethan model. Today's scheme did not evolve from that scheme but began as a reaction against its underlying poor law relief which, by the late nineteenth century, had degenerated into the harsh, demoralising, corrective and punative system of provision made familiar to everyone through Dickens' graphic descriptions of its treadmills and work-houses and their inmates and overseers. A realisation was borne in upon the late Victorians that there was a destitution in the land to which such measures were not an answer: one-third of the population was in real poverty and a socially acceptable alternative to the despised and morally-demeaning institutional relief had to be found. The answer that gradually emerged lay in a series of state schemes for the provision of benefits as of right once certain conditions of eligibility had been satisfied.

1.03   The Lloyd George reforms

The first of these new state schemes was introduced by Asquith's Old Age Pension Bill of 1908. This proposed a non-contributory pension of five shillings per week at the age of seventy, financed by general taxation and freed, by payment through the Post Office, from the stigma of poor law relief. The bill received the royal assent in August 1908 but cost, in the first year, eight million pounds rather than the six and a half million that had been forecast and thereby convinced Lloyd George (the Chancellor of the Exchequer who had the task of budgeting for its provision) that such schemes could never be implemented in other areas of need if they were to be financed by taxation alone. His famous 'People's Budget' of 1908 had already provoked the wrath and opposition of the Lords. Another way had to be found and the new German insurance scheme (the workings of which Lloyd George had seen at first hand) provided him with the answer. The idea of drawing on the funds of both earners and their employers to provide those earners with sickness and unemployment benefits was both socially acceptable and financially viable. Thus Part I of a bill introduced into the Commons in May 1911 proposed a national health insurance scheme to be administered on behalf of the government by 'approved' friendly societies, trade unions and industrial societies which were already engaged in the provision of health insurance and benefits, and which, if not allowed to run the state scheme, would have ensured that it could never come into existence. Under the scheme an accumulated fund was to be set up to which all employed earners would compulsorily contribute 4d, their employers 3d and the Treasury 2d ('9d for 4d' as Lloyd George put it) and from which insured earners would be entitled to sickness benefit of 10s per week in addition to free medical treatment. This part of the bill had a stormy passage through parliament. Even then 'insurance' was recognised as a euphemism for 'tax'; and not an income-related tax but a regressive poll tax the like of which had not been imposed in Britain for eighty years! Despite this recognition of the true nature of the new 'insurance', and the opposition it engendered, the bill did, however, eventually pass into law as the National Insurance Act 1911, including its second part which had proposed compulsory employment insurance in a limited and specified range of industries. This employment insurance aspect of the scheme was to be administered by the Ministry of Labour through the national network of labour exchanges which had been established under the Labour Exchange Act 1908 and set-up by William Beveridge (a name of great significance in any history of social security).

Plans for gradually extending the unemployment insurance aspect of the scheme were disrupted by the 1914–18 war but, in the face of the rising unemployment which followed that war, the scheme was precipitantly extended to virtually all employed earners by the Unemployment Insurance Act of 1920 in a largely unsuccessful attempt to avoid a return to a disguised form of poor relief, ie the dole. The fact that unemployment was rising, and continued to do so, undermined the insurance aspect of the extended scheme from its inception and led to both the annual 'action by crisis' manipulation of contribution rates to meet current claims and the supplementing of contributory benefits by a system of non-contributory benefits that have been features of all schemes since. These non-contributory benefits brought the country to near bankruptcy in the early 1930s and led to the cutting of the dole and the establishment of local authority Public Assistance Committees which imposed a stringent family means test before paying out non-contributory assistance ('transitional payment'). These committees acted inconsistently, however, and the whole unemployment benefit issue was rationalised by the Unemployment Act 1934. Essentially, that Act set out to segregate the insured unemployed and the uninsured unemployed. Part I of the Act further extended the coverage of the unemployment insurance scheme and revised the contribution rates in an attempt to make the scheme self-supporting. Part II established the Unemployment Assistance Board which would, independently of the unemployment insurance scheme, take responsibility for assisting the uninsured unemployed.

1.04 The Beveridge Report

If it is now noted that, by the Widows', Orphans' and Old Age Contributory Pensions Act 1925, the old non-contributory pension scheme had been integrated into the health insurance scheme and expanded into one financed in equal shares by employees and employers (with Treasury contribution as necessary), it will be seen that, by the outbreak of the Second World War, Britain had contributory schemes in each of the three areas of need referred to earlier: sickness, unemployment and old-age. These schemes were, however, administered by different government departments and therefore lacked co-ordination. Furthermore, their scope was limited and there were anomalies and inequities in both contributory requirements and benefit cover. The war itself now created the social climate for rationalisation and reform by arousing a public interest in reconstruction. In partial response to this, Sir William Beveridge was, in 1941, appointed chairman of an inter-departmental committee of civil servants to inquire into the whole area of social insurance. His controversial Report on Social Insurance and Allied Services (Cmd. 6404 (1942)) was published in December 1942 and, after much modification, became the basis for the National Insurance Act 1946 and the blueprint for our present welfare state.

Beveridge saw social insurance as the weapon by which the first of 'five giants'—Want, Disease, Ignorance, Squalor and Idleness—could be attacked and conquered. It is worth noting, however, that he regarded the creation and maintenance of full (ie 97%) employment as one of the prerequisites to the victorious use of that weapon! Given that the prerequisites were met, however, Beveridge envisaged a cradle-to-grave provision of flat-rate, non-means-tested, subsistence-level sickness, medical, unemployment, widows', orphans', old-age, maternity, industrial injury and funeral benefits in return for a single flat-rate contribution; the whole scheme to be uniformly administered by a Ministry of Social Security. Little reconsideration was given to the principle of contribution. It was 'what the people of Britain desire'; history and a deeply-rooted aversion to means-tested relief dictated it, and the possibility of alternatives which would avoid, on the one hand, means-testing and, on the other, contribution, were never considered. Ironically, of course, from that to the present day we have had both!

Beveridge's proposals (modified in some fundamentally damaging respects such as, for instance, the rejection of subsistence-level benefits) were implemented over the next few years. The Family Allowance Act 1945 brought into being another of his prerequisites for a successful social insurance scheme, and the National Insurance Act 1946 and the National Insurance (Industrial Injuries) Act 1946 would have completed the social security programme except that, by reason of the modifications referred to earlier, benefits did not match needs and supplementary benefits had to be provided on a means-tested basis through the National Assistance Board. This was a revamped Unemployment Assistance Board (later to be revamped again as the Supplementary Benefits Commission) created under the National Assistance Act 1948 which, while actually repealing the old poor law, ensured the perpetuation of something not greatly indistinguishable in its place.

1.05   The 'fifties to the present day

By the late 1950s a general desire for earnings-related benefits had been created by the credit-pattern of personal finances, and this reflected in a willingness to accept earnings-related contributions. Accordingly, the National Insurance Act 1959 (which took effect on 6 April 1961) introduced a system of graduated contributions which was intended to provide an element of earnings-related pension. Existing legislation was consolidated in the National Insurance Act 1965 and, during 1966, earnings-related supplements were added to basic unemployment and to basic sickness benefit, with invalidity benefits being introduced in 1971 by the new Conservative administration. The government decided, however, that the whole scheme should be revised and, by the Social Security Act 1973, flat-rate and graduated contribution schemes were to be abolished; all contributions from employers and employed earners were to be earnings-related; contributions from the self-employed were to be calculated on a new basis; and contributions from the non-employed were to become voluntary. These changes were to (and did) take effect on 6 April 1975 when the Social Security Act 1975 (which consolidated the 1973 Act and the National Insurance Acts 1965 to 1974) came into operation. Three years later, on 6 April 1978, the Social Security Pensions Act 1975 also took effect and brought in the full state scheme for earnings-related widows', retirement, and invalidity pensions, with provision for employers operating or wishing to operate occupational pension schemes of their own to contract-out of the state scheme once certain conditions relating to minimum guaranteed pension rights had been met.

Other developments in recent years have included the replacement (under the Ministry of Social Security Act 1966) of national assistance by supplementary benefits (current law relating to which is contained in the Supplementary Benefits Act 1976); the introduction by the Family Income Supplement Act 1970 of a scheme designed to assist lower-paid workers with families (FIS); and the superceding of family allowances by child benefits under the Child Benefit Act 1975. Other changes include a widening of the range of available benefits (mainly by amendment of existing legislation); the phasing out by 3 January 1982 of the earnings-related supplement to sickness and unemployment benefits; and many changes in employment protection law (which some regard as part of social security legislation). Present proposals will, if adopted, make it mandatory for employers to provide sickness benefit during the first eight weeks of an employee's illness and the benefit paid will be recoverable from contributions.

It is hoped that this highly, and, no doubt, over-simplified account of the history of social security in Great Britain is sufficiently comprehensive to at least place the scheme as we know it today (particularly its contributory aspect) in a new light and to reveal something of its complex origins.

SOCIAL SECURITY LAW

1.06 The relevance of the 'tax or premium' debate

The foregoing paragraphs—even those concerned with the history of the social security scheme—are part of a debate which has now been carried on for some seventy years and is still unresolved: Are social security contributions a tax or are they insurance premiums? Paragraph **1.01** above should leave no one in any doubt as to where this particular writer stands on the issue, but the relevance of the issue itself may, of course, be questioned. The answer must surely lie in the fact that our view on the nature of contributions will govern our approach to the payment of them. If the scheme were optional and such that a person, having joined it by choice, secured an entitlement to benefits by contributions, it would be morally and legally indefensible for him to reduce or avoid the payment of those contributions while still retaining his entitlement to benefit. If, on the other hand, the scheme is a thinly-disguised taxation scheme for the redistribution of earnings from the better-off to the worse-off, a potential contributor is (to borrow Lord Tomlin's dictum) 'entitled, if he can, to order his affairs so that the tax attaching under the appropriate Acts is less than it otherwise would be' (*IRC v Duke of Westminster* [1936] AC 1, 19 TC 490). The justification for such permissible 'avoidance' of contributions is the same as that for the permissible avoidance of any other tax: that, apart from statute, there is no antecedent relationship between the payer and the state. No one, in other words, is committed in general law to contribute to the National Insurance Fund, there being no contract, outside of statute, between a contributor and the DHSS.

Having made this point, however, it must be confessed that the ordering of one's affairs in such a way as to legitimately reduce or avoid contribution liabilities is no easy matter. A tax consultancy firm recently commented in one of its bulletins that the legislation relating to social security contributions is 'so convoluted as to make the Finance Acts appear paragons of clarity and simplicity by comparison' [and that it is] 'small wonder that for far too long people have just paid what they were told to pay' (Templegate Tax Planning Newsletter, 1981, Issue No. 4).

This book is an attempt to overcome the problem by providing a detailed, comprehensive, correlated exposition of all current legislation and relevant case law, with verbatim extracts from statutes, regulations, orders and DHSS explanatory notes wherever the precise wording is thought to be of some significance. Worked examples have been provided in the text to illustrate points of difficulty and appendices attempt to summarise and illustrate in a concise form matters given detailed coverage in the text.

1.07   The governing legislation

Before proceding to a general outline of the scheme, it is necessary to comment on the actual legislation which governs its contributory aspects. The principal act is the Social Security Act (SSA) 1975 which has been extensively amended by the Social Security Pensions Act (SSPA) 1975, the Social Security (Miscellaneous Provisions) Act (SS(MP)A) 1977, the Social Security Act (SSA) 1979, the Social Security Act (SSA) 1980, the Social Security (Contributions) Act (SS(C)A) 1981, the Social Security (Contributions) Act (SS(C)A) 1982 and by indirectly related statutes (eg the Employment Protection (Consolidation) Act (EP(C)A)) 1978 and the National Insurance Surcharge Act (NISA) 1976. Numerous regulations and orders are authorised by the statutes referred to and the principal regulations relating to the contributory side of the scheme are the Social Security (Contributions) Regulations, SI 1979, No. 591, though others presently in force are the Social Security (Determination of Claims and Questions) Regulations, SI 1975, No. 558; the Social Security (Credits) Regulations, SI 1975, No. 556; the Social Security (Credits) Amendment Regulations, SI 1977, No. 788; the Social Security (Contributions) (Employment Protection) Regulations, SI 1977, No. 622; the Social Security (Categorisation of Earners) Regulations, SI 1978, No. 1689; the Social Security (Contributions, Re-rating) (No. 2) Order, SI 1979, No. 1736; the Social Security (Contributions, Re-rating) Consequential Amendment Regulations, SI 1980, No. 13; the Social Security (Categorisation of Earners) Amendment Regulations, SI 1980, No. 1713; the Social Security (Contributions) Amendment Regulations, SI 1980, No. 1975; and the Social Security (Contributions) Amendment Regulations, SI 1981, No. 82.

It will be immediately apparent from the foregoing catalogue, that current legislation is not only extensive and fragmented but is also largely composed of delegated law, ie that created by the Secretary of State under powers given to him by statute. While this enables the law to be amended with ease and frequency and without the inevitable delays attendant upon the passage of what would usually be a highly technical bill through Parliament, it makes the task of analysis and exposition of current law extremely difficult and is open to

criticism in that the constitutional protective division of national administration between the legislature (ie Parliament), the executive (ie the government
of the day) and the judiciary (ie the courts) is inevitably weakened by the
transfer of function (in whatever degree) from one of those divisions (the
legislature) to another (the executive, of which the Secretary of State is part).
One 'check' on the delegated legislation which forms such a major part of social
security law is the Social Security Advisory Committee, the functions of which
are described at **1.11** post.

1.08   Construction

In dealing with this substantial body of legislation, various principles of
construction must be borne in mind. Before considering these, however, it must
be stated that, as social security contributions owe their existence to statute and
have no existence without it, the only principles of law applicable to such
contributions are those contained in the legislation itself. It is, of course, true
that general principles of law may be applicable to questions such as whether a
person is under a contract of service or not for the purposes of SSA 1975,
s. 2(1)(a), but such questions are antecedent to contribution law. Consequently,
caution is called for when considering provisions such as those relating to
residence and ordinary residence: concepts which, under tax law, have a
meaning derived partly from general principles of construction (which may be
validly carried over into this area of law) and partly by statutory definition
(which may not).

Subject to these strictures, it may be said that the same principles of
construction apply to social security statutes as apply to statutes generally.
When the Interpretation of Legislation Bill passes into law during the next few
months, certain principles will themselves acquire the force of law but, at the
present time, they and all others are simply judicially approved ways of
approaching a statute. The first of these principles of approach is that one must
look fairly at the words used, not reading anything into them and, in the
absence of a supplied definition, giving them their ordinary meaning on the
assumption that neither injustice nor absurdity is intended (*Mangin v IRC*
[1971] AC 739, [1971] 1 All ER 179). Secondly, to the extent that the statute
imposes a tax, the taxpayer (in this context, the contributor) has a right to
stand on a strict and literal interpretation of the words used (*Price v
Monmouthshire Canal and Rly Cos* (1879) 4 App Cas 197, HL). Thirdly, one must
not rely on punctuation as its insertion was begun in 1850 without statutory
authority and is probably not strictly part of an enactment (*IRC v Hinchy* [1960]
AC 748, [1960] 1 All ER 505). Fourthly, the social security acts and regulations
made under them form a single code and, accordingly, all current legislation
must be construed *in pari materia*; which is to say that the meaning and intention
of any provision must be ascertained by reading the words used in the light of
the statutes as a whole (*Penang and General Investment Trust Ltd v IRC* [1943] AC
486, [1943] 1 All ER 514). In cases of doubt or ambiguity, this principle may be
extended to former enactments and, where words are there used in the same
context as in the current statute, any judicial interpretation given under the

former enactment may be given legal currency (*Gartside v IRC* [1968] AC 553, [1968] 1 All ER 121).

These few selective notes on the principles of construction are by no means exhaustive but may be of assistance in following some of the arguments used in the main text of the book.

SCHEME ADMINISTRATION

1.09   The Department of Health and Social Security

The government department which is instrumental in giving effect to government policy on matters of health and social security as reflected in legislation passed by Parliament is the Department of Health and Social Security (DHSS) which was created on 1 November 1968 to combine the functions of the former Ministry of Health and the Ministry of Social Security. The department has wide responsibilities including not only the administration of the social security scheme in England, Scotland and Wales but also (in England) the administration of the National Health Service and the social services provided by local authorities.

The minister at the head of the DHSS (and the person politically responsible to Parliament for the administration of the law) is the Secretary of State for Social Services. This is a cabinet post and is presently occupied by Mr Norman Fowler. The Secretary of State is assisted in his task by two ministers of state: the Minister for Health (presently Dr Gerard Vaughan) and the Minister for Social Security (presently Mr Hugh Rossi); and three under-secretaries of state (presently Mrs Linda Chalker, Mr Geoffrey Finsberg and Lord Elton).

The department's address is Alexander Fleming House, Elephant and Castle, London SE1 6BY, though it operates through numerous divisions, the principal of which (so far as the contributory side of the social security scheme is concerned) are located at Central Office, Newcastle-upon-Tyne, NE98 1YX. Essential to the functioning of the department, however, are approximately 600 local DHSS offices which, under their managers and through their staffs of executive and clerical officers, administer the social security scheme on a day-to-day basis and carry the law into effect as regards the general public.

1.10   Inspectors

The staff of each local DHSS office includes inspectors who are appointed by the Secretary of State under SSA 1975, s. 144(1).

An inspector's powers are necessarily wide and include the right of entry at all reasonable times to any premises (except a private dwelling-house not used for trade or business purposes) where he has reasonable grounds for supposing that persons are employed or that an employment agency or similar business is being carried on (SSA 1975, s. 144(2)(a) and (3)). 'Premises' includes any place (SSA 1975, s. 144(6)) so that the right of entry will extend to building sites, farmland etc.

An inspector is also empowered to make any such examination or inquiry as he thinks necessary in order to ascertain whether or not social security legislation is being complied with (SSA 1975, s. 144(2)(b)) and to examine (alone if he thinks fit) anyone he finds on premises he has entered or anyone whom he has reason to believe is (or has been) liable to pay contributions (SSA 1975, s. 144(2)(c)). No one may be required to answer questions or give evidence which would tend to self-incrimination or the incrimination of his or her spouse but, apart from this, anyone who occupies premises which an inspector may enter, anyone who is (or has been) an employer, anyone carrying on an agency or similar business, anyone employed by any such persons, and anyone who is (or has been) liable to pay contributions, may be called upon by an inspector to furnish him with all such information and produce for his inspection all such documents as he might reasonably require for the purpose of ascertaining whether or not contributions are (or have been) payable, or have been duly paid (SSA 1975, s. 145(1) and (2)). Such documents will include wages sheets, deduction working sheets, and other documents and records relating to the calculation of earnings, all of which must be retained for at least three years after the end of the year to which they relate (SSA 1975, Sch. 1, para. 6(1)(a) and SI 1979, No. 591, Sch. 1, R. 32(1) as amended by SI 1981, No. 82, R. 8). The penalty for wilful delay or obstruction of an inspector in the exercise of his powers, or for refusal or neglect to answer questions, furnish information or produce documents when required to do so, is a fine of up to £50 on summary conviction and a fine of up to £10 a day thereafter while the offence continues (SSA 1975, s. 145(3) and (4)).

An inspector may exercise such other powers as may be necessary to enforce social security legislation (SSA 1975, s. 144(2)(d)).

When applying for admission to any premises, an inspector must, if required to do so, produce his certificate of appointment (SSA 1975, s. 144(4)) and it is a sound precaution to make this a requirement before an inspector removes any books or documents from business premises.

Where an inspector or officer of some other government department (the Inland Revenue or Customs and Excise, for example) is to enter premises, an arrangement may be made by the Secretary of State for that inspector or officer to be given all the powers of a DHSS inspector (SSA 1975, s. 144(5)).

1.11 The Social Security Advisory Committee

The Social Security Advisory Committee was created by SSA 1980, s. 9(1) to replace the National Insurance Advisory Committee. Its primary function is to give advice and assistance to the Secretary of State and to the Northern Ireland Department in connection with the discharge of their functions under the relevant enactments (SSA 1980, s. 9(1)(a) and (b)), and they, in turn, are to furnish the Committee with such information as it may reasonably require in order to properly discharge its functions (SSA 1980, s. 9(4)).

The committee consists of a chairman and between eight and eleven other members, all appointed by the Secretary of State. Of the members, one is appointed after consultation with employers' organisations, one after consultation with workers' organisations, one after consultation with the Head of the Northern Ireland DHSS and at least one with experience of work among, and the needs of, the chronically sick and disabled (SSA 1980, Sch. 3, paras. 1 and 3).

With some exceptions, none of which relate to the contributory side of the social security scheme, any proposals by the Secretary of State to make regulations under social security enactments must be referred to the committee (SSA 1980, s. 10(1)) unless the matters proposed are so urgent as to make it inexpedient to do so or the committee has agreed that the proposals should not be referred to it (SSA 1980, s. 10(2)). The committee must, after considering proposals, report and make such recommendations as it considers appropriate (SSA 1980, s. 10(3)) and a copy of that report must be laid before Parliament by the Secretary of State along with the draft regulations and a statement showing the extent to which the committee's recommendations have been given effect to and, insofar as effect has not been given, the reasons why that is so (SSA 1980, s. 10(4)).

1.12   Co-ordination with Northern Ireland

Joint arrangements are in force between the Secretary of State and the Head of the Northern Ireland Department whereby the operation of the British social security legislation is co-ordinated with that of Northern Ireland to an extent where the legislation provides a single system of social security for the United Kingdom (SSA 1975, s. 142(1)). Instrumental in these matters is the National Insurance Joint Authority, a body corporate constituted under the National Insurance Act 1965 and consisting of the two parties to the joint arrangements (SSA 1975, s. 142(2) and Sch. 17). The Joint Authority is empowered to effect financial adjustments between the two national insurance funds (SSA 1975, s. 142(3)(a)) and the Secretary of State may make regulations for adapting legislation so as to secure its reciprocal operation with Northern Ireland (SSA 1975, s. 142(4)(a)).

SCHEME FINANCE

1.13   The National Insurance Fund

On 1 April 1975 the National Insurance (Reserve) Fund and the Industrial Injuries Fund which had been established under the National Insurance Act 1946 and the National Insurance (Industrial Injuries) Act 1946 were wound up and their assets and liabilities were transferred to the National Insurance Fund. This fund (which has not yet been renamed and which, accordingly, still lends validity to the term 'national insurance contribution') is under the control and management of the Secretary of State (SSA 1975, s. 133(1)) and is the fund which receives all but a small percentage of social security contributions along with a Treasury supplement and other income (see below) and bears the cost of all contributory benefits and administration.

Periodically, accounts of the fund are prepared at Treasury direction and, after being examined, certified and reported on by the Comptroller and Auditor-General, are laid before Parliament (SSA 1975, s. 133(2)).

Every five years (or at more frequent intervals) the fund and the social security scheme in general are to be subjected to a review by the Government Actuary who, having regard to current contribution rates, expected future contribution yields, and other relevant factors, is to determine the extent to which the fund may be expected to bear a proper relationship to the demands made upon it in respect of benefits, and to report to the Secretary of State (SSA 1975, s. 137(1)(2) and (3)). The Secretary of State is then to lay the report before Parliament (SSA 1975, s. 137(4)).

1.14   Fund income

The National Insurance Fund has four sources of finance: contributions payable by earners, employers and others (SSA 1975, s. 1(1)); Treasury supplements (SSA 1975, ss. 1(1) and 134(3)); state scheme premiums received under SSPA 1975, Part III (SSPA 1975, s. 63(3)); and income arising from the investment of fund monies (SSA 1975, s. 133(3)). The fund's income from these sources in 1980 was £12,543 million (net of health service and employment protection allocations), £2,768 million, £183 million and £606 million respectively: a total of £16,100 million which excludes the national insurance surcharge payable by employers of £3,500 million as this supplements Exchequer funds.

Contributions are (as is explained more fully at **1.16** post) of four classes designated 1, 2, 3, and 4, with Class 1 having both a primary and a secondary element. Not the entire amount of such contributions is paid into the fund as there must first be deducted from contributions received an allocation towards the costs of the national health service and an employment protection allocation to the Redundancy Fund and the Maternity Pay Fund (SSA 1975, ss. 1(1)(b) and 134(1) as amended by the Employment Protection Act (EPA) 1975, s. 40(1) and (5)), each of which is subjected to a deduction (payable into the Consolidated Fund) to cover expenses of collection which may fairly be attributed to those allocations (SSA 1975, s. 134(5)(a)(b) and (c)). The net allocations in 1980 were £1,040 million to the National Health Service and £211 million to the Redundancy Fund and the Maternity Pay Fund.

From 6 April 1982, the national health service allocation has, in the case of primary Class 1, secondary Class 1 and Class 4 contributions, been 0.75%, 0.6% and 0.95% respectively of the amount determined to be that of the earnings in respect of which contributions have been paid, and, in the case of Class 2 and Class 3 contributions, 11.5% of the amount determined to be the total contributions of those classes (SSA 1975, s. 134(4) as amended by SS(C)A 1981, s. 3(2) and SS(C)A 1982, s. 3(2)). These percentages may, with Treasury consent, be varied by order of the Secretary of State, provided the increase or decrease is, in the case of primary or secondary Class 1 contributions, not more than 0.1% of the relevant earnings and, in the case of Class 4 contributions, not more than 0.2% of the relevant earnings and, in the case of Class 2 and Class 3 contributions, not more than 4% of the relevant contributions (SSA 1975 s. 134(4A) and (4B) as inserted by SS(C)A 1981, s. 3(3)). Variations which go beyond these limits require full legislation. Where secondary Class 1 contributions are reduced in the case of mariners (see **7.33** post), the national health service allocation is, by regulations made under SSA 1975, s. 134(6), reduced to 0.3% (SI 1979, No. 591, reg. 134(a)).

From 6 April 1982, the employment protection allocation has been 0.35% and 0.2% respectively of the amount determined to be that of the earnings in respect of which primary and secondary Class 1 contributions have been paid (SSA 1975, s. 134(4) as amended by EPA 1975, s. 40(5); SI 1979, No. 1736, art. 3 and SS(C)A 1982, s. 3(3)) and is divided between the Redundancy Fund and the Maternity Pay Fund in such shares as the Secretary of State (with Treasury consent) determines (SSA 1975, s. 134(5)(b) as amended by EPA 1975, s. 40(1) and (5)). Where the Secretary of State makes an order whereby he alters contribution rates or amounts, he may, if he thinks it expedient, also alter one or other, or both, of the employment protection allocation percentages (SSA 1975, s. 122(3)(b) as amended by SS(C)A 1981, s. 4(6) and SS(C)A 1982, Sch. 1, para. 1(2)). Furthermore, where he makes an order altering the primary or secondary Class 1 contribution rate for the purpose of adjusting the level at which the Redundancy Pay Fund or the Maternity Pay Fund stands, he must also alter the employment protection allocation specified in relation to that contribution by a corresponding percentage (SSA 1975, s. 122(5) as amended by EPA 1975, s. 40(1) and SS(C)A 1982, Sch. 1, para. 1(4)).

Regulations made under SSA 1975, s. 134(6) provide that, where Class 1 contributions in respect of registered dock workers are paid at a reduced rate (see **5.18** post), the employment protection allocation percentage is correspondingly reduced (SI 1979, No. 591, reg. 133(4)(a)); where Class 1 contributions in respect of mariners are paid at a reduced rate (see **7.33** post) no allocation is to be made in respect of the Redundancy Fund (SI 1979, No. 591, reg. 134(b)); and where Class 1 contributions in respect of members of the forces are paid at a reduced rate (see **7.52** post) no employment protection allocation is to be made at all (SI 1979, No. 591, reg. 134(c)).

The Treasury supplement has, from 6 April 1982, been an amount equal to 13% of so much of the contribution of all four classes as remains after deducting the national health service allocation and the employment protection allocation referred to above (SSA 1975, s. 1(5) as amended by EPA 1975, s. 40(2) and by SS(C)A 1982, s. 2(1)). For this purpose, contributions paid at contracted-out rate (see **5.18** post) are to be treated as amounting to such sum as they would have amounted to had they been paid at the normal rate (SSPA 1975, s. 27(6)).

At Treasury direction, monies in the National Insurance Fund may, from time to time, be paid over to the National Debt Commissioners for investment by them within a permitted range of securities (SSA 1975, s. 133(3)) and this gives rise to investment income which assists fund finance. Each year, the

National Debt Commissioners present to Parliament an account of the securities in which fund monies are invested (SSA 1975, s. 133(4)).

1.15 Fund expenditure

Benefits payable out of the National Insurance Fund include not only all contributory social security benefits but also guardian's allowance, industrial injuries benefits and benefits under the Industrial Injuries and Diseases (Old Cases) Act 1975 (SSA 1975, s. 1(1)(a) and (c) and s. 135(1)). Non-contributory benefits (other than guardian's allowance) are payable out of money provided by Parliament (SSA 1975, s. 135(3)(b)).

Contributory benefits and their cost to the fund in 1980 are unemployment benefit £1,097 million, sickness benefit £660 million, invalidity benefit £1,195 million, maternity allowance (and maternity grant for births before 4 July 1982) £163 million, widow's benefit, £637 million (including guardian's allowance), category A and B retirement pensions £10,277 million, child's special allowance and death grant £17 million (SSA 1975, s. 12(1) as amended by SSA 1980, s. 5(1)(i)).

Non-contributory benefits are attendance allowance, non-contributory invalidity pension, invalid care allowance, mobility allowance, maternity grant for births on or after 4 July 1982, guardian's allowance, category C and D retirement pensions (or an equivalent) and age addition (SSA 1975, s. 135(2) as amended by SSPA 1975, Sch. 4 para. 52 and SSA 1980, s. 5) and other benefits such as family income supplement (payable under the Family Income Supplements Act 1970), child benefit (payable under the Child Benefit Act 1975) and supplementary benefits (payable under the Supplementary Benefits Act 1976). The cost of these other benefits to the Exchequer in 1980 amounted to £21,047 million.

Industrial injuries benefits and their cost to the fund in 1980 are injury benefit £47 million, disablement benefit £282 million and industrial death benefit £41 million (SSA 1975, s. 50(2)).

Benefits paid out of the National Insurance Fund but recovered as a result of a reversed or varied decision or a review are paid back into the fund (SSA 1975, s. 135(6)(b)). Other recoveries are paid back to the Consolidated Fund (SSA 1975, s. 135(6)(a)).

Where benefits which would have been paid out of the National Insurance Fund are foregone in order that (under an approved arrangement such as that made between the Post Office and its members, officers etc) pay during absence from work (other than pay forming part of the National Insurance Fund's administrative or other expenses referred to below) is abated, amounts equivalent to the amounts of benefit foregone may, with Treasury consent, be paid by the Secretary of State from the National Insurance Fund to such persons or funds (eg the Post Office) as the Treasury directs (SSA 1975, s. 136(1), (2) and (4)). Where that other fund is the Consolidated Fund, the Secretary of State determines the amount to be transferred; otherwise the amount is by agreement with Treasury consent (SSA 1975, s. 136(3)).

Administrative and other expenses paid out of money provided by

Parliament but attributable to benefits payable from the National Insurance Fund are reimbursed, at Treasury direction, by payments from the National Insurance Fund into the Consolidated Fund (SSA 1975, s. 135(3)(a), (4) and (5)(a) and (b)). Other payments between the National Insurance Fund and the Consolidated Fund by way of adjustment are also permitted at Treasury direction or with Treasury consent (SSA 1975, s. 133(5) and (6)).

CONTRIBUTION CONDITIONS FOR BENEFIT ENTITLEMENT

1.16   The four classes of contribution

As has been explained in the preceding section, contributions payable by earners, employers and others are the main source of the National Insurance Fund's income. The remainder of this work will examine in detail the current law and practice relating to such contributions, but this is an appropriate point at which to distinguish between their four classes which are:

> 'Class 1, earnings-related . . . being . . . primary Class 1 contributions from employed earners, and . . . secondary Class 1 contributions from employers and other persons paying earnings; Class 2, flat-rate, payable weekly . . . by self-employed earners; Class 3, payable . . . by earners and others voluntarily with a view to providing entitlement to benefit, or making up entitlement; and Class 4, payable in respect of the profits or gains of a trade, profession or vocation, or . . . in respect of equivalent earnings' (SSA 1975, s. 1(2)).

The amounts and rates of contributions are set by parliament but are subject both to regulations made by the Secretary of State as regards certain special classes of earner and to alteration by his orders from year to year (SSA 1975, s. 1(3)(a) and (b)). Detailed provisions have effect as regards the computation, collection and recovery of contributions (SSA 1975, s. 1(4)(a) and (b)) and the conditions of residence or presence under which liability or entitlement to pay contributions is to arise (SSA 1975, s. 1(6)(a) and (b)). Contributions in excess of liability may only be paid to the extent permitted by regulations (SSA 1975, s. 1(6)(c)).

Contribution receipts in 1980 (net of national insurance surcharge and of the allocations referred to at **1.14** ante) were: Class 1 primary (employees) £4,703 million, Class 1 secondary (employers) £7,547 million, Class 2 and Class 4 (self-employed) £284 million and Class 3 (non-employed) £9 million.

It should be noted that secondary Class 1 contributions only are allowable as a deduction in computing profits or gains for tax purposes (ICTA 1970, s. 219).

1.17   The two conditions

The contributory conditions which must be fulfilled before any entitlement to contributory benefits can arise are summarised in Appendix 1. Any contribution planning exercise which disregards such conditions or deliberately reduces contributions below minimum levels leaves a great deal to be desired. For that reason the precise statutory wording of those conditions is reproduced here although, a detailed study of the benefit side of the social security scheme is beyond the scope of this work.

In order that a claim for unemployment benefit, sickness benefit, maternity allowance, widow's allowance, invalidity pension, invalidity allowance or death grant might be considered

'. . . the claimant must in respect of any one year have actually paid contributions of a relevant class, and those contributions must have been paid before the relevant time; and . . . the earnings factor derived from those contributions must be not less than that year's lower earnings limit multiplied by 25' (SSA 1975, Sch. 3, para. 1(2) etc).

This is known as the 'first condition' and the multiplier is increased to 52 where claims to widowed mother's allowance, widow's pension and Category A or B retirement pensions are in question. For child's special allowance the multiplier is 50. The 'relevant class' is, in the case of unemployment benefit, Class 1; in the case of sickness benefit and maternity allowance, Class 1 or Class 2; and in the case of the remaining benefits, Class 1, 2 or 3 (SSA 1975, s. 13). The 'relevant time' is the day in respect of which benefit is claimed (SSA 1975, Sch. 3, para. 1(4)(a)); an 'earnings factor' is fully described at **5.26** post; and the 'lower earnings limit' is explained at **5.15** post.

In order to fulfil what is known as the 'second condition' for unemployment benefit, sickness benefit, maternity allowance, invalidity pension or invalidity allowance

'. . . the claimant must in respect of the relevant past year have either paid or been credited with contributions of a relevant class; and . . . the earnings factor derived from those contributions must be not less than that year's lower earnings limit multiplied by 50' (SSA 1975, Sch. 3, para. 1(3) etc).

The 'relevant past year' is the last complete tax year (ended 5 April) before the beginning of the relevant benefit year (SSA 1975, Sch. 3(1)(4)(b) etc) and the 'relevant benefit year' is the year beginning on the first Sunday in January in which there falls the beginning of the period of interruption of employment which includes the day in respect of which benefit is claimed (SSA 1975, Sch. 3, para. 1(4)(c)).

There is no second condition to be fulfilled in connection with a claim to widow's allowance, child's special allowance or death grant. Where a claim for widowed mother's allowance, widow's pension or a Category A or B retirement pension is in question, however, the multiplier is 52 instead of 50 and the condition must have been fulfilled for a certain number of years before the allowance becomes payable or pensionable age is reached. The required number of years is ascertained by reference to the length of the contributor's 'working life' which is the number of tax years between (and including) that in which he attained the age of sixteen and (but excluding) that in which he attained pensionable age or died under that age (SSA 1975, s. 27(2)). The following table shows how the requirement is to be determined (SSA 1975, Sch. 3, para. 5):

| If the working life is | | The requirement is the |
more than:	but not more than:	working life reduced by:
—	10 years	1 year
10 years	20 years	2 years
20 years	30 years	3 years
30 years	40 years	4 years
40 years	—	5 years

Pension rights may, however, be protected for any year from 1978–79 onwards by home responsibilities protection for anyone who is unable to work because of certain home responsibilities such as having a child under the age of sixteen or looking after someone who is old or ill (The Social Security Pensions (Home Responsibilities and Miscellaneous Amendments) Regulations, SI 1978, No. 508, reg. 2).

It should be noted that, although the first contribution condition must be fully satisfied for any benefit to be payable, the second contribution condition, even if only partially satisfied, may yield partial benefits.

CHAPTER 2

Categorisation of earners, employers and others

2.01 Introduction

In the tradition of most taxing and similar statutes, the Social Security Act 1975 begins by casting a net sufficiently wide to leave but few fish in the pond, and only later—once it has landed its catch—becomes discriminatory as to which fish should remain caught and which should be allowed to swim away. The net is s. 1(1) of the Act which states that

'. . . funds required . . . shall be provided by means of contributions payable . . . by earners, employers and others . . .'

and, even after SSA 1975, s. 1(2) has revealed that the 'others' are merely others paying earnings and others voluntarily paying Class 3 contributions, the initial catch is still seen to be very great indeed. Subject to points raised in the succeeding paragraphs, the only fish avoiding the net are, in fact, those who neither employ others nor are themselves employed or self-employed (other than on a voluntary and non-gainful basis). All the rest are caught and have a potential liability to pay contributions.

EARNERS

2.02 An 'earner' defined

The definition of 'earner' is itself wider than might generally be supposed, for

'. . . "earnings" includes any remuneration or profit derived from an employment; and "earner" shall be construed accordingly' (SSA 1975, s. 3(1))

while the term 'employment' itself includes

'. . . any trade, business, profession, office or vocation' (SSA 1975, Sch. 20)

which, for the purposes of the contribution scheme, includes the exercise and performance of the powers and duties of a public or local authority (SSA 1975, Sch. 20).

The manner and basis of an earnings calculation is prescribed by regulation, as are certain specific classes of payment which may be disregarded (SSA 1975, s. 3(2) and (3)), but such matters fall to be discussed in Chapters 4 and 5. The point to be made here is that, in line with the Act's definition of earnings and the rule of construction prescribed, an earner must minimally be defined as 'anyone who derives remuneration or profit from any trade, business, profession, office or vocation.'

It should be evident, from this definition alone, that (to echo dicta delivered almost a century ago by Denman J in connection with the meaning of the word 'employment') the term 'earner' cannot be confined merely to those

> '... set to work by others to earn money; a man may employ himself so as to earn profit in many ways' (*Partridge v Mallandaine (Surveyor of Taxes)* (1886) 18 QBD 276, 2 TC 179)

He may, in other words, be either employed or self-employed; and statutory recognition of this possibility is clearly given by s. 2(1) of the Act (see **2.05** and **2.09** post).

2.03   The force of the term 'gainfully'

Unfortunately, SSA 1975, s. 2(1) does not stop at its recognition of the distinction between the employed and the self-employed, but proceeds to introduce a qualification which, in the light of what has already been said, might, on first reading, be considered quite unnecessary: it limits each category of earner to those in each class who are 'gainfully employed'. The adverb is, in fact, a borrowing from earlier (and now repealed) legislation where it appeared both in the equivalent of its present context and (adjectively) in the definition of earnings now found in SSA 1975, s. 3(1) and quoted at **2.02** ante. In that definition, the word 'employment' has been substituted for the phrase 'gainful occupation' (National Insurance Act (NIA) 1965, s. 114) and 'gainfully employed' in SSA 1975, s. 2(1) has replaced 'gainfully occupied in employment' (NIA 1965, s. 1(2)(a)).

Since the word has been dispensed with in one instance, why, we might ask, should it have been retained in the other? Simply, it would seem, to ensure the continued applicability, where necessary, of a body of case law which, over the years, has grown up around the term and which has been useful to the DHSS in blocking a possible avenue of escape from the net of potential liability by offering precedent for the construing of 'gainful' as 'for the purposes of gain' (*Vandyk v Minister of Pensions and National Insurance* [1955] 1 QB 29; [1954] 2 All ER 723). The principle of construing *in pari materia* (see **1.08** ante) permits the assumption that, where a word is used in the same context as that in which it was used in a previous statute and that word has received judicial interpretation, the word is used in the same sense as it was used previously (*Gartside v IRC* [1968] 1 All ER 121, [1968] 2 WLR 277).

The relevance of such case law under current legislation falls to be considered in greater detail later, but it is of sufficient application for the term 'earner' to now be more fully re-defined as 'anyone who derives or expects or intends to derive remuneration from any trade, business, profession, office or vocation.' To put it another way: mere failure to realise profit or to receive remuneration will not, per se, remove a person from the Act's circle of coverage if the realisation of profit or the receipt of remuneration is the ultimate aim he has in view. All such persons, and any by whom they are employed or remunerated are potentially within the scope of the contribution requirements of social security law. The seaside landlady does not cease to be an 'earner' merely because she has no paying guests in winter!

2.04 The crucial distinction

Having now arrived at a comprehensive definition of 'earner', we may return to the point made earlier; namely that the Act affords statutory recognition to the distinction between those who are employed and those who are self-employed. In intention at least, however, it does more. Those who drafted it would seem to have been instructed to draw a dividing line between the two categories of earner of such precision that all possible ambiguity would be avoided; and motivating such instruction would doubtless be the considerable consequentiality of any incorrect categorisation that could ensue. For the distinction is of great consequence. Not only do the earnings of a self-employed earner attract liability to contributions of a different class and on quite a different basis to those of an employed earner, but the contributions paid by a self-employed earner carry entitlement to a restricted and potentially far less costly range of benefits.

EXAMPLE 2(A)

On 6 April 1982, D. Mollish, a contractor, engages six labourers to carry out work for him on the understanding that each of them is, from that date, to be treated as a self-employed earner for tax and social security purposes.

By 5 April 1983, each will have profited from his engagement to the extent of £6,000 and will pay Class 2 and Class 4 contributions amounting to £351.75. The cost to D. Mollish will have been £36,000 and the state will receive:

	£
Class 2 contributions: $6 \times 53 \times £3.75$	1,192.50
Class 4 contributions: $6 \times 6\% \times (£6,000 - £3,450)$	918.00
	2,110.50

Although an entitlement to sickness and other contributory benefits will have been secured, none of the labourers will have fulfilled the contribution conditions necessary to an unemployment benefit entitlement in the relevant benefit year (ie that beginning 1 January 1984) and, consequently, the state will have been relieved of a contingent liability for that year amounting to (assuming none of the labourers has dependents), say, £9,360.00 (ie $6 \times 52 \times$ say, £30)—though each labourer could, in fact, become a charge on the Exchequer by resorting to supplementary benefit should he become unemployed in circumstances sufficiently extreme for him to qualify for such assistance.

If, however, each labourer had, at 5 April 1982, been categorised as an employed (rather than a self-employed) earner, the situation would have been entirely different. By 5 April 1983 each would receive his £6,000 less a deduction of primary Class 1 contributions of £525.00. The cost to D. Mollish would be £36,000 plus secondary Class 1 contributions (including surcharge) of £4,932.00, and the state would receive:

	£
Primary Class 1 contributions: $6 \times £6,000 \times 8.75\%$	3,150.00
Secondary Class 1 contributions: $6 \times £6,000 \times 13.7\%$	4,932.00
	8,082.00

In other words, each labourer would suffer by a change in categorisation only to the extent of £173.25 and would be able to console himself with the thought that he was thereby securing for himself an entitlement to unemployment benefit (should he be in need of it) of up to, say, £1,560 in the year commencing 1 January 1984. The state would benefit from the change to the extent of £5,971.50 (and would recognise her corresponding liability for unemployment benefit of, say, £9,360 to be a mere contingency which would be unlikely to crystallise in full, if at all). D. Mollish, however, would suffer by the change to the extent of £4,932.00 and would have no prospect of potential benefits whatsoever with which to console himself. In his view, the £4,932.00 would simply be a large, unproductive, additional charge on his profits; and, for this reason, he and others like him will, at times, be found appearing as the appellant in categorisation cases coming before the courts.

As the distinction between an employed earner and a self-employed earner is of such demonstrable importance, we shall now consider carefully the definition of each.

2.05   An 'employed earner' defined

An 'employed earner' is defined by s. 2(1)(a) of SSA 1975 as:

'a person who is gainfully employed in Great Britain either under a contract of service, or in an office (including elective office) with emoluments chargeable to income tax under Schedule E.'

The syntax (and the punctuation, if it is permissible to heed it—see **1.08** ante) is here of some importance and should, therefore, be noted. Reinforced by the comma after 'service,' the scope of the adjectival phrase 'with emoluments chargeable to income tax under Schedule E' is clearly limited to 'office' so that the schedule (if any) under which earnings derived from gainful employment under a contract of service are chargeable to tax is of no relevance for social security contribution purposes. It will not be possible, therefore, to exclude someone from the category of employed earner merely because earnings derived by him under a contract of service have not been charged to tax at all or have been charged to tax under Schedule D or some other Schedule apart from Schedule E.

2.06 Place of employment

Even where a person is gainfully employed under a contract of service, or in an office with emoluments chargeable to tax under Schedule E, he will not be categorised as an 'employed earner' unless he is employed 'in Great Britain'. The phrase is somewhat vague. A person may enter into a contract of employment in Great Britain and be placed on the payroll of an employer here but may nevertheless perform the duties of the employment abroad. Where is he gainfully employed? The Act itself provides no answer, but regulations made under the Act and described in Chapter 3 ensure that, even in cases where the duties of an employment are, for up to a year, continuously carried out abroad, the person carrying out the duties will be treated as an employed earner whether, because of his absence from Great Britain, he escapes categorisation under s. 2(1)(a) of the Act or not.

2.07 The meaning of 'contract of service'

A distinction must, at all times, be maintained between a contract *of* service and a contract *for* services. Both are common law concepts of antiquity, though the former has now been defined by statute and is the type of contract whereby a person is, for social security contribution purposes, drawn into the category of 'employed earner' (see **2.05** ante). The latter, however, is indicative of self-employment and is fully discussed later at **2.09**.

A contract of service is defined by the Act as:

> 'any contract of service or apprenticeship, whether written or oral and whether expressed or implied' (SSA 1975, Sch. 20).

It is, accordingly, to these intents and purposes, synonymous with a 'contract of employment' as defined in current employment legislation:

> 'a contract of service or apprenticeship, whether express or implied, and (if it is express) whether it is oral or in writing' (Employment Protection (Consolidation) Act (EP(C)A) 1978, s. 153(1));

and, being based on the offer-acceptance-consideration structure of any simple contract, connotes the usual arrangement between two parties where an employer has offered employment and a person has agreed to work for him as an employee. A contract of this kind exists

> '. . . where there is a mutual agreement or understanding that, in return for some specific remuneration in money or in kind or some other benefit or privilege, the employee shall personally render services subject to the right on the part of the employer to control or direct him in the work he does and the method and performance of his duties' (DHSS Leaflet NI39).

In the light of this description, it will be clear that no one factor is going to be determinative when deciding whether such a contract governs a particular relationship. Method of remuneration, for example, does not itself show whether such a contract exists (DHSS Leaflet NI39) and, even though persons employed under a contract of service are usually paid by weekly wage or salary, a person

> '. . . may be paid by a piece-rate, or by the hour or day, or receive payment in kind (for example, board and lodging) and still be an employee under contract of service' (DHSS Leaflet NI39).

Thus, under earlier legislation (see **2.03** ante), a person whose remuneration was insufficient to cover even his out-of-pocket expenses was held to be 'gainfully occupied in employment' under a 'contract of service' (*Vandyk v Minister of Pensions and National Insurance* [1955] 1 QB 29, [1954] 2 All ER 723), as was an articled clerk who received no actual wage but from time to time received small gratuitous sums of money (*Benjamin v Minister of Pensions and National Insurance* [1960] 2 QB 519, [1960] 3 WLR 430) and two other articled clerks who, likewise, received no remuneration but were merely reimbursed for the cost of lunches and travel (*Re J. B. Griffiths, Quinn & Co* 5 KIR 128). A married woman who was only intermittently engaged in market research and then at a fixed fee for each engagement was also held to be employed under a contract of service (*Market Investigations Ltd v Minister of Social Security* [1968] 3 All ER 732, [1969] 2 WLR 1).

Another non-critical factor is lack of form. The law looks at substance; so that a person to whom written particulars of the main terms of a contract of service ought, under current employment protection legislation (see **9.16** post), to have been given, but have not, may nevertheless still be employed under a contract of service, provided the essential structure of the contract as described above is unimpaired. Failure to provide written particulars of a contract or to reduce it to writing may contravene legislation requiring that to be done but it will not invalidate the contract in question.

Even an agreed description of a contract as something other than what, in reality, it is, will not prevent the law from looking beyond that description:

> 'If the true relationship of the parties is that of master and servant under a contract of service, the parties cannot alter the truth of that relationship by putting a different label on it . . .' (*Massey v Crown Life Insurance Co* [1978] 2 All ER 576 per Lord Denning).

A contract which is never intended to be acted upon cannot have effect for categorisation purposes because the basis of such categorisation would not be genuine. This holds true even where no bad faith on the part of the persons involved is in evidence (*Reade v Brearley (Inspector of Taxes)* (1933) 17 TC 687, 12 ATC 96).

If, however,

> '. . . the parties' relationship is ambiguous . . . then the parties can remove that ambiguity . . . The agreement itself then becomes the best material

from which to gather the true legal relationship between them . . .'
(*Massey v Crown Life Insurance Co* [1978] 2 All ER 576, [1978] ICR 590 per
Lord Denning).

Because, on occasions, people do, for various reasons, attempt to disguise the
true nature of the contract between them, and because, too, contractual
relationships are often obscure or vague, a series of tests has evolved in the
courts whereby the truth of a relationship may be established. These are
discussed at **2.11** et seq post.

2.08   The meaning of 'office'

The point was made many years ago that it is important to distinguish between
one who holds an office and one who 'merely sits in one' (*Great Western Rly Co v
Bater* [1922] 2 AC 1; 8 TC 231 per Lord Sumner)! Most typists fall into the
latter category but are not office holders, being employed under contracts of
service. 'Office' is, in fact, a term which, though never statutorily defined, has
acquired

> '. . . a signification coloured over the years by legal construction in a
> technical context such that return to the pure source of common parlance
> is no longer possible' (*Edwards (Inspector of Taxes) v Clinch* [1981] STC
> 617).

Even the Social Security Act 1975 does no more than state that 'elective
office' is included among its meanings. This being the case, one must have
recourse to the constructions which the courts have, at various times, placed on
the word. The two most long-standing and widely accepted of those state that
the word signifies

> '. . . a subsisting, permanent, substantive position, which had an existence
> independent of the person who filled it, which went on and was filled in
> succession by successive holders' (*Great Western Rly Co v Bater* [1920] 3 KB
> 266, (1922) 8 TC 231 per Rowlett J)

and

> '. . . a position or place to which certain duties are attached, especially one
> of a more or less public character' (*McMillan v Guest* [1942] 1 All ER 606,
> 24 TC 190 per Lord Wright, quoting from the New English Dictionary).

Intrinsic to these definitions is the existence of a sufficient degree of
continuance for the post to be capable of being held by successive incumbents.
Thus a civil engineer appointed from time to time to hold public local inquiries
on an ad hoc basis for the Crown is not an office holder and his emoluments are
not assessable under Schedule E (*Edwards v Clinch* [1980] 3 All ER 278, [1980]
STC 438; affd. [1981] 3 All ER 543, [1981] STC 617).

In the *Clinch* case, Buckley LJ expressed the view that an office, in the context
of Schedule E, is

> '. . . a post which can be recognised as existing, whether it be occupied for

the time being or vacant, and which, if occupied, does not owe its existence in any way to the identity of the incumbent or his appointment to the post . . .'.

Given these definitions, we can see that a bishop of the Church of England, for example, is clearly such an office holder, and, as his emoluments are chargeable to tax under Schedule E, he is, therefore, an employed earner for social security contribution purposes (DHSS Leaflet NP21). So, too, is a company director:

'There can be no doubt that the director of a company holds such an office as described' (*McMillan v Guest* [1942] 1 All ER 606, 24 TC 190 per Lord Atkin, referring to the description of 'office' by Rowlett J quoted above).

This is true whatever the status of the company (*Berry v Farrow* [1914] 1 KB 632, 83 LJKB 487) and notwithstanding the fact that the director may own its entire share capital. This follows from the fact that a limited company is a separate legal entity; and, on the same premise, a director may, therefore, also be employed by a company under a contract of service and may even negotiate such a contract with himself on behalf of the company (*Lee v Lee's Air-Farming Ltd* [1961] AC 12, [1960] 3 All ER 420 (PC)). Such matters have become of some importance in recent months and are fully discussed in Chapter 8.

Members of Parliament, Ministers of the Crown and judges have been cited as additional examples of the category of office holder in a parliamentary reply by the Secretary of State for Social Services (Hansard, 16 December 1975, Vol. 902, No. 20, col. 578).

It should perhaps be noted before leaving this section that the charge to tax under Schedule E (referred to in SSA 1975, s. 2(1)(a)) arises under section 181 of the Income and Corporation Taxes Act 1970 and (subject to various rules relating to 'residence') extends to emoluments from any office or employment. Originally, the Schedule only applied to public offices and public employments of profit (Income Tax Act 1918, reg. 6, Sch. E Rules) and to certain annuities, pensions and stipends payable by the Crown. Other employed persons were brought within the Schedule by the Finance Act 1922, but, in linking Schedule E with 'office', the Social Security Act would seem to have the original category of charge in mind. This is perfectly logical when one considers that the original Schedule E was intended to impose a charge to tax on those who were neither engaged under a contract of service on the one hand, or under contracts for services on the other (both of which groups came, at that time, within the charge to tax under Schedule D).

2.09   A 'self-employed earner' defined

SSA 1975, s. 2(1)(b) negatively defines a self-employed earner as:

'a person who is gainfully employed in Great Britain otherwise than in an employed earner's employment (whether or not he is also employed in such employment)'.

In other words, gainful employment which is neither under a contract of service, nor in an office with emoluments chargeable to income tax under Schedule E, is self-employment; and a person in such employment will be categorised as a self-employed earner, even if he falls to be categorised as an employed earner in connection with some other employment.

The 'location' question (see **2.06** ante) arises here too and reference should be made to Chapter 3 in this connection. It must, however, be said now that, unless a persons self-employment is centered 'in Great Britain', categorisation as a self-employed earner is unlikely to ensue.

It is worth noting here that the DHSS takes the view that most professional or fee earning foster parents who receive a separate or distinct 'reward element' will be self-employed earners for social security purposes (Foster Care Allowances and Income Tax: National Foster Care Association booklet). Such a reward element consists of payments made over and above reimbursement of costs in recognition of the time and skill used by the foster parent in caring for a difficult or handicapped child.

It should also be noted that, in reply to a parliamentary question, the Secretary of State has confirmed that possession of a sub-contractor's tax exemption certificate is normally accepted as evidence of self-employment unless investigation reveals that a contract of service is in existence (Hansard, 13 November 1981, Vol. 12, No. 8, Pt. II, col. 188).

In the majority of cases, categorisation according to the above definition presents no difficulties at all. A man who invests his capital in purchasing a shop in the high street and stocking it with electrical goods which he proceeds to retail to the public, is clearly neither under a contract of service nor in an office. He is, therefore, a self-employed earner. But what of a man who, armed merely with a few screw-drivers and a great deal of technical expertise, describes himself as a self-employed electrical engineer and undertakes to repair television receivers for a TV rental company? Is there or is there not a contract of service and is he truly self-employed? Is his contract, in fact, for services, as he maintains it to be?

2.10 The meaning of 'contract for services'

'For the last 100 years the law has drawn a distinction between a "contract of service" on the one hand and a "contract for services" on the other; or, as it is sometimes put, between a master and servant relationship on the one hand, and between an employer and independent contractor on the other' (*Massey v Crown Life Insurance Co* [1978] 2 All ER 576, [1978] ICR 590 per Lord Denning).

The difficulty, however, is how to distinguish between the two. If, as a matter of fact, a person

'. . . has undertaken certain work, but is free to make whatever arrangements he pleases for getting it done and is not bound to render services in person . . .' (DHSS leaflet NI39)

that person is a party to a contract for services. So, too, is

> '. . . a person engaged to render services on the understanding that he will do the work personally but not subject to a right of control over his method of working' (DHSS Leaflet NI39).

In many instances, however, the issue is not so clearly cut. It is then that matters of law arise:

> 'The question of whether a contract is one of service—or is a contract for services, is a question of fact. It is, however, a question of law as to what are the right tests to be applied in determining whether a contract falls into the one or the other class' (*Construction Industry Training Board v Labour Force Ltd* [1970] 3 All ER 220 per Fisher J).

Such tests are of two main kinds: tests of 'control' and tests of 'integration'.

2.11   The 'control' test

The primary test to be applied centres on the degree of control which one party to the contract may, if he wishes, exert over the other:

> 'Although not conclusive in itself the existence of this right of control (even if seldom or never exercised) is a strong indication that there is a contract of service' (DHSS Leaflet NI39).

Before it will be indicative of the existence of such a contract, however, the right of control must go beyond mere specification of the work to be performed, and must extend to the time, place, means, method and manner of performance of that work. Thus, an actor who was a part-time teacher at a school of music and drama was held not to be employed under a contract of service as his choice of teaching material and his method of teaching were almost entirely uncontrolled and his remuneration was either at an hourly rate or at a fee per session (*Argent v Minister of Social Security* [1968] 3 All ER 208, [1968] 1 WLR 1749). A 'lump labourer', however, who regarded himself as a self-employed earner and had been treated as such for tax and social security purposes by his employers, was found by the Court of Appeal to be under a contract of service as his employers controlled not only the work he did but also the method and manner in which he did it and even provided him with the necessary tools (*Ferguson v John Dawson & Partners (Contractors) Ltd* [1976] 1 WLR 1213, [1976] 3 All ER 817). Similarly, a driver of hired-out industrial plant regarded himself as a self-employed earner and paid tax and social security contributions accordingly. He became engaged to supply services to a company under a contract which purported to give him freedom to work when he chose and to send a suitably qualified substitute to work in his stead. In practice, however, he worked the normal hours of a full-time employee, attending sites at times dictated by the company and being paid at an hourly rate of remuneration based on the number of hours worked. He drove the company's machines on, and only on, sites selected by the company and under the control of the company's site foreman, and behaved in all respects as would an employee of the company. Accordingly, the Secretary of State for Social Services looked behind the form of the 'contract for services' and found that, in reality, there was a contract of service. His decision was upheld on appeal by the company (*Global Plant Ltd v Secretary of State for Health and Social Security* [1972] 1 QB 139, [1971] 3 All ER 385) for the control test had been properly applied.

2.12 The 'integration' test

'Under a contract of service a man is employed as part of the business and his work is done as an integral part of the business; whereas under a contract for services his work, although done for the business, is not integrated into it but only accessory to it' (*Stevenson, Jordan and Harrison v Macdonald and Evans* [1952] 1 TLR 101, 69 RPC 10 (CA) per Lord Denning).

The integration test seeks, therefore, to determine whether or not a person is 'part and parcel' of an organisation (*Bank Voor Handel en Scheepvaart, NV v Slatford* [1953] 1 QB 248, [1952] 2 All ER 956, CA, per Lord Denning) and among the relevant factors to be considered are: whether he provides his own equipment or has equipment provided for him by the organisation; whether he hires his own helpers or has assistants supplied; and whether or not he undertakes personal financial risk, assumes investment and management responsibilities, and has the opportunity to profit from sound management in the performance of his tasks (*Market Investigations Ltd v Minister of Social Security* [1969] 2 QB 173, [1968] 3 All ER 732, CA).

Of course . . .

'. . . no magic formula can be propounded for determining which factors should, in any given case be treated as the determining ones . . . In a large number of cases, the court can only perform a balancing operation, weighing up the factors which went in one direction and balancing them against those pointing in the opposite direction . . . This operation cannot be performed with scientific accuracy' (*Construction Industry Training Board v Labour Force Ltd* [1970] 3 All ER 220 per Fisher J, quoting with approval Professor Atiyah).

Nevertheless, the courts have decided that a consultant surgeon appointed to a NHS Hospital Board was a servant of the Board because, despite a lack of control, he had been 'integrated' into the business of the Board in the manner described above (*Cassidy v Minister of Health* [1951] 2 KB 343, [1951] 1 All ER 574) and that a part-time 'sick-steward' of an AEU branch was a servant of the union for the same reason—despite the fact that his contract precluded the union from controlling his movements or the manner in which his duties were performed (*Amalgamated Engineering Union v Minister of Pensions* [1963] 1 All ER 864, [1963] 1 WLR 441).

A person contracting to carry concrete in a vehicle provided by himself for the purpose has, however, been held not to be under a contract of service, even though he was obliged to wear the uniform and colours of the concrete manufacturer and to work to the manufacturer's orders. The contract was thought to be inconsistent with a contract of service in that neither integration nor control extended far enough for the owner-driver to cease to be an independent contractor (*Ready Mixed Concrete (South East) Ltd v Minister of Pensions* [1968] 2 QB 497, [1968] 1 All ER 433).

Similarly, an associate player and three additional players were held not to be employees of the London Philharmonic Orchestra, even though they had obligations of personal attendance, dress and discipline which were appropriate to employees. They were paid sessional fees and certain expenses but were held to have had no special relationship or commitment to the orchestra, remaining essentially freelance musicians pursuing their own professions as instrumentalists and contributing their own skills and interpretative powers to the orchestra as independent contractors (*Addison v London Philharmonic Orchestra Ltd* (1980) Times, 21 October). This decision was followed in a similar case a few weeks later (*Midland Sinfonia Concert Society Ltd v Secretary of State for Social Services* (1980) Times, 10 November) and both may owe something to the dicta delivered in a slightly earlier case:

> 'Making music is an art, and the co-operation required for a performance of Berlioz's Requiem is dissimilar to that required between the manufacturer of concrete and the truck driver who takes the concrete where it is needed . . . In deciding whether you are in the presence of a contract of service or not, you look at the whole of the picture. The picture looks to us . . . like a co-operative of distinguished musicians running themselves with self and mutual discipline, and in no sense like a boss and his musician employees' (*Winfield v London Philharmonic Orchestra Ltd* [1979] ICR 726).

2.13   Caveat

The importance of the distinction between a contract of service and a contract for services is not confined to social security matters. It is central to employment law, and also to the law of torts for. . .

> 'a master is liable for all the wrongdoings of his servant in the course of his employment; but an employer is not liable for all the wrongdoings of an independent contractor' (*Massey v Crown Life Insurance Co* [1978] 2 All ER 576, [1978] ICR 590 per Lord Denning).

Indeed, it would seem that it was in this latter area that the category of 'contract of service' was first established. Be that as it may, the fact that the distinction is now of such widespread relevance makes it necessary for us to approach decisions of the court on such matters with a degree of caution for there can, of course, be no absolute certainty that any particular decision would have been the same had the area of law involved been different.

As none of the cases cited in the preceding paragraphs have concerned vicarious liability to third parties, it is, in fact, unlikely that any of the decisions reached would have been reversed had the issue been contribution liability instead of, say, wrongful dismissal or an entitlement to benefits. All are related to the protection of the employee in much the same way. In tort law, however, the protection of third parties is at stake, and, where cases come before the courts on such matters, we should expect a leaning towards the integration test which would not necessarily be found were the correct categorisation of an earner for social security purposes to be in question.

Though both the tests described are, as has been explained, of widespread application in determining whether an earner is employed or self-employed for social security contribution purposes, the courts have tended, in such cases as have come before them, to favour the control test wherever this has proved capable of application. This is surely as it should be, for the issue at the root of all questions of categorisation is whether or not a person should be insured against unemployment. If a person is categorized as an employed earner, he will be so insured; if he is categorised as a self-employed earner, he will not. For social security purposes, therefore, 'employed' ought essentially to connote 'capable of being dismissed' and the control test is, in most circumstances, more likely than the integration test to indicate whether, in a given relationship, such dismissability is a present factor.

2.14 Determination of doubtful cases

Although questions of categorisation frequently arise, very few, in fact, ever reach the courts, for the Act provides for their resolution at a much earlier stage wherever possible.

Initially, it is to be

'. . . determined by the Secretary of State . . . whether a person is an earner and, if he is, as to the category of earners in which he is to be included' (SSA 1975, s. 93(1)(a)).

Under regulations made by virtue of SSA 1975, ss. 114(1) and 115(1), however, a person wishing to obtain a decision by the Secretary of State on a question of categorisation may apply to him in an approved form but must supply him with all such particulars as he requires (SI 1975, No. 558, reg. 6(1)). Anyone making such an application must be 'interested' in the decision (SI 1975, No. 558, reg. 6(6)), which is to say that he must have an interest which is under, or for the purposes of, the social security legislation and which relates to his own liability under the legislation or his actual or potential rights under it (SI 1975, No. 558, reg. 6(7)(a) and (b)). Once an application has been made, the Secretary of State will bring it to the notice of any person who appears to him to be an interested party and will obtain additional particulars from that person (SI 1975, No. 558, reg. 6(2)). The Secretary of State's decision will then be notified in writing to all interested parties (SI 1975, No. 558, reg. 6(5)).

If he thinks fit, the Secretary of State may, before determining any such question, arrange for an inquiry into the question itself and any related matters (SSA 1975, s. 93(3)). Anyone appointed to hold such an inquiry may, by summons, require persons to attend and give such evidence or produce such documents as may reasonably be required for the purpose (SI 1975, No. 558, reg. 6(3)). The applicant, anyone notified of the application and anyone else who appears to the person holding the inquiry to be 'interested', has the right to attend and be heard, and is to be given reasonable notice of the time and place at which the inquiry is to be held (SI 1975, No. 558, reg. 6(4)). Furthermore, anyone who has the right to be heard may be represented by some other person who need not be professionally qualified (SSA 1975, s. 115(6) and SI 1975, No. 558, reg. 3(1)(b)). Witnesses may be examined on oath (SSA 1975, s. 115(4)).

The machinery of these two provisions is capable of resolving most of the doubtful cases which arise and, subject to what is said in the following paragraphs, the decision arrived at is final (SSA 1975, s. 117(1)), though a finding of fact in connection with such a decision is not conclusive for the purpose of any further decision (SSA 1975, s. 117(2)).

There are occasions, however, when—although the facts are not in dispute—uncertainty arises over a question of law: whether, for example, the control test should be applied or whether the integration test is more appropriate. The Secretary of State is empowered to refer such a point of law to the High Court (or, in Scotland, the Court of Session) for decision (SSA 1975, s. 94(1)) but, if he declines to do so, 'any person aggrieved' by his decision is entitled to appeal to that court (SSA 1975, s. 94(3)). If the Secretary of State does decide to refer to the court, he is obliged to give written notice of his intention to anyone who appears to him to be concerned (SSA 1975, s. 94(2)(b)) and this would include not only the person whose categorisation is at issue but also that person's employer.

It will be observed that, where a categorisation question has been determined without reference to the court, the way is open for persons quite unrelated to the parties involved to appeal against the ruling by the Secretary of State—provided they are 'aggrieved' by that ruling. A legitimate grievance would doubtless include becoming a secondary contributor were the categorisation decision to be generally applied.

As has been noted above, however, the grounds for any such appeal are limited. Hearing an appeal against the findings of an industrial tribunal (where similar provisions for appeal on a question of law exist under EP(C)A 1978, s. 136(4)) the appellant court made it clear that

> '. . . the question of whether a contract is one of service—or is a contract for services, is a question of fact. It is, however, a question of law as to what are the right tests to be applied in determining whether a contract falls into the one or the other class. A decision of the tribunal could be upset by this court if it was of the opinion that the tribunal had applied the wrong tests—in other words, that they had misdirected themselves in law' (*Construction Industry Training Board v Labour Force Ltd* [1970] 3 All ER 220);

but not otherwise, even if that court's decision might have been different:

> 'Of course, a decision of the Tribunal may be such that the court will say that they could not possibly have come to their decision of fact unless they

had misdirected themselves in law; and in those circumstances, this court could interfere' (ibid).

In order that any interested party may determine whether any question of law has arisen on which he may appeal to the court, the Secretary of State must, on request, provide that interested party with a statement of the grounds of his decision (SI 1975, No. 558, reg. 7).

Appeals under the provisions of the Act are subject to rules of court as regards conduct, time limits etc (SSA 1975, s. 94(5)), but requirements of the Supreme Court of Judicature (Consolidation) Act 1925 which require an appeal to be heard by a divisional court do not apply (SSA 1975, s. 94(6)).

The Secretary of State is entitled to appear and be heard on any reference or appeal to the court (SSA 1975, s. 94(4)); but, whether he appears or not, he may be ordered to pay any other person's costs (in Scotland, expenses) even though the decision may be in the other person's favour (SSA 1975, s. 94(8)). A decision of the court on reference or appeal is final (SSA 1975, s. 94(7)).

2.15   Revision of categorisation decisions

Where the Secretary of State has decided a question of categorisation, he may,

> '. . . on new facts being brought to his notice, or if he is satisfied that the decision was given in ignorance of, or was based on a mistake as to, some material fact, review any decision given by him . . .' (SSA 1975, s. 96(1)),

provided no appeal against his decision is already pending and that the time for so appealing has expired (SSA 1975, s. 96(2)).

Anyone who has been given notice of a categorisation decision by the Secretary of State and who wishes to raise a question leading to a review of that decision may, within three months of receiving notice (or of receiving a statement of grounds, if one has been requested) apply for a review (SI 1975, No. 558, reg. 8(1)). The procedure is then identical with that described at **2.14** ante as following on application for a decision (SI 1975, No. 558, reg. 8(2) and (3)(a)).

Regulations provide for the special categorisation of a person following such a revised decision or following a decision of the court, if this would be in the interests of the person concerned.

The effect of such regulations is for the person to be treated

> '. . . as though he had been included in the category of earners corresponding to the contributions paid during the period for which contributions appropriate to that other category were so paid before the date on which the decision of the High Court was given . . .' (SI 1978, No. 1689, reg. 4(1))

or before the date on which the Secretary of State revised his previous determination (SI 1978, No. 1689, reg. 4(2)). Thus, for example, a person who has paid primary Class 1 contributions in the belief that he is an employed earner will, even if the court or the Secretary of State now decides he is in fact a self-employed earner, be treated as if he has been an employed earner until the date the decision is made and will be eligible for benefits accordingly. From the date of the decision, however, he will, of course, be treated as a self-employed earner and will be liable to contribute as such.

2.16   Exclusion from and reversal of categories

From time to time, problems of categorisation have arisen which neither the courts nor DHSS administrators have been able to resolve satisfactorily, and sometimes, too, anomalous situations have been created by a precise application of the categorisation provisions. ˍ

In anticipation of such difficulties, the Act permits regulations to be made which may provide

> 'for employment of any prescribed description to be disregarded in relation to liability for contributions otherwise arising from employment of that description' (SSA 1975, s. 2(2)(a))

and

> 'for a person in employment of any prescribed description to be treated . . . as falling within one or other categories of earner . . . notwithstanding that he would not fall within that category apart from the regulations' (SSA 1975, s. 2(2)(b)).

Thus, for example, the question brought before the court in *Market Investigations Ltd v Minister of Social Security* [1969] 2 QB 173, [1968] 3 All ER 732, CA, as to whether or not someone intermittently engaged in market research at a fixed fee per engagement could rightly be held to be under a contract of service was finally resolved by Sch. I of The Social Security (Categorisation of Earners) Regulations 1975, No. 528, which declared that employment as an interviewer for the purpose of obtaining information about the habits or opinions of members of the public or any particular category or description of persons was to be treated as an employed earner's employment.

Categorisation regulations currently in force are contained in SI 1978, No. 1689 (which revokes and consolidates earlier regulations) and The Social Security (Categorisation of Earners) Amendment Regulations 1980, No. 1713 (which augments the consolidating regulations). Together these provide for categorisation or exclusion from categorisation as described in Chapter 7, except that self-employed earners who would be affected by the regulations are to continue to be treated as self-employed earners until their current self-employment ceases (SI 1978, No. 1689, reg. 3 and Sch. 2).

EMPLOYERS AND OTHERS

2.17   Secondary contributors

Although, as has been noted in the introduction to this chapter, the s. 1 net scoops up all 'employers', employers do not, as such, constitute a category within the contribution scheme and some, in fact, escape categorisation altogether under the detailed provisions of the Act.

The category that is created is one of 'secondary contributors' and to this most (but no all) employers belong as well as certain other specified persons.

The category exists only

'. . . in relation to any payment of earnings to or for the benefit of an employed earner . . .' (SSA 1975, s. 4(4))

so that, unless a person is either directly or indirectly involved in the making of such payments, he cannot fall into the category of secondary contributor.

In normal circumstances, the secondary contributor will, in the case of an earner employed under a contract of service (see **2.07** ante), be his employer (SSA 1975, s. 4(4)(a)) and, in the case of an earner employed in an office with emoluments chargeable to tax under Schedule E (see **2.08** ante), any person who is prescribed in relation to the office (under, for example, the charter, statute, declaration of trust or other instrument creating the office) (SSA 1975, s. 4(4)(b)(i)). If no such person is prescribed, the government department, public authority or body of persons responsible for paying the emoluments of the office will be the secondary contributor (SSA 1975, s. 4(4)(b)(ii)).

Where circumstances are not quite normal, as, for example, where an employed earner is paid earnings in a tax week by more than one person in respect of different employments or where an employed earner works under the general control or management of a person other than his immediate employer, regulations made under SSA 1975, s. 4(5) prescribe who the secondary contributor is to be. Such regulations are presently contained in SI 1978, No. 1689 and SI 1979, No. 591. In all but two cases, they concern persons falling in one or other of the special classes of earner described in Chapter 7 and are, accordingly, discussed there. The two remaining cases concern, firstly, employment in chambers as a barrister's clerk where the head of chambers is prescribed as the secondary contributor (SI 1978, No. 1689, Sch. 3, para. 5) and, secondly, employment (other than through an agency) by a company which is in voluntary liquidation but is carrying on business under a liquidator. In this latter case, the person who at the time of the employment holds the office of liquidator is prescribed as the secondary contributor (SI 1978, No. 1689, Sch. 3, para. 4).

A person who would otherwise fall to be categorised as a secondary contributor may escape such categorisation if he fails to fulfil prescribed conditions as to residence or presence in Great Britain (see **3.14** post).

2.18 Voluntary contributors

A consideration of matters discussed in the preceding section will show that certain of the 'others' caught in the SSA 1975, s. 1 net are persons other than employers who are involved in the payment of earnings to or for the benefit of employed earners. The remainder are those who are entitled, if they so wish, to pay Class 3 contributions.

Entitlement to certain benefits is, as has been explained at **1.17** ante, contingent upon the satisfaction of certain contribution conditions. In order to enable persons whose contribution record is deficient in this respect to make up that deficiency (but for no other reason), the Act provides that Class 3 contributions may be paid (SSA 1975, s. 8(2)) subject to conditions imposed by regulation (SI 1979, No. 591, reg. 27(1)) and statute (SSPA 1975, s. 5(1)) as regards age, and by regulation (SI 1979, No. 591, reg. 119) as regards residence. These restrictions are dealt with at **3.15, 3.17** and **3.18** post.

CHAPTER 3

Residence, age and marital status

3.01 Introduction

The last chapter was devoted to a consideration of the wide net thrown by the Social Security Act 1975 and, in particular, its resultant catch of 'earners, employers and others' (s. 1). It is now appropriate to examine the main criteria by which the Act, as it begins a complex process of discrimination, decides which elements of that initial catch should remain enmeshed and which should be restored, unscathed, to the pool.

RESIDENCE

3.02 General exclusion

S. 1(6) of the Act provides that a person shall be neither liable to pay Class 1 or Class 2 contributions nor entitled to pay Class 3 contributions

> '. . . unless he fulfills prescribed conditions as to residence or presence in Great Britain',

though SSA 1975, s. 131 provides that the Secretary of State may make regulations modifying the Act in its application to persons who are, or have been, outside Great Britain at any prescribed time or in any prescribed circumstance (see **3.09** post).

No reference is made to Class 4 contributions in this connection as such contributions are firmly linked to the assessability of profits and gains to income tax under Schedule D (SSA 1975, s. 9).

The prescribed conditions as to residence or presence to which SSA 1975, s. 1(6) refers are contained in SI 1979, No. 591, reg. 119. That regulation employs three terms all of which are undefined and at least two of which are, therefore, a potential source of difficulty. The terms are 'resident', 'ordinarily resident' and 'present', and, because of the lack of statutory definition, each term must take its meaning from normal usage as illumined by relevant pronouncements of the courts.

3.03 Presence

'Present' is the narrowest of the terms and, because its meaning is reasonably transparent, it calls for least discussion. The Concise Oxford Dictionary defines the word as 'being in the place in question' and to this it would seem that nothing need be added.

3.04   Residence

Being 'resident' is, however, something more than merely being in a particular place, though physical presence at some point during the relevant period is certainly a prerequisite of 'residence' (*Lloyd v Sulley (Surveyor of Taxes)* 1884 11 R (Ct. of Session) 687, 2 TC 37). It is beyond dispute that someone who has never set foot in Great Britain during a given period cannot be held to have been 'resident' in Great Britain for that period. The questions as to when 'present' becomes 'resident' and when 'resident' becomes 'ordinarily resident' are, however, questions which cannot be easily answered.

Perhaps the most important case which bears upon the problem is *IRC v Lysaght* [1928] AC 234, HL, for there the House of Lords authoritatively established the rule that questions of residence and ordinary residence are questions of 'degree' and 'fact', and that the terms are not ones to which any special or technical meaning should be attached.

It must first be stated that, if actual, physical 'presence' at some point is a prerequisite of 'residence', the maintenance of a fixed place of abode is not (though, before *IRC v Cadwalader* 1904 7 F (Ct. of Session) 146, 5 TC 101 it had been thought to be the determinant factor). Thus, in the *Lysaght* case, a British subject whose home had once been in Great Britain but who now kept an establishment abroad, was held to be resident here because, though he stayed in hotels, he returned here each year for domestic, medical and religious purposes. This followed the decision in *Reid v IRC* (1926) 10 TC 673, 5 ATC 357 where another person moving from hotel to hotel and having no fixed place of abode was nevertheless held to be resident in Great Britain. If, however, a person does maintain a fixed place of abode here, or have accommodation available for his use, he will become resident should he make any visit, however brief (the *Cadwalader* case); and non-ownership of the accommodation will not prevent this (*Loewenstein v de Salis* (1926) 10 TC 424).

Two other important points were established in the *Lysaght* case. Firstly, that a person may be 'resident' in more than one place at one time. Secondly, that a persons intentions and wishes as to where he is resident have no bearing on whether or not he is, in fact, 'resident' in a particular place:

> '. . . though a man may make his home elsewhere and stay in this country only because business compels him, yet none the less, if the periods for which and the conditions under which he stays are such that they may be regarded as constituting residence, it is open . . . to find that in fact he does so reside' (per Lord Buckmaster).

This dictum represented a departure from previously held views but has since been followed, notably in *Lord Inchiquin v IRC* (1948) 31 TC 125, CA, where a person prevented by military service in Great Britain from residing as he wished at his ancestral home in Eire was held to be nevertheless resident here. The notion of residence connotes, it would seem, association with a particular place

> '. . . with some degree of continuity and apart from accidental or temporary absence' (*Levene v IRC* [1928] AC 217, 13 TC 486 per Viscount Cave LC).

Family ties may, therefore, indicate where a person is resident, though they on their own are not conclusive (*Turnbull v Foster* (1904) 6 TC 206, 7 F (Ct. of Session 1)); and, certainly, the residential status of one spouse does not depend on that of the other.

In the *Levene* case, residence was equated with being, to some extent and for some period of time, 'at home' in a particular place:

> 'The appellant elected in each . . . year to adopt a regular system of life in accordance with which he and his wife made their abode and lived in this country for a period of between four and five months in each year . . . they were therefore resident . . . not merely in the sense of being present here but in the fuller sense of making their home here' (per Sagant LJ).

3.05 Ordinary residence

It is clear that differentiation between being 'resident' and being 'ordinarily resident' is intended by the social security regulations referred to earlier, as (in reg. 119(1) for example) the latter is prescribed as an alternative condition of liability where the former condition is not met. In other words, a person may be 'ordinarily resident' though not 'resident' or 'present'. The consensus of judicial thought on these matters is that 'ordinary' contrasts with 'casual' or 'occasional' (Lawrence J in the *Lysaght* case) or 'extraordinary' (Viscount Sumner in the same case) and that 'ordinarily resident' means residence which is part of the habitual, usual, regular order of a person's life in contrast with 'residence' which is special, occasional or casual. It follows that a person may, in fact, be away from this country for extensive periods of time and still be 'ordinarily resident' in Great Britain. Indeed, the DHSS regard a person as continuing to be 'ordinarily resident' where he is absent abroad for up to three years, provided the intention to return is not abandoned, though, where the absence extends, or is likely to extend, beyond three years, the DHSS consider each case individually taking into account the intended length of absence, whether a home or accommodation is being maintained in the UK and whether furniture and personal effects are being stored or being disposed of (DHSS Leaflet NI38).

With the preceding discussion in mind, we may now consider the regulations themselves.

3.06 Employed earner's employment in Great Britain

SI 1979, No. 591, reg. 119(1)(a) states that the residence conditions under which an employed earner will become liable to pay primary Class 1 contributions in respect of earnings from an employed earner's employment are

'. . . that the employed earner is resident or present in Great Britain (or but for any temporary absence . . . would be present . . .) at the time of that employment or is then ordinarily resident in Great Britain.'

The principal grounds of liability contained in this regulation present no real problem:

EXAMPLE 3(A)

Manuel, a waiter, obtains summer employment in a London hotel. His home is in Spain and he intends to return there in early autumn. He is not 'resident' in Great Britain but he is 'present' and that is sufficient to create a liabilty for him to pay primary Class 1 contributions on his earnings. Nationality does not enter into the matter except to the extent that it indirectly bears on the (in this instance irrelevant) question of whether or not he is 'ordinarily resident' here.

The remainder of the regulation is not, however, without its difficulties. Clearly, 'ordinarily resident' is inserted so as to provide an alternative ground for liability where the grounds of 'residence' and 'presence' fail. Yet, if a person is absent from Great Britain to a degree where he is actually non-resident, it must surely follow that, if employed, he is employed outside Great Britain. He is thus removed from the category of 'employed earner' to which the regulation refers and placed within a special category of earners working abroad (see **3.09** post) who are merely 'treated' as employed earners with a limited degree of liability. If the logic of this argument is sound, the clause 'or is ordinarily resident in Great Britain' is without effect and a liability is imposed only on employed earners who are 'present' or 'resident' at the time of their employment. If the logic is unsound then reg. 120 (see **3.09** post) is superfluous and liability should, under reg. 119(1)(a), continue not merely for one but for three years, ie, until 'ordinary residence' as well as 'presence' and 'residence' has ceased or been lost.

EXAMPLE 3(B)

Frank, a British subject whose home is in Great Britain, is employed by a British manufacturer of widgets. The company (having recently developed a super-widget) asks Frank to launch it on the overseas market by organising promotional campaigns in the United States and working from their Chicago branch. Frank is engaged in this activity from March 1981 until August 1982 when, for the first time in eighteen months, he sets foot in Great Britain. Although neither 'present' nor 'resident' during 1981–82, Frank (because his home has remained in Great Britain) is, however, 'ordinarily resident' for that year and is, therefore, under reg. 119(1)(a), liable to pay primary Class 1 contributions on his earnings throughout his period abroad. Under reg. 120, however, he is only so liable for the first fifty-two weeks of his term of duty in the States!

Perhaps the paradox illustrated by the above example is to be resolved by assuming that, out of a concern to prevent any true resident slipping out of the liability net, the draftsmen have attempted to forestall the interpretation of 'residence' as something akin to mere 'presence' by lending the supposed weight of 'ordinary residence' to the regulation? If so, they would seem to have created something of an anomaly.

3.07   Temporary employment in Great Britain

Under certain circumstances, the rule in reg. 119(1)(a) is to be modified, and those circumstances are described in reg. 119(2) and (3).

The first is the situation where a person who is not ordinarily resident in the UK and normally works abroad is sent to work here temporarily by his overseas employer (who may or may not have a place of business here). Such a person falls to be categorised as an employed earner according to the principles set out in the preceding chapter and, but for a modification to the rule in reg. 119(1)(a), would, therefore, be liable to pay primary Class 1 contributions from the start of his period of employment here.

Similarly placed would be any non-ordinarily resident student who, though pursuing a course of full-time studies overseas, takes up temporary vacational employment in Great Britain similar to or related to his course of studies abroad, and such students form the second group to whom the modified rule applies.

The third group consists of non-ordinarily resident persons who, being in a relationship with someone outside the UK comparable with that between an apprentice and his master in Great Britain, take up employment here of a similar nature to (or related to) that under their relationship abroad and do so before reaching the age of twenty-five.

It is provided that, with regard to any such person

'. . . no primary or secondary Class 1 contribution shall be payable . . . before he has been resident in Great Britain for a continuous period of 52 contribution weeks . . .' (SI 1979, No. 591, reg. 119(2)).

A contribution week is a period of seven days beginning with midnight between Saturday and Sunday (SI 1979, No. 591, reg. 1) and the period of fifty-two such weeks referred to begins at the start of the contribution week following a person's last entry into Great Britain (SI 1979, No. 591, reg. 119(2)).

EXAMPLE 3(C)
Pak-lok, a Malay accountant who works mainly in Kuala Lumpur for his Malay employers, is sent to Great Britain for a nine-month period of service in an associated British company. Shortly after his return to Malaysia his presence is again required in Britain and he spends a further four months here. Although he falls to be categorised as an employed earner for each period, he is not liable to pay primary Class 1

contributions as he is neither ordinarily resident here nor employed here for a *continuous* period of fifty-two or more weeks.

Where a person of any class to which the modified rule applies comes to Great Britain from another EEC country or a country with which Great Britain has a reciprocal agreement, the modified rule may be further modified (see **3.12** and **3.13** post).

3.08   Self-employment in Great Britain

The conditions as to residence and presence with respect to a self-employed earner's liability to pay Class 2 contributions are stated by reg. 119(1)(d) to be:

'. . . that the self-employed earner is ordinarily resident in Great Britain or . . . that before the period in respect of which . . . contributions are to be paid he has been resident for . . . at least 26 out of the immediately preceding 52 contribution weeks . . .'

though such an earner may pay Class 2 contributions, if he wishes to do so, for any contribution week during which he is merely 'present' in Great Britain (reg. 119(1)(c)).

EXAMPLE 3(D)
Bill and Ben are in partnership and run a pottery in Staffordshire. Bill goes abroad for a year while Ben looks after the business in Great Britain. As Bill has not ceased to be 'ordinarily resident' he continues to be liable to pay Class 2 contributions.

EXAMPLE 3(E)
Jacques arrives in Great Britain from France on 1 September 1981. He takes a short lease on a flat (intending to return to France within a year or two) and starts up in business as a general tradesman. As he is not 'ordinarily resident', the first week for which he can possibly be liable to pay a Class 2 contribution is that ending on 13 March 1982 for not until then will he have been resident for twenty-six out of the immediately preceding fifty-two weeks. He is, however, entitled to pay Class 2 contributions, if he so wishes, from the day he begins to trade. It should be noted that if Jacques had already been resident (and not merely present) in Great Britain at any time during the period from 1 September 1980, the date of his earliest liability to pay contributions will be advanced by one week for each week of previous residence.

3.09   Overseas employment

Any person who, while remaining ordinarily resident in Great Britain, begins a period of gainful employment overseas may find himself still liable to pay primary Class 1 contributions in respect of earnings from his new employment. This will be so whenever the person concerned is resident in Great Britain immediately before taking up his overseas employment and his overseas employer has a 'place of business' here. In those circumstances a person will fall to be treated as an employed earner (even though under the Act he is not such an earner) and will be liable to pay primary Class 1 contributions on his earnings for the period of fifty-two contribution weeks (see **3.06** ante) beginning with that in which his overseas employment commences, to the same extent that such contributions would be payable were his employment in Great Britain (reg. 120(1) and (2)).

This and the other regulations described in this section are made under SSA 1975, s. 131 whereby the Secretary of State is empowered to modify the Act in its application to persons who are or have been outside Great Britain at any prescribed time or in any prescribed circumstances, and to treat a person as being an employed earner even though his employment is outside Great Britain.

In practical terms, reg. 120(1) and (2) merely operates so as to extend (for their own protection) the liability of persons who, though going abroad for temporary (even if substantial) periods of duty, remain on a British payroll. Anyone who directly obtains employment overseas and is placed on an overseas payroll will, even though his employer may have a place of business in Great Britain, be relieved of any liability to pay contributions for, in most such cases, the 'residence' link will have been broken. Indeed, the absence of any of the circumstantial factors mentioned will be sufficient to snap the chain of continued liability.

EXAMPLE 3(F)

Albert, who works for the UK branch of an Australian company, feels he has no future in Great Britain. He requests and obtains a transfer to the head office in Sydney, buys a house there, moves there with his family, severs all his ties here and vows never to return. Even though his new employer has a branch in Great Britain and even though Albert was resident here immediately before taking up employment in Australia, he will not be liable to pay primary Class 1 contributions as he has ceased to be 'ordinarily resident' in Great Britain.

A 'place of business' is regarded by the DHSS as meaning any place from which an employer can, as of right, conduct his business, or from which his agent has power to conduct business on his own behalf. The registered office of a limited company will not necessarily be such a place of business (DHSS Leaflet NI132).

If, during the fifty-two week liability period described above, a person changes his employment for other employment abroad, his liability to pay primary Class 1 contributions will cease with the last payment of earnings made to him by his first employer abroad (DHSS Leaflet NI132).

Where a fifty-two week liability to pay primary Class 1 contributions arises as described, those weeks will include any weeks of sickness or leave for which the person employed abroad is remunerated. Weeks or unpaid leave and weeks of temporary duty in Great Britain are not included, however; though, by concession, where a period of temporary duty in the UK extends over no more than twenty-six weeks and that period of duty plus the number of reckonable weeks already spent abroad together exceed fifty-two weeks, any remaining period of liability abroad will be cancelled (**DHSS** Leaflet NI132).

If, once his initial fifty-two week period of liability has come to an end, a person returns to Great Britain on paid leave or temporary duty for a period in excess of twenty-six weeks, a further period of liability to primary Class 1 contributions will arise and will consist of the excessive weeks of paid leave (or the whole of any period of temporary duty) plus a further fifty-two weeks commencing with the week in which the person resumes his duties abroad (**DHSS** Leaflet NI132).

The regulations described above in relation to persons entering periods of employment overseas may be modified where the country of employment is another EEC member state (see **3.12** post) or a country to which a reciprocal agreement applies (see **3.13** post).

3.10   Overseas self-employment

Any person leaving Great Britain and becoming self-employed overseas may, in certain circumstances, pay Class 2 contributions if he so wishes. There is, however, no liability for him to do so. The conditions for voluntary payment are that, immediately before leaving Great Britain, the person was ordinarily either an employed earner or a self-employed earner and that he has, at some time, been resident here for a continuous period of at least three years or has, in each of any three years, paid contributions yielding an earnings factor (see **5.26** post) at least equivalent to fifty-two times the appropriate lower earnings limit (see **5.15** post) (reg. 121(1)(2) and (3)).

There is automatic exception from liability for Class 4 contributions for anyone who is not resident in the United Kingdom for income tax purposes in a year of assessment (SI 1979, No. 591, reg. 58(b)).

3.11   The continental shelf

For the purposes of s. 132 of the Act and SI 1979, No. 591, reg. 85 (each of which relates to employment in continental shelf operations and is discussed at **7.21** post), any area designated under s. 1(7) of the Continental Shelf Act 1964 is to be regarded as being in Great Britain (reg. 85(2)).

3.12   The European Economic Community (EEC)

So far as social security matters are concerned, the EEC presently consists of Belgium, Denmark, France (including Corsica), the Federal Republic of Germany, Gibraltar, Greece, the Irish Republic, Italy (including Sardinia),

Luxembourg, the Netherlands, and the United Kingdom of Great Britain and Northern Ireland. Between Great Britain and each of the other member states (apart from, at the present time, Greece) there are reciprocal agreements which relate to social security and these, along with EEC Regulations No. 1408/71 and 574/72 (as amended), bear on social security matters so far as persons moving between member states are concerned.

The general rule described at **3.06** ante whereby, under reg. 119(1)(a), anyone who becomes present or resident (though not necessarily ordinarily resident) in Great Britain is liable to pay primary Class 1 contributions in respect of earnings from an employed earner's employment, is, for instance, modified where the person has been sent here by an employer in another EEC state. So long as the tour of duty is not expected to last for a period in excess of twelve months and the person has not been sent to replace another person whose tour of duty is at an end, no liability to pay primary Class 1 contributions will arise. The person will continue to be insured in the country from which he has been sent and either he or his employer's representative in Great Britain should have obtained a certificate E101 in confirmation of this. In the event of the term of duty in Great Britain unexpectedly exceeding twelve months, the arrangement may continue for up to a further twelve months if an extension is approved by the DHSS prior to the expiry of the first period of exemption (DHSS Leaflet SA29).

Similarly (and in conformity with reg. 120 described at **3.09** ante), where a person who is ordinarily resident in Great Britain is sent to work in another EEC member state for a period of duty which is not expected to exceed twelve months, he will, unless he is sent to replace a person whose period of duty is at an end, continue to be liable to pay primary Class 1 contributions under the British social security scheme. This will be so even where the period overseas is not preceded by a period of employment in Great Britain by the employer concerned, provided that employer continues to operate similar businesses in both Great Britain and the other member state. A certificate E101 confirming the continued liability must be obtained by the person or his employer from the DHSS Overseas Branch at Newcastle upon Tyne, NE98 1YX and, in the event of the period of duty abroad unexpectedly exceeding twelve months, application for an extension of the arrangement for a further period of up to twelve months may be made to that address on form E102 (DHSS Leaflet SA29).

A special rule applies to travelling or flying personnel who are employed in two or more EEC states by an employer whose business involves the carriage of goods or passengers by road, rail, air or inland waterway. If the person in question is ordinarily resident in Great Britain and mainly employed here or if his employer's main office is in Great Britain or if the employer has only a branch office or permanent agency in Great Britain but the person is employed by that branch or agency, then (but not otherwise) will the person be liable to pay primary Class 1 contributions on his earnings under the British scheme (DHSS Leaflet SA29).

Persons employed in two or more EEC states in circumstances other than those described in the immediately preceding paragraph are also liable to pay primary Class 1 contributions on their earnings if they are either ordinarily resident in Great Britain and are either employed in Great Britain as well as other states or employed by several employers based in different EEC states or though not ordinarily resident in any EEC state in which they are employed, have their employer in Great Britain (DHSS Leaflet SA29).

3.13   Reciprocal agreement countries

Great Britain has reciprocal agreements concerning social security matters with various countries other than those which are members of the EEC. These agreements provide, so far as possible, that arrangements similar to those between Great Britain and other EEC states shall apply to persons taking up temporary employment here or abroad. The agreements themselves vary considerably, however, and, before it can be established whether or not there is a continuing liability to Class 1 contributions under the terms of any particular one, it is necessary to look not only at the status of the person being sent overseas and his expected term of duty in the reciprocal agreement country, but also at the status of his UK employer. Appendix 10 provides a quick guide in this connection, but it is essential to consult the reciprocal agreements themselves in specific cases. It should be noted that the term of continuing liability stated in Appendix 10 may (on application by the employer before the expiry of the stated term) be extended in most cases if this is desirable, though, so far as Jersey, Guernsey, Spain and Portugal are concerned, no extension beyond an additional year will be countenanced.

3.14   Secondary contributors

The residence conditions under which a secondary contributor's liability to pay secondary Class 1 contributions will arise are that he

> '. . . is resident or present in Great Britain when such contributions become payable or then has a place of business in Great Britain . . .' (SI 1979, No. 591, reg. 119(1)(b)).

The DHSS interpretation of the term 'place of business' has been stated at **3.09** ante.

It should be noted that, where an employed earner (or anyone who falls to be treated as such) is excepted from liability to pay primary Class 1 contributions for fifty-two weeks as described in the foregoing sections, the secondary contributor is similarly relieved of any liability (SI 1979, No. 591, reg. 119(2) and (3)). A secondary contributor may, however, if he wishes, pay contributions where he has no legal obligation to do so (SI 1979, No. 591, reg. 119(1)(b)).

3.15 Voluntary contributors

The residence condition whereby a person will become entitled to pay Class 3 contributions for any year is that the person is

> '. . . resident in Great Britain during the course of that year' (SI 1979, No. 591, reg. 119(1)(e))

or that he is working overseas in circumstances which give, or have given, rise to a continued Class 1 liability (see **3.09** ante) (SI 1979, No. 591, reg. 120(2)(b)). A person who (though not necessarily becoming self-employed overseas) meets the conditions as to previous residence or contribution record as described in **3.10** ante is also entitled to pay Class 3 contributions for any year during which he is outside Great Britain (SI 1979, No. 591, reg. 121(1)(b)).

AGE

3.16 The working life

Having returned to the pool of non-liability all such persons as do not fulfil the requirements of residence and presence described in the foregoing sections of this chapter, the Act now subjects those who remain in the net to the test of age. The contributory scheme is built around a person's working life and the parameters of this are generally set by, on the one hand, leaving school and, on the other, retirement.

3.17 The lower age limit

The Act begins by providing under s. 4(2)(a) (as amended by the Education (School Leaving Dates) Act 1976, s. 2(4)) that a liability to primary and secondary Class 1 contributions is only to arise where earnings are paid to an employed earner who is 'over the age of sixteen' and extends this same age limitation to any self-employed earner's liability to pay Class 2 contributions (SSA 1975, s. 7(1)). The entitlement of earners and others to pay Class 3 contributions is similarly restricted (SSA 1975, s. 8(1)) and, as regards Class 4 contributions (which are linked to the tax system and charged for years of assessment) it is provided that any person who, at the beginning of the year of assessment, is under the age of sixteen may, if he wishes, claim exception from liability to pay such contributions (SI 1979, No. 591, reg. 60(6)).

It should be noted that, while the age of 16 has been deliberately selected with the basic school-leaving age in mind, the fact that a person may remain at school after attaining that age will not relieve such a person of a liability to pay contributions where he becomes an employed or a self-employed earner (by reason of gainful week-end, evening or vacational employment, for example) during the time he so continues his education.

3.18   The upper age limit

At the other end of the age-scale, any self-employed earner who 'attains pensionable age' is relieved of liability to pay Class 2 contributions (SSPA 1975, s. 4(2)) and any employed earner is similarly relieved of any liability to pay primary Class 1 contributions on all earnings properly paid on or after the relevant date, even if they relate to a period before (SSPA 1975, s. 4(1); SI 1979, No. 591, reg. 20). Likewise, there is no entitlement to pay Class 3 contributions in respect of the year in which pensionable age is attained, nor any year following (SI 1979, No. 591, reg. 28(1)(e)); and any person who, at the beginning of a year of assessment is 'over pensionable age' is excepted from liability for Class 4 contributions by regulations made under SSA 1975, ss. 9(7)(a) and 9(8)(b) (SI 1979, No. 591, reg. 58).

'Pensionable age' is, in the case of a man, sixty-five; in the case of a woman, sixty (SSA 1975, Sch. 20), and it should be noted that a person is deemed to attain a given age at the commencement of the relevant anniversary of the date of his birth (Family Law Reform Act 1969, s. 9(1)).

It will be observed that the cessation of liability described above is to no extent conditional upon actual retirement taking place. Prior to 6 April 1978, however, actual retirement 'from regular employment' was required except where the person concerned did not qualify for a category A retirement pension or was a woman over sixty years of age who, at the date of her sixtieth birthday, was married to that husband (and had been so before her fifty-fifth birthday) but was unable to satisfy the contribution requirements for a category A retirement pension (SSA 1975, s. 6 now repealed). Under the repealed provisions, retirement was deemed to take place at seventy (sixty-five for a woman) even where regular employment continued (SSA 1975, s. 27(5) now repealed).

3.19   Age exemption

Where a person who has attained retirement age continues in, or takes up, employment as an employed earner, it will be necessary for him to obtain a certificate of age exemption, CF384, as evidence to his employer of his non-liability to pay primary Class 1 contributions. Prior to 5 April 1981, such certificates were referenced CF381 and known as certificates of non-liability. Application for a CF384 should be made to the local DHSS office.

It should be noted that age exemption from liability extends no further than the employed earner himself. The secondary contributor continues to be liable to pay contributions on the employed earner's earnings.

MARITAL STATUS

3.20   Reduced rate elections

It must be said at the outset that marital status is not, per se, a relevant factor in determining whether or not any employed or self-employed earner who does not fall to be relieved of contributory liability on the grounds of non-residence or age should be relieved of such liability or be eligible for its reduction. Until 11 May 1977 (SI 1979, No. 591, reg. 100(4)), however, it was open to certain married women and widows to elect that this should be so, and many such elections continue in force, subject to regulations contained in SI 1979, No. 591 and made under SSA 1975, s. 130(1) and SSPA 1975, s. 3.

The women to whom the making of such an election was open were those who, on 6 April 1977, were married or were widows entitled to either a widow's benefit under the social security scheme (ie widowed mother's allowance, widow's pension or age-related widow's pension) or an industrial or war widow's pension at a rate equivalent to, or greater than, the standard rate of basic widow's pension (£29.60 per week from 23 November 1981) (SI 1979, No. 591, reg. 100(1) and (8)).

The effect of the election was (and is, where still in force) to relieve its maker of liability to pay Class 2 contributions; to convert any liability to pay primary Class 1 contributions at standard rate into a liability to pay such contributions at a reduced rate (SI 1979, No. 591, reg. 100(1)); and to render the woman concerned almost completely dependent for benefit on her husband's contribution record. It also precluded (and, where still in force, precludes) her from paying Class 3 contributions (SI 1979, No. 591, reg. 105); being credited with contributions during periods of sickness or unemployment; and obtaining 'home responsibilities protection' of basic pension (DHSS Leaflet NI1). Class 4 liability was and is unaffected.

Such elections were no 'box-ticking' formality but had to be in writing to the Secretary of State (SI 1979, No. 591, reg. 100(5)), on a form CF9 supported by a marriage certificate and other relevant documentation (SI 1979, No. 591, reg. 100(7)). They resulted in the issue of certificates of election (CF383) (SI 1979, No. 591, reg. 106(1)) which, in the event of their holders becoming employed earners, had to be handed to their secondary contributors as the authority for the deduction of primary Class 1 contributions from earnings at a reduced rate (SI 1979, No. 591, reg. 106(3)). It is most unlikely, therefore, that any woman who does not know whether or not she has such an election in force has ever made such an election.

Elections similar to those described above but made under reg. 91 or reg. 94 of the Social Security (Contributions) Regulations 1975 (and evidenced by certificates of reduced liability, CF380A) were continued under current regulations (SI 1979, No. 591, reg. 102), as were elections made, or deemed to have been made, prior to 6 April 1975 under the old National Insurance scheme (SI 1979, No. 591, reg. 108).

3.21 Cessation of elections

Any election made on or before 11 May 1977 remains effective until one or other of several possible events takes place.

The first of these is a woman ceasing to be married other than by reason of her husband dying (SI 1979, No. 591, reg. 101(1)(a)). This covers both divorce and annulment and necessitates immediate cancellation of the certificate of reduced liability, which should be returned to the local DHSS office.

The second terminating event is the ending of the year in which a woman ceases to be a widow who fulfills the conditions as regards entitlement to widow's benefit etc as set out in **3.20** ante (SI 1979, No. 591, reg. 101(1)(b)). If, however, a woman in this situation has remarried or again become a qualifying widow before the end of the year, her election continues in force (unless, of course, some other terminating event befalls her) (SI 1979, No. 591, reg. 101(2)).

The third terminating event is the ending of any two consecutive years beginning on or after 6 April 1978 in which a woman has no earnings on which primary Class 1 contributions are payable and in which she is at no time a self-employed earner (SI 1979, No. 591, reg. 101(1)(c)). This is known as the 'two year test'. The fact that a woman may have earnings from an employed earner's employment during the two years will not prevent the terminating event taking place if those earnings at no time exceed the lower earnings limit.

The fourth terminating event is the ending of a year in which notice of revocation is given, unless the revocation has been cancelled before the end of the year (SI 1979, No. 591, reg. 101(1)(d)). Revocation is to be by notice in writing to the Secretary of State (SI 1979, No. 591, reg. 100(5)) but may be effected at any time simply by returning the certificate of reduced liability to the local DHSS office and completing another form CF9 (SI 1979, No. 591, reg. 99(2) and (3)). It must, however, extend to both Class 1 and Class 2 contributions (SI 1979, No. 591, reg. 100(2)). A revocation may itself be cancelled by submitting a further CF9 to the DHSS before the end of the contribution year in which the notice of revocation is given (SI 1979, No. 591, reg. 100(6)).

The fifth and final terminating event is the ending of a year in which a payment of a standard rate primary contribution is made in the erroneous belief that such contributions were due and the woman concerned wishes to pay standard rate contributions (SI 1979, No. 591, reg. 101(1)(d)).

3.22   Newly-widowed women

Where a woman who, at 6 April 1977, was married (or was then a widow but has since remarried) becomes (or again becomes) a widow and an election as described above is still in force at the time of her bereavement, that election will continue to be effective until the end of a certain prescribed period (SI 1979, No. 591, reg. 102(1)). Where the husband's death occurs before 1 October in a year, the prescribed period is the period to the end of that year (SI 1979, No. 591, reg. 103(2)(b)(i)). Where, however, the husband's death occurs after 30 September in a year, the prescribed period is the end of the year next following that year (SI 1979, No. 591, reg. 103(2)(b)(ii)).

EXAMPLE 3(G)

Gert and Daisy both have reduced rate elections in force and are widowed within a few days of each other. Gert's husband dies on 28 September 1981; Daisy's husband dies on 3 October 1981. Gert's election would continue to be effective only until 5 April 1982 but Daisy's election will continue in force until 5 April 1983.

The prescribed period will be extended if, at the date when the prescribed period would otherwise end, a claim or application for any widow's benefit under the social security scheme (ie widowed mother's allowance, widow's pension or age-related widow's pension) or an industrial or war widow's pension at a rate equivalent to, or greater than, the standard rate of basic widow's pension (currently £29.60 per week) made by or on behalf of the widow within 182 days of her husband's death, is still pending. Such extension will be to the end of the year in which the claim or application is determined (SI 1979, No. 591, reg. 103(3)).

Where, at the end of the prescribed period (or any extension made to it) a woman is a qualifying widow or has remarried, her election will continue to be effective unless any of the last three terminating events described in **3.21** ante occurs (SI 1979, No. 591, reg. 103(4)).

3.23 The revocation option

From time to time the question arises as to whether a woman who has an election in force should revoke it, despite the fact that no terminating event has taken place nor is likely to do so. No definitive answer can be given because of the many variable factors present in each individual case, all of which will be of some relevance: the amount and class of contributions which have been paid by the woman and her husband; whether a need for the woman to claim sickness benefit, maternity allowance, unemployment benefit or invalidity benefit in her own right is likely to arise; whether, if the woman is a member of a contracted-out occupational pension scheme, she wishes her pension under that scheme to be inflation-proofed by the state scheme; whether the woman still has time to contribute towards a worthwhile pension in her own right; whether she will be able to benefit from 'home responsibilities protection' of her pension rights; the respective ages of herself and husband; and whether she is prepared, or can afford, to pay (currently) at least £85 per annum more in contributions. Reduced contributions carry no entitlement to benefit, and the only contributory benefits to which a woman is entitled by virtue of her husband's contributions are maternity grant (which is, in any case, non-contributory as regards births on or after 4 July 1982), a 60% basic pension once her husband retires (at age sixty-five or over) if she is then sixty or more years of age, death grant, widow's benefit and child's special allowance.

What may be said, in general terms, is that any woman over the age of forty who is younger than her husband and has not established a substantial contribution record prior to making her election is unlikely to gain from its revocation, but that any woman under forty years of age who is older than her husband and has paid contributions prior to her election may well find revocation advantageous if she intends to continue in employment.

Chapter 4

Identification of earnings

4.01 Introduction

In the two preceding chapters we have considered the catch of earners which the Social Security Act lands by the sweep of its s. 1 net and the way in which it segregates the employed and the self-employed. We have seen, too, how, by applying criteria of residence, age and marital status, it identifies and releases certain elements in each group and concedes to others a restricted level or term of liability. We must now, therefore, look at the way in which the Act quantifies the earnings of those who remain, as all further restriction of liability is directly related to the level of such earnings.

Earnings are to be defined (see **2.02** ante) as any remuneration or profit derived from any trade, business, profession, office or vocation (SSA 1975, s. 3(1) and Sch. 20). The quantum of such earnings is, however, to be calculated or estimated in such manner or on such basis as is prescribed by regulation (SSA 1975, s. 3(1)) and regulations may also prescribe that certain payments are to be disregarded or deducted in performing the calculation (SSA 1975, s. 3(3)). In practical terms, of course, the earnings of an employed earner and those of a self-employed earner are quite dissimilar in both nature and composition. Accordingly, separately applicable regulations have been introduced for each class and those relating to the earnings of an employed earner will first be considered.

EMPLOYED EARNERS' EARNINGS

4.02 Gross pay

The starting point for any calculation of an employed earner's earnings is stated by SI 1979, No. 591, reg. 18:

> '. . . the amount of a person's earnings shall . . . be calculated on the basis of that person's gross earnings from the employment . . . concerned.'

This is not necessarily as straightforward as it may at first appear, largely because of the false equation that is often drawn between gross earnings as specified in the regulation quoted and gross earnings for income tax purposes under the PAYE scheme. Despite the fact that the explanatory booklets of both schemes consistently refer to 'gross pay' (Employer's Guide to PAYE (P7), April 1981, para. 45; Employer's Guide to National Insurance Contributions (NP15),

January 1980, para. 19), the term does not embrace identical concepts. Gross pay for PAYE scheme purposes is to be identified with

'. . . any payment of, or on account of, any income assessable to income tax under Schedule E' (Income and Corporation Taxes Act (ICTA) 1970, s. 204);

such income to be

'. . . income . . . after the deduction of allowable superannuation contributions' (Income Tax (Employments) Regulations 1973, SI 1973, No. 334, reg. 2(1)).

Gross pay for the purposes of the social security earnings-related contributions scheme, however, is to be identified with

'. . . earnings paid to or for the benefit of an earner in respect of an employed earner's employment (SI 1979, No. 591, reg. 1(2)),

but only in so far as those earnings are not 'excluded from the computation' by the operation of SI 1979, No. 591, reg. 19.

4.03   Advances and payments on account

A comparison of these various provisions and regulations will reveal, firstly, that gross pay for PAYE purposes includes payments on account of income:

'. . . payments in advance or on account (including drawings in advance or on account of director's remuneration) should be entered in the pay column of the Deductions Working Sheet for the week or month in which the advance or payment on account was made . . .' (Employer's Guide to PAYE (P7), April 1981, para. 61).

Such payments are not, however, gross pay for earnings-related contribution purposes and may not be treated as such. In the case of directors' fees, for instance, a liability for contributions

'. . . arises only when the directors' fees are voted unconditionally by the company in general meeting' (DHSS Leaflet NI35, April 1981)

for not until then is there an entitlement to the fees, as of right, by the directors concerned.

EXAMPLE 4(A)

On 5 April 1981, Arthur is appointed to the office of director of B Ltd. He is not, however, under a contract of service to the company. During 1981–82 he draws a 'salary' of £700 per month (£8,400 in total) which is voted to him by the company in general meeting in May 1982 along with a 'bonus' of £1,600. From 5 April 1982 his 'salary' is increased to £800 per month though nothing has, as yet, been voted to him for 1982–83. For taxation purposes, his gross pay is £700 per month throughout 1981–82, £800 in April 1982, £2,400 (ie £800 + £1,600) in May 1982 and £800 for each of the ten remaining months in 1982–83. For earnings-related Class 1 contribution purposes, however, his gross pay is nil for 1981–82 and £10,000 (ie £8,400 + £1,600) for 1982–83. If the £800 per month Arthur is drawing during 1982–83 is ultimately voted to him at some time during 1983–84, it will then (but not until then) become gross pay for social security purposes.

This applies not only to directors but to any employed earner who receives 'subs' or other advance payments on account of his regular remuneration. Where, however, an employed earner's regular remuneration is, as a term of his employment, 'in advance', the amounts are to be treated as gross earnings paid at the time of payment (DHSS Leaflet NP15, para. 25).

Payments on account of earnings which have already been assessed for earnings-related contribution purposes (such as drawings against fees previously voted and included in gross pay) do not, of course, fall to be included in gross pay a second time (SI 1979, No. 591, reg. 19(1)(a)).

4.04 Superannuation contributions and overseas earnings

Further comparison of the provisions detailed in **4.02** ante will reveal that gross pay for PAYE scheme purposes is, in fact, net pay after allowable superannuation contributions made within the terms of the Income and Corporation Taxes Act 1970, s. 208(1) have been deducted. This 'net pay arrangement' is, on application, extended to remuneration which includes or consists of overseas earnings qualifying for Finance Act 1977, s. 31 relief of 25% (IR Statement A17, 3 August 1977). In neither case, however, can the reduction of the true gross pay be admitted for social security contribution purposes.

EXAMPLE 4(B)

Brian's salary for the month of May 1982 is £660 gross under his contract of service with C Ltd. His approved superannuation contributions for the month are £50 and, during the month, he has been in France on business for four of his twenty-two working days. The tax office has approved a net pay arrangement with regard to Brian's overseas earnings. Accordingly, Brian's gross pay for PAYE purposes in May is £580, viz:

	£	£
Contractual salary		660
less:		
Overseas earnings relief: 25% × (4/22 × £660)	30	
Superannuation contributions	50	
		80
Gross pay		580

His gross pay for earnings-related Class 1 contributions is, however, the full £660.

4.05   Holiday pay

Holiday pay is part of earnings and generally falls to be included in gross pay when paid. There are two exceptions to this general rule, however. The first arises where holiday pay is directly or indirectly derived from (or reimbursed out of) a central fund to which a number of employers contribute but do not manage or control. Such schemes are particularly widespread in the building and civil engineering, electrical contracting and heating, ventilating and domestic engineering industries, and pay arising under them is to be excluded from gross pay (SI 1979, No. 591, reg. 19(1)(b)) as are amounts expended in the purchase of the special stamps which are used to build up entitlement under such schemes (DHSS Leaflet NP15, para. 22(d)). Holiday pay provided by a participating employer for any employed earners (eg permanent staff) not within the scope of the scheme is, of course, gross pay according to the normal rules (DHSS Leaflet NP15, para. 22(d)). For tax purposes, such pay has, from 1 January 1982, been subject to a basic rate deduction (Income Tax (Holiday Pay) Regulations 1981, No. 1648).

The second exception arises when an employer operates a holiday credit scheme under which, with the employed earner's consent, he sets aside from earnings to which an employed earner has an underlying present right, amounts to be paid in a lump sum when that earner eventually takes his holidays. In such cases, the sums set aside should be included in gross pay at the time when they are placed to the employed earner's credit. This is in conformity with the treatment of payments on account described at the end of section **4.03** ante. Where, however, the employed earner's right to the accrued amount is restricted to such time as he takes his holiday, the amounts set aside should be excluded from gross pay until that time arrives (DHSS Leaflet NP15, para. 104(b)).

The treatment of holiday pay described above is parallel to that prescribed for holiday pay under the PAYE scheme (IR Booklet P7, para. 55).

4.06   Gratuities and offerings

Where gratuities, tips, offerings or 'service charges' are allocated or paid, directly or indirectly, to an employed earner by his employer, such amounts are earnings and must be included in gross pay for both tax and earnings-related contribution purposes. Where, however, such amounts are paid to an employed earner either directly or through a tronc (ie pooling scheme) operated independently of the employer (with a paying point separate from the employer's payroll), the amounts are to be disregarded for earnings-related contribution purposes (though, if paid through a tronc, they will be subject to PAYE tax deductions at the hands of the troncmaster) (SI 1979, No. 591, reg. 119(1)(c); DHSS Leaflet NP15, paras. 21(i) and 22(e); DHSS Leaflet NI232; IR Booklet P7, para. 58).

Offerings made to, and received directly by, a minister of religion are, provided they do not form part of his stipend or salary, not to be regarded as earnings for social security purposes (though they may be so regarded for tax purposes). They are not, therefore, to be included in gross pay when calculating earnings-related contributions (DHSS Leaflet NP21). Reference should be made to **4.11** and **7.07** post.

4.07 Benefits in kind

Income chargeable to tax under Schedule E is, by definition, wider than earnings to be taken into account under the social security scheme. The former includes 'perquisites' (ICTA 1970, s. 183(1)) whereas the latter does not, so that

> 'any payment in kind or by way of the provision of board or lodging or of services or other facilities' (SI 1979, No. 591, reg. 119(1)(d))

is to be disregarded for earnings-related contribution purposes.

Cash payments made in lieu of benefits in kind cannot be so disregarded, however, and are part of gross pay (DHSS Leaflet NP15, para. 21(h)).

Various benefits in kind provided to 'lower-paid' employees who are not directors are, in practice, disregarded for tax purposes also, and these include the private use of a motor vehicle (provided there is some business use), board and lodgings, private sickness insurance cover (after 5 April 1982), interest-free loans, outings, luncheon vouchers of up to fifteen pence per day, and the private use of assets placed at the employee's disposal. Certain other benefits do fall to be taxed even in the hands of such employees, however, but will, under the regulation quoted above, be disregarded from a Class 1 liability point of view. Such benefits are the provision of a company house (unless it is needed for the purposes of the employment), clothing, private sickness insurance premiums (until 5 April 1982), share options, cash vouchers, and the use of credit cards (after 5 April 1982). Directors and higher paid employees are, of course, liable to tax on virtually all of the benefits mentioned but they too will be free of any liability to earnings-related contributions in respect of such benefits. It will be apparent, therefore, that remuneration by way of benefits holds distinct advantages over remuneration by way of salary from the contribution point of view of both an employed earner and his employer.

4.08 Payments to or by trustees

Where a payment to which an employed earner is entitled is, instead, paid to trustees (eg in connection with a profit-sharing scheme or an insured sick pay scheme) at their discretion or as the performance of a duty arising under the trust, that payment is to be disregarded in calculating the employed earner's earnings for contribution purposes. Likewise, any payment to an employed earner by trustees exercising discretion or performing duties arising under the trust is also to be disregarded (SI 1979, No. 591, reg. 19(1)(e)).

4.09 Payments under SI 1973, No. 1854, reg. 3(2)(e)

Certain payments of earnings which an employer is required by the

Occupational Pension Schemes (Recognition of Schemes) (No. 2) Regulations 1973, reg. 3(2)(e) to make in connection with the approval of certain retirement annuity contracts and trust schemes are to be excluded from gross pay for earnings-related contribution purposes (SI 1979, No. 591, reg. 19(1)(f)).

4.10   Pensions

Any payment by way of a pension is to be disregarded for earnings-related contribution purposes, even though it may be part of gross pay for taxation purposes (SI 1979, No. 591, reg. 19(1)(g)). The term 'pension' is, of course, confined to an allowance made to someone who has either retired, been disabled, reached old age, been widowed or been orphaned. It cannot relate to present services.

4.11   Fees receivable by ministers of religion

Any fees which are paid directly to a minister of religion and which do not form part of his stipend or salary (eg wedding, baptism and funeral fees) are to be disregarded for earnings-related contribution purposes (SI 1979, No. 591, reg. 19(1)(h)). Ministers of religion are a special class of earner and are dealt with at **7.07** post.

4.12   Travelling expenses

Although specific and distinct payments of (or contributions towards) expenses actually incurred by an employed earner in carrying out the duties of his employment are to be excluded from gross pay for earnings-related contribution purposes (SI 1979, No. 591, reg. 19(4)(b)), payments in respect of the cost of travelling between his home and his normal place of employment are not (DHSS Leaflet NP15, para. 21(j)). An exception to this rule arises, however, where the employed earner is a disabled person for whom training or employment facilities are provided under the Disabled Persons (Employment) Act 1944, s. 15 (ie sheltered workshops). Payment of (or contributions towards) such a person's costs of travel in availing himself of the facilities provided is not to be included as earnings for contribution purposes (SI 1979, No. 591, reg. 19(1)(i)) despite the fact that it may be travel between home and place of business.

4.13   Profit-sharing schemes

Under the provisions of the Finance Act 1978, Pt. III, Chap. III, a company is enabled to establish a trust which, for the benefit of directors and employees, acquires ordinary shares in the company (or a related company) and holds them for the participants to whom it ultimately transfers them. Payments by way of, or derived from, shares appropriated under such a scheme are not to be regarded as earnings for contribution purposes (SI 1979, No. 591, reg. 19(1)(j)).

4.14 Value added tax

Where an employed earner supplies vatable goods or services to his employer and his remuneration includes VAT on those goods or services (under the provisions of the Finance Act 1972, s. 45(4), for example), the VAT element of earnings paid is to be excluded in arriving at the gross pay for earnings-related contribution purposes (SI 1979, No. 591, reg. 19(2)).

EXAMPLE 4(C)

Charles, a practicing solicitor is appointed to the board of D Ltd, a client company. On 31 May 1982, fees of £2,000 are voted to him. Charles is VAT registered and his services to the company are a supply. C Ltd must, therefore, pay Charles £2,000 + VAT £300. Class 1 contributions are, however, to be calculated on only £2,000.

4.15 Social security benefits

Where an employed earner is entitled to sickness benefit, invalidity benefit, maternity allowance or injury benefit but, under a DHSS-approved arrangement made between him (or her) and his (or her) employer, undertakes not to claim the benefit and, in consequence, receives unabated pay, the amount of benefit foregone is to be excluded from gross pay for the purpose of calculating earnings-related contributions (SI 1979, No. 591, reg. 19(3)). Similarly, where an employed earner does obtain one of the benefits mentioned but hands it over to the employer and, in return, receives unabated pay, the amount of the benefit is to be excluded from gross pay for Class 1 contribution purposes (DHSS Leaflet NP15, para. 26). The net amount of pay so arrived at is to be used for PAYE purposes also (IR Booklet P7, para. 54).

If the proposals contained in the Social Security and Housing Benefits Bill (presently before Parliament) become law, short-term sickness benefit will cease to be payable from 6 April 1983 and employers will be legally obliged to provide sick pay to their employees during the first eight weeks of illness. Employees earning £60 per week or more will receive £37 per week and others will receive £25 per week. Employers will be able to recover from their contribution remittances the payments made, but the sick pay will be treated in the same way as other earnings for contribution purposes and will thus carry an irrecoupable primary and secondary Class 1 liability.

4.16 Leaving payments

Any regular payment of earnings made to an employed earner (under pensionable age) after he has left his employment will still fall to be treated as gross pay for earnings-related contribution purposes whether, at the time of payment, he is then receiving pay from a new employer or not (DHSS Leaflet NP15, para. 33). So also will any additional payment such as deferred bonus, pay arrears from a back-dated pay increase or an accrued holiday pay entitlement (DHSS Leaflet NP15, para. 35). Redundancy pay does not, however, form part of earnings (SI 1979, No. 591, reg. 19(4)(a)) and neither do payments in lieu of notice (DHSS leaflet NP15, para. 22(h)). Compensation payments for loss of office and ex gratia payments will also fall to be disregarded as there is no contractual right to their receipt.

4.17   Sick pay

Pay which continues while an employed earner is sick (or otherwise absent from work) is gross pay for both tax and social security purposes (subject to reduction by the amount of any social security benefits foregone or passed to the employer (see **4.15** ante) (DHSS Leaflet NP15, para. 21(e)). Where, however, sick pay is provided by means of insurance, such pay will not be part of earnings if the employed earner is the beneficiary under the policy (even though the employer may have paid the premiums) or the payment is made through a properly constituted trust (see **4.08** ante) or the payment relates to a period after the contract of service has ended (ill-health pension payments, for example). Where the contract of service has not ended, however, and the employer is the beneficiary under the policy, sick pay is part of gross pay in accordance with the normal rule (DHSS Leaflet NP15, para. 23). The Finance Act 1981, s. 30, ensures that sick pay under an insurance scheme will be taxable for 1982–83 (in the case of schemes entered into before 4 June 1981) or 1983–84 (in the case of schemes entered into after 4 June 1981) and future years, even where the employed earner is the beneficiary and the payments are not earnings for social security purposes. Reference should also be made to **4.15** ante.

4.18   Payments under employment protection legislation

Regulations 2(a) and (b) of the Social Security (Contributions) (Employment Protection) Regulations 1977, No. 622, provides that certain sums specified in s. 18(2) of the Social Security (Miscellaneous Provisions) Act 1977 are to be treated as earnings for earnings-related contribution purposes. Such sums arise under the Employment Protection Act 1975 and the Employment Protection (Consolidation) Act 1978 and relate to guarantee payments, medical suspension payments, maternity pay, arrears of pay under an order for reinstatement or re-engagement, pay due as a result of an order for the continuation of a contract of employment and pay due as a result of a protective award.

In the case of guarantee payments and medical suspension payments, the actual amount paid is the amount to be treated as earnings (DHSS Leaflet NI224).

So far as maternity pay is concerned, the amount to be included in earnings is the actual amount of maternity pay, where it is the only payment made; the gross wage where normal wages are paid; or the gross wage net of maternity pay where normal wages are paid but the employed earner hands her maternity pay to her employer (DHSS Leaflet NI224).

In the case of the awards made by industrial tribunals, the amount to be treated as earnings is always the gross amount of the award, even if the net amount actually payable is very small or non-existent (where, for instance, the tribunal has taken certain amounts into account in deciding the actual amount to be paid by the employer, and because of PAYE deductions). The gross amount in respect of an order for reinstatement or re-engagement will include wages in lieu of notice, ex gratia payments and such other benefits as the tribunal thinks appropriate. The gross amount in respect of an order for the continuation of a contract of employment will include payments under the contract of employment, damages for breach of the contract in respect of any part of the pay period covered by the order and any lump sum payment in lieu of notice. The gross amount in respect of a protective award will include payments made under the contract of employment and damages for breach of the contract in respect of a period falling within the protected period (DHSS Leaflet NI224).

Where there is difficulty in ascertaining the gross amounts of any tribunal awards, the clerk to the tribunal which made the award should be consulted.

4.19 Payments under the temporary short-time working scheme

Payments made to employed earners under the temporary short-time working scheme (which came into operation on 2 April 1979) are earnings for earnings-related contribution purposes even though the employer is partially reimbursed by the state for the payment of such earnings (DHSS Leaflet NP15, para. 21(k)).

4.20 Gifts

Payments made to employed earners on a personal and non-contractual basis (eg as a wedding present or in recognition of an examination success) are not earnings for social security purposes.

4.21 Payments to serving members of the forces

Regulation 117(1) of SI 1979, No. 591, provides that earnings as a serving member of the forces are not to include payments of an Emergency Service grant, payments of liability bounty in recognition of liability for immediate call-up in times of emergency, or the allowances, bounties and gratuities referred to in ICTA 1970, s. 366. Members of the forces constitute a special class of earner and are dealt with at **7.48** et seq post.

4.22 Payments to mariners

Regulation 94(1)(b) of SI 1979, No. 591, provides that earnings as a mariner are not to include 'special payments' (as defined by the National Maritime

Board) which shipowners make to mariners left abroad on account of illness or injury or for the purpose of preventing infection, or payments made to a mariner by the Department of Trade and Industry (with the consent of the mariner's employer) in respect of wages deposited with the Department by reason of that mariner having failed to rejoin his ship (DHSS Leaflet NI25, para. 16). Mariners constitute a special class of earner and are dealt with at **7.25** et seq post.

4.23   Nominee directors' fees foregone to nominating company

If, by virtue of its shareholding in (or other formal agreement with) another company, a company appoints someone as a nominee director of that other company and the nominee is required to forego the fees of the directorship to the nominating company and does, in fact, do so, those fees are not earnings for social security contribution purposes. A useful guide as to whether a nominee director's fees fall within this category is whether the Inland Revenue regard the income foregone as that of the nominating company or of the director personally (DHSS Leaflet NI35, April 1981).

4.24   Other remuneration

Subject to the various qualifications, exceptions and inclusions described in the foregoing paragraphs, earnings consist of any gross salary, wage, overtime pay, commission, fee or bonus paid to an employed earner in respect of an employed earner's employment (DHSS Leaflet NP15, para. 21(a) and (b)).

4.25   The meaning of 'payment'

Before concluding this examination of what constitutes earnings so far as an employed earner and his earnings-related contributions are concerned, it is worth noting that the Act speaks of payments made to an employed earner or 'for his benefit' (SSA 1975, s. 3(2)) and that the Regulations speak similarly of earnings paid to or 'for the benefit of' an earner (SI 1979, No. 591, reg. 1(2)). The force of those words must not be overlooked. It is not necessary that an employed earner should personally receive monies for them to become earnings; it is sufficient that they are paid for his benefit. If, for example, a man authorises his employer to pay a proportion of his salary to his wife from whom he is separated, the payment is for his benefit and will not, therefore, escape related contribution liability. Furthermore, to 'pay' a sum of money to someone has been judicially interpreted as meaning to place a sum of money unreservedly at a person's disposal (*Garforth v Newsmith Stainless Ltd* [1979] 1 WLR 409, [1979] STC 129), so that the crediting of amounts to an account on which the employed earner is free to draw is payment for the purposes of the Act and the Regulations.

SELF-EMPLOYED EARNERS' EARNINGS

4.26 Determination of basis

A self-employed earner's earnings are essentially all profits and gains which he derives from the exercise of any trade, profession or vocation in which he is engaged, but the basis on which such profits or gains are to be calculated depends on the purpose for which the calculation is being made. If the question at issue is whether the self-employed earner may be excepted from his liability to pay Class 2 contributions on the grounds of small earnings from self-employment, earnings are to be calculated on the basis described at **4.27** post. If, however, the object is to ascertain the amount on which a liability for Class 4 contributions arises, the basis and rules described at **4.28** et seq post apply.

4.27 Earnings for exception purposes

A self-employed earner may, as explained at **5.22** post, be excepted from liability to pay Class 2 contributions on the grounds that his earnings are only small (SSA 1975, s. 7(5)) and SI 1979, No. 591, reg. 24(1)). Earnings for this purpose are

'. . . net earnings from employment as a self-employed earner' (SI 1979, No. 591, reg. 25(2)).

This is interpreted by the DHSS as meaning the figure which would appear in a profit and loss account prepared in accordance with normal accounting principles, ie deductions may be made from gross earnings for expenses incurred in running the business and an allowance may be made for depreciation, but no deduction may be made for income tax payments or for Class 2 and Class 4 contributions payable; income from any source other than self-employment is to be disregarded; and adjustment should be made for the amount of any drawings from the business and the value of any withdrawals from stock for the person's own use (DHSS Leaflet NI27A).

The profits or losses of all self-employments exercised by a self-employed earner must be aggregated in arriving at earnings for this purpose and, where accounting periods overlap 5 April, the profits or losses are to be apportioned on a time-basis (DHSS Leaflet NI27A).

EXAMPLE 4(D)

David runs a taxi business and is also a free-lance photographer. Recent trading results (adjusted in accordance with the above rules) have been as follows:

			£
Taxi owner:	Year ended 5.10.80	Profit	3,400
	Year ended 5.10.81	Profit	3,800
Photographer:	Year ended 5.06.80	Profit	2,400
	Year ended 5.06.81	Loss	(3,600)

His earnings for Class 2 exception purposes, apportioned and aggregated according to DHSS practice are, for the year ended 5 April 1981:

	£
1/2 × £4,300	1,700
1/2 × £3,800	1,900
1/6 × £2,400	400
5/6 × (£3,600)	(3,000)
	1,000

4.28   Earnings for Class 4 purposes

A self-employed earner's earnings for Class 4 contribution purposes are

> '. . . all annual profits or gains immediately derived from the carrying on or exercise of one or more trades, professions or vocations, being profits or gains chargeable to income tax under Case I or Case II of Schedule D for any year of assessment beginning on or after 6 April 1975 . . .' (SSA 1975, s. 9(1))

subject to various deductions, additions and reliefs specified in SSA 1975, Sch. 2, paras. 2 and 3 and described in the following paragraphs.

It should be noted that the effect of this provision is to exchange the normal actual basis of earnings under the social security scheme for, in the case of earnings for Class 4 purposes, whatever basis is adopted with regard to those earnings for Schedule D purposes. In the opening and closing years of a business this may be an actual basis or a combination of actual and preceding year bases dependent on the application of ICTA 1970, ss. 116 and 118. In the intermediate years it will normally be a preceding year basis, though a change of accounting date could result in 'averaged' profits under ICTA 1970, s. 115. Averaged profits may also arise if a farmer or market gardener so elects under Finance Act 1978, s. 28. Earnings falling to be assessed for Class 4 purposes will, therefore, normally be unrelated to the actual profits or gains in a year.

4.29   Capital allowances

First-year, initial, writing-down and balancing allowances which, under the Capital Allowances Act (CAA) 1968, s. 70(2) fall to be made as a deduction in charging profits or gains to tax, are a permissible deduction for Class 4 purposes also (SSA 1975, Sch. 2, para. 2(a)(i)), as are agricultural buildings allowances which, under CAA 1968, s. 71, fall to be given by way of discharge or repayment of tax (SSA 1975, Sch. 2, para. 2(a)(ii)). In both cases, the deduction is conditional upon the allowances having arisen from the activities of the relevant trade, profession or vocation.

Balancing charges which, under CAA 1968, s. 70(6), fall to be made for tax purposes are to be added to profits for Class 4 purposes also (SSA 1975, Sch. 2 para. 2(b)).

4.30   Stock relief

Where, in computing the amount of the profits or gains of a trade, deductions in respect of stock relief (or additions in respect of stock relief recovery) fall to be made in charging those profits or gains to income tax under Schedule D, Case I or II, such deductions (or additions) are to be made for Class 4 purposes also (FA 1976, Sch. 5, para. 8; FA 1981, Sch. 9, para. 11). Stock relief under earlier legislation was given by way of a reduction in the closing stock of a business and was thus taken into account automatically for both tax and Class 4 purposes.

4.31   Loss relief

Loss relief available for tax purposes under ICTA 1970, s. 171 by carry-forward against subsequent profits is available for Class 4 purposes also, as is carry-back of terminal loss relief under ICTA 1970, s. 174 (SSA 1975, Sch. 2, para. 3(1)(c) and (d)). It is worth noting here that the year in which a loss presently being carried forward first arose is irrelevant—even though that year may, in fact, pre-date the introduction of the Class 4 scheme.

If it is remembered that, with one exception, the treatment of trade losses for Class 4 purposes follows whatever treatment is adopted for the purposes of Schedule D, no difficulties will be encountered. The exception concerns loss relief available under either ICTA 1970, s. 168 or FA 1978, s. 30 whereby trade losses may be set off, for tax purposes, against general income. The relief afforded by both provisions is available for Class 4 purposes also (where the losses arise from activities of which any profits or gains would have been earnings for Class 4 purposes) (SSA 1975, Sch. 2, para. 3(1)(a); FA 1978, s. 30(7)(c)) and may be augmented for Class 4 purposes, as it may for tax purposes under ICTA 1970, s. 169, by capital allowances (SSA 1975, Sch. 2, para. 3(1)(b)) and by stock relief (FA 1976, Sch. 5, para. 8; FA 1981, Sch. 9, para. 11). In most cases, however, it will not be possible for relief to be given for Class 4 purposes in the same manner in which it is given for tax purposes. Indeed, it is provided that where, in any year beginning on or after 6 April 1975, a deduction in respect of a loss falls to be made in computing a person's total income (or that of his spouse) for tax purposes and all or part of the loss falls to be deducted from income other than his trading profit or gains, the loss is, to that extent, to be carried forward for Class 4 purposes and set off against his first available trading profit or gains for subsequent years (SSA 1975, Sch. 2, para. 3(3)).

Section 168 and FA 1978, s. 30, though popular because they generally provide earlier and more advantageous relief for trade losses than the carry-forward provisions, are complex in application and can create problems from a Class 4 point of view.

There are statutorily two (but effectively four) possible claims under s. 168. Subsection 1 enables a loss to be set off against income of the year in which the loss was incurred, while subsection 2 enables a loss to be set off against income of the year following that in which the loss was incurred. Statutorily, the loss should be quantified by apportioning figures shown in the accounts on a time-basis to 5 April where the accounting date is other than 5 April; in practice, however, the Inland Revenue grant relief on the concessional basis that the loss for a particular tax year is the loss for the accounts year ended within the tax year. Where the total income against which the loss relief is given consists only of trading profits or gains of the claimant himself, no Class 4 problems arise.

EXAMPLE 4(E)

David (who is single and has no other income) owns a craft shop. His trading results (adjusted for Schedule D, Case I purposes) have been as follows:

		£
Year ended 5 July 1979	Profit	8,000
Year ended 5 July 1980	Profit	7,200
Year ended 5 July 1981	Loss	(4,000)
Year ended 5 July 1982	Profit	8,400

Assessable profits are:

	£
1980–81	8,000
1981–82	7,200
1982–83	—
1983–84	8,400

The loss of £4,000 may, on the concessional basis, be relieved under s. 168(1) against the 1981–82 assessment, in which case the profits chargeable to tax and the Class 4 earnings for 1981–82 will both be £3,200. Alternatively, on the statutory basis, the loss of £1,200 (3/4 × £4,000 − 1/4 × £7,200) for the year ended 5 April 1981 may, under s. 168(1) be relieved against the 1980–81 assessment in which case the profits chargeable to tax and the Class 4 earnings for 1980–81 will both, instead, be £6,800.

Where, however, a self-employed earner's total income includes income other than profits or gains arising from the trade, profession or vocation in which he is engaged, the situation becomes much more complex.

EXAMPLE 4(F)

Eric owns a garage. His trading results (adjusted for Schedule D, Case I purposes) are as follows:

	£
Year ended 5 July 1979 Profit	2,000
Year ended 5 July 1980 Profit	4,000
Year ended 5 July 1981 Loss	(7,200)
Year ended 5 July 1982 Profit	8,400

Eric is single but has other income and the assessable amounts of that income and his trading profits are as follows:

	Sch. D	Inv. Inc.
	£	£
1980–81	2,000	1,500
1981–82	4,000	1,700
1982–83	—	1,800
1983–84	8,400	2,200

The loss of £7,200 may, on the concessional basis, be regarded as being for the year ended 5 April 1982 and may, under s. 168(1), be relieved against 1981–82 total income of £5,700 and, under s. 168(2), against 1982–83 total income to the extent of the balance of £1,500. For Class 4 purposes, this would reduce earnings to nil for 1981–82 but would necessitate a carry-forward to 1983–84 of the £3,200 loss relieved against other income for tax purposes where Class 4 earnings for that year would become £5,200.

Alternatively, on the statutory basis, the loss for the year ended 5 April 1981 would be £4,400 (3/4 × £7,200 − 1/4 × £4,000) and could be relieved, under s. 168(1), against the 1980–81 total income of £3,500 and, under s. 168(2), against the 1981–82 total income of £5,700 to the extent of the balance of £900. For Class 4 purposes, however, the 1980–81 earnings would be reduced to nil and the 1981–82 earnings would become £1,600.

Matters may, of course, be further complicated if loss relief is first claimed under s. 168(2) and only secondly under s. 168(1) on the balance of the loss. The principle to be followed remains the same in all cases, however: to whatever extent a loss is relieved against the claimant's (but not his spouse's) trading profits or gains for tax purposes, the loss is also to be relieved against those profits or gains for Class 4 purposes, but, to whatever extent the loss is relieved against other income for tax purposes, the loss is to be relieved for Class 4 purposes against the earliest successive profits or gains available.

Under the provisions of FA 1978, s. 30, trade losses may be relieved against general income for the three years of assessment last preceding that in which the loss has been sustained, beginning with the earliest of the years. This is effectively an extension of s. 168 relief and the principles described above apply equally to both s. 168 relief and s. 30 relief.

No relief is to be given for Class 4 purposes of any constructive losses available in respect of annual payments carried forward for tax purposes under ICTA 1970, s. 173 or interest carried forward or back under s. 175 (SSA 1975, Sch. 2, para. 3(2)(d) and (e)).

4.32   Interest and annual payments

Although personal reliefs, premiums (or other consideration) under retirement annuity contracts and trust schemes, interest allowable under FA 1972, s. 75 so far as not incurred wholly or exclusively for business purposes, and relief in respect of periods spent overseas may not be deducted from trading profits or gains for Class 4 purposes (SSA 1975, Sch. 2, para. 3(2)(a)(b) and (c); FA 1978, Sch. 4, para. 8), relief is to be given for interest, annuities, patent royalties or other annual payments subject to deduction of tax under ICTA 1970, ss. 52 or 53 and for interest paid under FA 1972, s. 75 to the extent that such expenses are incurred wholly or exclusively for the purposes of the relevant trade, profession or vocation (SSA 1975, Sch. 2, para. 3(4)(a) and (b)). It should be noted that relief is to be given by a deduction of the gross amount of the actual payments made in the tax year concerned. Any such amounts which, because of an insufficiency of profits or gains, cannot be relieved in the year of payment are to be carried forward and relieved as soon as possible (SSA 1975, Sch. 2, para. 3(4)).

In order to prevent interest and other annual payments being deducted twice for Class 4 purposes, their deduction in arriving at Class 4 profits other than under this provision is prohibited (SSA 1975, Sch. 2, para. 3(2)(d) and (e)).

EXAMPLE 4(G)

Frank is a dental surgeon. His tax assessment for 1981–82 is as follows:

	£	£
Schedule D Case II profit		13,400
Deduct:		
Capital allowances	3,400	
Superannuation contributions	655	
Retirement annuity premiums	200	
Building society mortgage interest	3,000	
		7,255
		6,145
Less: Personal allowance	2,145	
Chargeable to tax		4,000

One-third of Frank's house is used as his surgery.

His earnings for Class 4 contribution purposes are:

	£	£
Schedule D Case II profit		13,400
Deduct:		
Capital allowances	3,400	
1/3 Building society mortgage interest	1,000	
		4,400
Assessable for Class 4		9,000

Had Frank's Schedule D Case II profits been less than £4,400, so much of the building society mortgage interest as could not be relieved in 1981–82 would be carried forward to 1982–83 and, if then still unrelieved, to future years.

4.33   Husband and wife

In accordance with the general principle that husband and wife are wholly separate individuals for social security contribution purposes, SSA 1975, Sch. 2, para. 4(3) provides that a wife's profits and gains are to be computed for Class 4 contribution purposes as if ICTA 1970, s. 37 (whereby a wife's income is deemed to be that of her husband for income tax purposes) is of no application. A husband will, however, be liable to pay any Class 4 contributions arising on his wife's income unless an application for separate assessment under ICTA 1970, s. 38 has been approved or an election for separate taxation of his wife's earnings under FA 1971, s. 23 is in force (SSA 1975, Sch. 2, para. 4(1)), though it is not permissible to make such an application or election for Class 4 purposes only (SSA 1975, Sch. 2, para. 4(2)).

It follows from these provisions that, while the trading loss of one spouse may be relieved for tax purposes under ICTA 1970, s. 168 against the trading profits of the other, no such utilisation of losses may be made for Class 4 purposes. It also follows that, in a husband and wife partnership, each spouse's earnings must be assessed separately for Class 4 purposes on the basis of their individual entitlement to a share in the Schedule D Case I or II profits.

EXAMPLE 4(H)

Fred runs a dancing school and his profits (adjusted for Schedule D Case I purposes) for the year ended 31 August 1981 are £14,000. He takes his wife, Ginger, into partnership on 1 September 1981 on a 50:50 basis and they jointly elect to be assessed on a continuing basis for tax purposes under ICTA 1970, s. 154(2). The 1982–83 assessment will consequently be on the £14,000 which was earned by Fred alone but, as the profit sharing ratio between 6 April 1982 and 5 April 1983 is 50:50, Fred's earnings for Class 4 purposes in 1982–83 will be reduced to £7,000 while Ginger will find herself with Class 4 earnings for that year of £7,000 which she has never earned at all!

4.34 Partnership

As will be apparent from Example 4(H) above, the earnings of a partner for Class 4 purposes consist of his share of the profits or gains of the partnership adjusted in accordance with the rules described in the foregoing paragraphs. Furthermore, for Class 4 purposes, that share is to be aggregated with any other profits or gains derived by him from any other trade, profession or vocation (SSA 1975, Sch. 2, para. 5(1)).

EXAMPLE 4(I)

The facts are as stated in Example 4(H) except that Ginger also owns and runs a boutique of which the Schedule D Case I adjusted profits for the year ended 31 December 1981 were £4,000.

Ginger's earnings for Class 4 contribution purposes in 1982–83 are £11,000 (£4,000 + £7,000).

Chapter 5

Calculation of contributions

5.01 Introduction

The three preceding chapters have been devoted to a detailed consideration of the 'earners, employers and others' caught by the SSA 1975, s. 1 net; the criteria of residence, age and marital status to be applied in determining which of the individuals in each of those groups should remain within that net; and the rules whereby the earners' earnings are to be identified and quantified. It is now appropriate to examine the principles of assessment to be applied in relation to those earnings and the rules for calculation of contributions.

CLASS 1 CONTRIBUTIONS

5.02 Class 1 contributions defined

Class 1 contributions are entirely earnings-related and consist of a primary contribution payable by employed earners and a secondary contribution payable by their employers or by such other persons as pay their earnings (SSA 1975, s. 1(2)).

5.03 Earnings periods

Of fundamental importance to the assessment of Class 1 contributions is the 'earnings period'. This is the period of time to which earnings paid to, or for the benefit of, an employed earner are deemed to relate (irrespective of the actual period involved) and it is determined by the regularity of such payments or, if there is no regular pay interval, by the application of arbitrary rules provided by regulations made under SSA 1975, Sch. 1, para. 2.

Regular intervals are intervals of substantially equal length at which, in accordance with an express or implied arrangement between an employed earner and a secondary contributor, payments of earnings normally fall to be made (SI 1979, No. 591, reg. 1(2)) and a regular pay pattern is established when there is a succession of such intervals, each of which begins immediately upon the ending of the period which precedes it (SI 1979, No. 591, reg. 3(1)(b)). Where there is but one such pay pattern the earnings period is simply the normal pay interval.

EXAMPLE 5(A)
Abigail and Barbara work in a hairdressing salon. Abigail, an assistant, is paid £40 per week but Barbara, the cashier, is paid £200 per month. Abigail's earnings period is one week and Barbara's is one month.

An earnings period cannot be less than seven days in length (SI 1979, No. 591, reg. 3(1)(a)(ii)) and the first earnings period in any tax year is deemed to begin on the first day of that tax year (SI 1979, No. 591, reg. 3(1)(b)). Where the normal pay interval is a week or a month (or a multiple of a week or a month) the end of any earnings period will, therefore, correspond with the end of either a tax week or tax month in the PAYE calendar. Thus, to refer back to Examples 5(A) above, a payment to Abigail on 15 April 1982 will fall within, and be related to, her earnings period of one week ended 19 April 1982 (PAYE week 2), and a payment to Barbara on 7 January 1982 will fall within, and be related to, her earnings period of one month ended 5 February 1982 (PAYE month 10).

5.04   Multiple pay intervals

It can be seen that a single regular pay pattern gives rise to no particular difficulty. Problems do arise, however, where an employed earner has two or more regular pay patterns running concurrently. As only one earnings period is permissible, it becomes necessary in each such case to decide which of several pay intervals is to be regarded as that single earnings period, and to this end regulations provide that

'... where any part of ... earnings ... is paid or treated ... as paid at regular intervals, the earnings period in respect of those earnings shall ... be the period ... the length of which is ... the length of the shortest interval at which any such part is paid or treated as paid ...' (SI 1979, No. 591, reg. 3(1)(a)(i))

except in certain circumstances where earnings from more than one employment fall to be aggregated for Class 1 contribution purposes (see **5.10** post).

EXAMPLE 5(B)
Clifford is a sales representative for Dee Ltd. He receives a monthly salary (£500 per month throughout the year ended 5 April 1982), quarterly commission (30 June 1981 £920, 30 September 1981 £870, 31 December 1981 £1,300, 31 March 1982 £910), and an annual bonus (31 March 1982 £1,000). There are three regular pay intervals: one month, one quarter and one year. As the shortest of these is one month, the earnings period for *all* earnings paid is one month (irrespective of the fact that some of those earnings have been earned over longer intervals) and assessment for Class 1 purposes would take place on the following basis:

Month ended	£	Month ended	£	Month ended	£
5 May	500	5 September	500	5 January	1,800
5 June	500	5 October	1,370	5 February	500
5 July	1,420	5 November	500	5 March	500
5 August	500	5 December	500	5 April	2,410

In certain circumstances, however, the Secretary of State is empowered to modify the rule described by merely notifying the earner and the secondary contributor that he is doing so (SI 1979, No. 591, reg. 3(2)). Such modification may take place

'. . . if the Secretary of State is satisfied that the greatest part of the earnings . . . is normally paid at intervals of greater length than the shortest . . .' (SI 1979, No. 591, reg. 3(2))

and, in effect, will identify the earnings period with that longer pay interval.

EXAMPLE 5(C)
The facts are as stated in Example 5(B) except that the salary is £350 per month; commission is £1,920 at 30 June 1981, £1,870 at 30 September 1981, £2,300 at 31 December 1981 and £1,910 at 31 March 1982. The bonus remains £1,000. Total earnings are, therefore, £13,200 and of these £4,200 are paid at intervals of one month, £8,000 at intervals of one quarter and £1,000 at an interval of one year. The greatest part of earnings is clearly paid at a quarterly interval and it will be open to the Secretary of State to notify Clifford and Dee Ltd that, in future, that will be the earnings period.

It should be noted that the regulation refers to the 'greatest' part of earnings, not the greater part. No modification of the earnings period will, therefore, be possible solely on the grounds that two or more parts of total earnings are together greater than the remaining part or parts. If in the above example, for instance, bonus and commission together accounted for over half of the total earnings, but neither bonus nor commission separately exceeded salary, no modification of the earnings period rules would be supportable on that ground alone.

It must also be stressed that unless and until a notification is made by the Secretary of State under SI 1979, No. 591, reg. 3(2), the earnings period continues to be the shortest pay interval irrespective of the distribution of earnings over different pay cycles, and, furthermore, that such notification cannot be retrospective:

. . . the length of that longer period shall *thereafter* be the length of the earnings period . . .' (SI 1979, No. 591, reg. 3(2), author's italics).

But for the 'thereafter', Clifford's earnings as detailed in Example 5(C) above should have become assessable as follows:

	£
Quarter ended:	
5 July 1981	2,970
5 September 1981	2,920
5 January 1982	3,350
5 April 1982	3,960

The importance of the point being underlined here may not be fully appreciated at this stage in the explanation of the Class 1 rules, but, as is shown at **8.02** post, lies in the fact that savings in contributions almost invariably accrue from the retention of a short earnings period, wherever this is possible.

5.05   End of year gap

Where in any year there is a period between the end of the last earnings period of normal length and the beginning of the next tax year, that bridging period is itself to be treated as an earnings period of normal length, however short it may in fact be (SI 1979, No. 591, reg. 3(3)). The last normal weekly earnings period in 1981–82, for instance, ended on 3 April 1982 and, in consequence of the rule now stated, 4 and 5 April 1982 (though only two days) were to be treated as an earnings period of one week as regards any earnings paid on those dates.

5.06   Earnings paid after termination of employment

Where an employment under which earnings have been paid according to a regular pay pattern comes to an end and, after the end of the employment, a payment of earnings is made additionally to those paid before the employment ended, an earnings period of one week is to apply to those additional earnings regardless of what the regular pay interval has been (SI 1979, No. 591, reg. 3(4)).

5.07   Earnings paid at irregular intervals

In certain circumstances, payments of earnings are (by regulations made under SSA 1975, Sch. 1, para. 2) to be treated as made at regular intervals even though they have not been so made. This will be so where, for instance, a payment of earnings which would normally fall to be made at a regular interval is made at some other interval (SI 1979, No. 591, reg. 6(1)(a)). In such a case the payment of earnings is to be treated as being made on the date on which it would normally fall to be made (SI 1979, No. 591, reg. 6(2)(a)).

EXAMPLE 5(D)
Eddie works for Fred, a self-employed joiner, and is paid £50 per week. Fred falls ill and for three weeks Eddie is unpaid. In the fourth week, however, Fred is once again able to attend to his business and Eddie receives his £200. For Class 1 contribution purposes, however, he is treated as having received £50 on each normal pay day and his earnings period remains one week.

Likewise, earnings paid at irregular intervals will be treated as paid at regular intervals if the pay arrangement ensures that one and only one payment is made in each of a succession of periods consisting of the same number of days, weeks or calendar months (SI 1979, No. 591, reg. 6(1)(b)). The deemed date of payment in such a case will be the last day of the deemed regular interval (SI 1979, No. 591, reg. 6(2)(b)).

EXAMPLE 5(E)

Gill is paid £120 on the last Thursday in each calendar month. Her earnings period is, therefore, one month and the payment made on 27 May 1982, for instance, will be treated as made on 5 June 1982.

Where earnings are similarly (but in other circumstances to these) paid in respect of regular intervals but at irregular intervals, each payment is to be treated as made on the last day of the regular interval in respect of which it is due (SI 1979, No. 591, reg. 6(1)(c) and (2)(b)).

EXAMPLE 5(F)

Henry is a computer programmer. He is paid £1,000 per month but only at the end of each assignment when the programme is shown to run. On 31 March 1982 he completes and proves a programme which he began on 1 January 1982 and is paid £3,000. His earnings period is, however, one month and he is treated as being paid £1,000 on 5 February 1982, £1,000 on 5 March 1982 and £1,000 on 5 April 1982.

The one and only circumstance in which these rules for treating certain irregular payments of earnings as being paid at regular intervals is not to apply is where, as a result, a payment of earnings made in one tax year would be treated as made in another (SI 1979, No. 591, reg. 6(3)). In such a case, the employed earner may apply to the Secretary of State for the contributions paid to be allocated to that other year for benefit entitlement purposes (SSA 1975, Sch. 1, para. 6(1)(d) and SI 1979, No. 591, reg. 37).

EXAMPLE 5(G)

The facts are as in Example 5(F) except that Henry is paid on 30 April 1982 and work on the programme began on 1 February 1982. If the normal rule were applied £2,000 of the payment made in the 1982–83 year would be treated as if it had been made in the 1981–82 year and this is not permissible. Instead, the whole £3,000 would be treated as paid for the one month earnings period ended on 5 May 1982.

There are, of course, pay arrangements and situations the nature of which is such that no degree of regularity can or does underly either the pay interval or the period for which the payments are made. Where the employment giving rise to such a wholly irregular pay pattern is one in which earnings are paid by reference to services which are to be rendered on one or more occasions and, on each occasion, within a fixed period (though in the earner's own time and at his convenience), the earnings period is to be the length of the fixed period or a week, whichever is the longer (SI 1979, No. 591, reg. 4(a)(i) and (ii)).

EXAMPLE 5(H)
On 15 July 1981, Ian became employed by Jay TV Productions Ltd as a research assistant. He was paid £4 per hour and worked in his own time and at his own convenience, but had to meet deadlines as follows:

'Social Services' material   31 August 1981
'Third World' material   28 October 1981
'Christmas' filler material   31 October 1981

He worked 106 hours on the first project, 151 hours on the second and 12 hours on the third. Earnings periods and earnings would be as follows:

	£
47 days from 15 July to 31 August 1981	424.00
58 days from 1 September to 28 October 1981	604.00
Week ended 1 November 1981 (PAYE Week 30), even though only a three day fixed period	48.00

Where, in any other circumstances, earnings are normally paid otherwise than at regular intervals and are not to be treated as paid at regular intervals, the earnings period is to be the length of that part of the employment for which the earnings are paid or a week, whichever is the longer (SI 1979, No. 591, reg. 4(b)(i)).

EXAMPLE 5(I)
Kevin is employed by Landscapes Ltd as a gardener. He is paid on an irregular basis for occasional attendance at various locations at such times and for such periods as he himself considers necessary. His rate of pay is £4 per hour. Part of his work record was as follows:

23 October to 5 November 1981   80 hours
18 November 1981   6 hours
30 November to 10 December 1981   63 hours

Kevin's earnings and earnings periods would be:

	£
14 days to 5 November 1981	320.00
Week ended 22 November 1981 (PAYE week 33)	24.00
11 days to 10 December 1981	252.00

Where it is not reasonably practicable to determine the period of that part of the employment for which earnings are paid, the earnings period is to be the period from the date of the last preceding payment of earnings in respect of the employment to the date of payment. Where there has been no previous payment, the period is to be measured from the date the employment began, and, if the employment has ended before payment is received, the period is to be measured to the date of termination. In any event, the minimum length of the earnings period will be one week (SI 1979, No. 591, reg. 4(b)(ii)).

5.08   Sessional fees

Each session of a person in a sessional fee-paid office is to be treated as a separate employment to which a weekly earnings period applies (DHSS Leaflet NP15, para. 66(c)).

5.09   Employment protection payments

Special earnings period rules apply in relation to payments (other than guarantee payments and medical suspension payments) under employment protection legislation as described at **4.18** ante.

   In the case of maternity pay, the earnings period is to be the period in respect of which the payment is made (SI 1979, No. 591, reg. 5(a)(i)). Where maternity pay is paid with the last payment of wages (whether before or after the employed earner leaves), the maternity pay must be assessed separately with an earnings period determined in accordance with the stated rule (DHSS Leaflet NI224).

   In the case of awards under orders for reinstatement or re-engagement or for the continuation of a contract of employment, the earnings period is to be the period to which the award relates or a week, whichever is the longer (SI 1979, No. 591, reg. 5(a)(ii)). The fact that certain amounts due under the order may be payable by instalments does not alter this rule. For the purpose of calculating the contributions due, all instalments are to be aggregated and related to an earnings period equal to the period to which the award relates (DHSS Leaflet NI224). If the award is paid along with the first regular payment of earnings following reinstatement or re-engagement, the award must, for contribution purposes, be assessed separately and an earnings period applied in accordance with the stated rule (DHSS Leaflet NI224).

   In the case of a protective award, the earnings period is to be the protected period or that part of it for which the sum is paid or a week, whichever is the longer (SI 1979, No. 591, reg. 5(a)(iii)). Where, therefore, earnings have been paid to an employed earner for part of the protected period, the earnings period to be applied in relation to wages paid for the remaining part of the protected period is to be that remaining part of the protected period (DHSS Leaflet NI224). Any earnings (such as overtime arrears) paid during the period covered by an award are to be added to the award payment for contribution purposes (DHSS Leaflet NI224).

It may be that, in consequence of the earnings period rules relating to payments under employment protection legislation, an earnings period falls wholly or partly in a tax year (or years) other than that in which relevant contributions are paid. The effect of this may be to impair an employed earner's contribution record from a benefit-eligibility point of view and it is, therefore, provided that, on request, contributions may be treated as paid proportionately in respect of the year or years in which the earnings period falls (SI 1979, No. 591, reg. 5(b)).

5.10   Pay interval on aggregation

Where earnings paid in respect of two or more employed earner's employments fall to be aggregated (see **5.13** post) and the earnings periods in respect of those earnings are, after application of whichever rules described above are relevant, of different lengths, the earnings period to which the aggregated earnings are to relate is to be the shorter or shortest of those earnings periods (SI 1979, No. 591, reg. 5A(1)(a)(b), (2)(b) and (3) as inserted by SI 1980, No. 1975, reg. 2). Where, however, the earnings are derived from employments which include both contracted-out and non-contracted-out employments, the common earnings period is to be the shorter or shortest of the contracted-out employments (SI 1979, No. 591, reg. 5A(2)(a) as inserted by SI 1980, No. 1975, reg. 2).

5.11   Change of regular pay interval

Where, because of a change in the regular interval at which any part of an employed earner's earnings is paid or treated as paid, an earner's earnings period is changed and the new earnings period is longer than the old, it may happen that a payment of earnings at the old interval falls within the first new earnings period. In that event, contributions on all payments made during the new earnings period are not to exceed the contributions which would have been payable had all those payments been made at the new interval (SI 1979, No. 591, reg. 14).

EXAMPLE 5(J)

Mark is paid £150 per week until 7 May 1982 when he becomes salaried at £1,100 per month. His first month's salary is due on 31 May but, to take account of the fact that he has already been paid £150 in the month, the May salary is reduced to £850. In the absence of the rule stated above, contributions in the first new earnings period (ie PAYE Month 2 – to 5 June) would be:

	Primary £	Secondary £
PAYE Week 5 (to 8 May 1982):		
Primary Class 1: £150 × 8.75%	13.12	
Secondary Class 1: £150 × 13.7%		20.55

	£	£
PAYE Month 2 (to 5 June 1982):		
Primary Class 1: £850 × 8.75%	74.37	
Secondary Class 1: £850 × 13.7%		116.45
	87.49	137.00

The reg. 14 rule, however, restricts contributions to:

	£	£
PAYE Month 2 (to 5 June 1982):		
Primary Class 1: £1,000 limited to £953.33 being monthly upper earnings limit (see **5.15** post) × 8.75%	83.42	
Secondary Class 1: £1,000 also restricted to £953.33 × 13.7%		130.61
	83.42	130.61

5.12 Holiday pay

Where a payment of earnings includes a payment in respect of one or more weeks holiday, the earnings period may be determined in accordance with the length of the interval in respect of which the payment is made (SI 1979, No. 591, reg. 15). Alternatively, the holiday pay may simply be treated for contribution purposes as pay in the weeks in which earnings would normally have been paid.

> EXAMPLE 5(K)
> Nancy received gross pay of £180 on 15 August 1981. £60 represented earnings for the week ended on that date; the remainder represented two weeks holiday pay. Oswald, her employer, calculated contributions on the whole £180 using a three-week earnings period ended 30 August 1981, but he could have calculated contributions on £60 in each of the weeks ended 16 August, 23 August and 30 August 1981 using a one week earnings period.

The reg. 15 procedure is not applicable to monthly-paid employed earners, nor to employed earners who will continue working during their holiday period (DHSS Leaflet NP15, para. 106). Where the reg. 15 option is available and applied, only complete weeks should be taken into account, any pay relating to the remaining fraction of a week being added to the pay relating to complete weeks (DHSS Leaflet NP15, para. 107). Subject only to this last point, holiday pay is always to be spread evenly over the period of holiday, regardless of the basis of its calculation (DHSS Leaflet NP15, para. 108).

5.13 Aggregation of earnings

For the purpose of calculating the amount of any Class 1 contributions payable in respect of an employed earner's earnings paid in any earnings period (SI 1979, No. 591, reg. 10), the general rule is that

'. . . all earnings paid to him or for his benefit . . . in respect of one or more employed earner's employments under the same employer shall be aggregated and treated as a single payment of earnings . . . (SSA 1975, Sch. 1, para. 1(1)(a))

except where such aggregation is not reasonably practicable because the earnings in the respective, concurrent employments are separately calculated (SI 1979, No. 591, reg. 11).

This rule of aggregation is, in certain circumstances, extended to situations where, in an earnings period, earnings are paid to or for the benefit of an employed earner by different persons in respect of different employed earner's employments (SSA 1975, Sch. 1, para. 1(1)(b)). The first of such circumstances is where the different persons paying earnings are

'. . . different secondary contributors who in respect of those employments carry on business in association with each other and the amount of earnings paid in respect of one or more of those employments is less than the current lower earnings limit . . .' (SI 1979, No. 591, reg. 12(1)(a)).

Earnings limits are discussed at **5.15** post, but the significance of the reference to the lower earnings limit here lies in the fact that earnings falling below that limit escape the contribution net entirely. Were it not for this rule of aggregation, therefore, it would be possible (and extremely advantageous) for an employer to fragment his employee's earnings into appropriately small amounts and to pay each of those amounts through a separate but associated company, thus avoiding contributions entirely. It should be noted in this connection that carrying on business in association is not synonymous with being a group member or an associated company within the terms of ICTA 1970, ss. 272 or 302. For the purpose of this regulation, the DHSS regards companies as carrying on business in association where those companies are, to a significant degree, interdependent and linked by a common purpose. Such a relationship is a matter of fact rather than law, and one which may be evidenced in various ways: the sharing of facilities, accommodation and resources; the interchange of personnel; mutual customers and sources of supply.

In this circumstance, but not in those described in the following paragraphs, aggregation may be avoided if 'it is not reasonably practicable' to aggregate (SI 1979, No. 591, reg. 12(1)), though no specific departmental guidance is available on this matter.

The second circumstance in which the aggregation rule is to apply is where the different persons paying earnings are different employers of whom one is treated by virtue of SI 1978, No. 1689, Sch. 3 as the secondary contributor in respect of each of the employments concerned (SI 1979, No. 591, reg. 12(1)(b)). The practical application of this regulation appears very limited indeed. The circumstances in which a person is to be treated as a secondary contributor under the statutory instrument specified are described at **2.17** ante but it is difficult to conceive of many situations where such a person will also be an employer of an employed earner with regard to whom he is treated as secondary contributor. A possible example follows:

EXAMPLE 5(L)
Oliver is employed by Pickwick Ltd, Quill Ltd and Rudge. Pickwick Ltd and Quill Ltd both enter into voluntary liquidation and Rudge is appointed liquidator. Oliver is paid earnings by different employers of whom one (Rudge) is, by virtue of SI 1978, No. 1689, Sch. 3, treated as the secondary contributor of each employment. Accordingly, all Oliver's earnings fall to be aggregated for contribution purposes.

The third circumstance in which the aggregation rule is to apply is where the different persons paying earnings are persons for whom work is performed in respect of the earnings but where some other person is by virtue of SI 1978, No. 1689, Sch. 3 to be treated as the secondary contributor (SI 1979, No. 591, reg. 12(3)). This regulation is of particular reference to persons employed through agencies (see **7.04** post) and ensures that the earnings of such persons, though possibly from several different unconnected sources and of relatively small individual amounts, are nevertheless aggregated for contribution purposes. Avoidance of contributions is thus precluded.

EXAMPLE 5(M)
Sam obtains employment through Temp Ltd in the week ended 15 May 1982 as follows:

		£
U Ltd	7 hours	14
V Ltd	5 hours	10
W Ltd	10 hours	20
X Ltd	6 hours	12
Y Ltd	11 hours	22
Z Ltd	8 hours	16
		94

Assuming that none of the companies carry on business in association with each other, Sam would (but for the regulation described) avoid all payment of contributions as each part of his earnings is below the lower earnings limit. As Temp Ltd falls to be treated as Sam's secondary contributor, however, contributions must be calculated on the aggregated sum of £94.

Where, in any of the circumstances described, earnings are aggregated, liability for any secondary contributions payable in respect of those earnings is, by regulation made under SSA 1975, Sch. 1, para. 1(3), to be apportioned between the secondary contributors in such proportions as they agree amongst themselves. In the absence of agreement, the proportions are to be those which the earnings paid by each bear to the aggregated earnings (SI 1979, No. 591, reg. 12(2)).

5.14   Apportionment of earnings

Where a single payment of earnings is made in respect of two or more employed earner's employments under different secondary contributors and those secondary contributors are (in respect of those employments) carrying on business in association with each other (see **5.13** ante), contributions are, by regulations made under SSA 1975, Sch. 1, para. 1(2), to be determined by treating the entire payment as due from the secondary contributor by whom it is made (SI 1979, No. 591, reg. 13(a)). Where, however, the secondary contributors are not carrying on business in association with each other, the payment is to be apportioned to the secondary contributors in proportion to the earnings due from each (SI 1979, No. 591, reg. 13(b)).

> EXAMPLE 5(N)
>
> Alec is employed by Bee Ltd and Cee Ltd which are the manufacturing and distribution sides of one business. He receives a single payment of £600 per month from Cee Ltd in respect of his earnings from both employments (£50 Bee Ltd, £550 Cee Ltd). Because the companies are clearly associated, the payment of £600 is to be treated as due entirely from Cee Ltd (as Cee Ltd is the secondary contributor making the payment) and contributions are accordingly payable on the full amount. Were the companies not associated, however, £50 of the payment would be apportioned to Bee Ltd and, as this is below the lower earnings limit, no contributions would be payable thereon. The remaining £550 would be apportioned to Cee Ltd.

It will be clear that this regulation is, like reg. 12(1)(a) described at **5.13** ante, framed in such a manner as to prevent avoidance of contributions by fragmentation of earnings where the secondary contributors are associated.

Apportionment of earnings may also be necessary in a situation where a husband and wife share an employed earner's employment (eg as wardens of a hostel) and earnings are paid to them jointly. The basis of apportionment in such cases is to be that applied for income tax purposes or, in the absence of such tax apportionment, a basis approved by the Secretary of State (SI 1979, No. 591, reg. 16).

5.15   Earnings limits

For every tax year there is set both a lower and an upper earnings limit for Class 1 contribution purposes. The lower earnings limit (LEL) is

'. . . the level of weekly earnings at which employed earners become liable for such contributions in respect of the earnings from their employments . . .' (SSA 1975, s. 4(1)(a))

and the upper earnings limit (UEL) is

'. . . the maximum amount of weekly earnings in respect of which such contributions are payable . . .' (SSA 1975, s. 4(1)(b)).

Both limits are set annually by regulations made under SSPA 1975, s. 1 and both are linked to the amount of the basic component of the Category A retirement pension at the start of the tax year for which the earnings limits are being set (or the immediately following 6 May if an increase in the basic component is to take effect by then). In the case of the LEL, the weekly amount set must be an amount equal to, or not more than forty-nine pence lower than, the basic component (SSPA 1975, s. 1(2)(a) and (b)). In the case of the UEL the weekly amount set must be an amount of between six and half and seven and half times the basic component (SSPA 1975, s. 1(3)(a) and (b)). Thus, for example, as the basic component was £29.60 at 6 April 1982, the weekly LEL could have been set at between £29.11 and £29.60, and the UEL could have been set at between £192.40 and £222.00. In fact, the limits have been set at £29.50 and £220.00 respectively (SI 1979, No. 591, reg. 7 as amended by the Social Security (Contributions) Act (SS(C)A) 1982, s. 1(1)(b)).

It must be stressed at this point that the LEL does not create a contribution-free band of earnings. It merely sets the level of earnings which, once reached, renders the employed earner liable to contributions on all his earnings to the UEL.

EXAMPLE 5(O)

Diana and Eve are employed by Frank. In the week ended 15 May 1982, Diana earns £29.49 and Eve earns £29.50. Diana's earnings have not reached the LEL (by 1p!) and, accordingly, neither she nor Frank is liable to pay Class 1 contributions in respect of those earnings. Eve's earnings, however, have reached the LEL and both she and Frank are, therefore, liable to pay contributions calculated as follows:

			£
Eve:	Class 1 primary:	£29.50 × 8.75%	2.58
Frank:	Class 1 secondary:	£29.50 × 13.7%	4.04

Eve's 1p of earnings in excess of those of Diana have, in fact, cost £6.62—though Eve has, of course, added a contribution to her record for benefit eligibility purposes.

The foregoing example makes it clear that there is a band of earnings immediately above the LEL which is not only absorbed by contributions but actually effects a reduction in net pay. The break-even level of earnings at which this effect ceases may be determined by applying the formula:

LEL + (LEL × Class 1 primary rate/(1 − Class 1 primary rate)).

Given the 1982–83 LEL of £29.50, for example, the break-even level of earnings is £32.33, ie:

$$£29.50 + (29.50 \times .0875/.9125)$$

A person earning £29.49 per week in 1982–83 will, therefore, require an increase of at least £2.85 to be better off by even 1p! This point will be touched upon again in Chapter 8.

Where an employed earner's earnings period is other than a week (see **5.03** ante) equivalent amounts of the LEL and the UEL are to be applied in accordance with regulations prescribed under SSA 1975, s. 4(2)(b). Where the earnings period is a multiple of a week, the equivalent limits are to be the weekly limits multiplied by that multiple (SI 1979, No. 591, reg. 8(1) and (2)(a)). Where the earnings period is a month, the equivalent limits are to be the weekly limits multiplied by four and one-third (SI 1979, No. 591, reg. 8(2)(b)) and where the earnings period is a multiple of a month, the equivalent limits are to be the monthly limits multiplied by that multiple (SI 1979, No. 591, reg. 8(2)(c)). In any other case, the equivalent limits are to be calculated by dividing the weekly limits by seven and multiplying the quotients by the number of days in the earnings period concerned (SI 1979, No. 591, reg. 8(2)(d)). All calculations are to be to the nearest penny and any amount of less than one-half penny is to be disregarded (SI 1979, No. 591, reg. 8(3)).

5.16   Incidence of contributions

Having ascertained the amount of earnings paid to (or for the benefit of) an employed earner (see Chapter 4); the earnings period to which those earnings relate (see **5.03** to **5.12** ante); and the relevant LEL and UEL (see **5.15** ante), the latter are to be applied to the former. If the earnings paid exceed the LEL, a primary contribution is to be paid by the earner and a secondary contribution by the secondary contributor (SSA 1975, ss. 2 and 3). The amount of the contributions is, in each case, to be a percentage of so much of the earnings paid as does not exceed the UEL (SSA 1975, s. 6). Matters are complicated, however, by the fact that the percentage rates to be applied to earnings from contracted-out employments are not the same as those applicable to earnings from non-contracted-out employments.

5.17   Contracted-out employments

On 6 April 1978 the contribution provisions of SSPA 1975 came into effect with the introduction of the state scheme for earnings-related pensions. The scheme provides for a two-tier retirement, widow's and invalidity pension consisting of a 'basic component' (which is a continuation of the former 'old age pension') and an 'additional component' (which is an additional pension related to any 'upper band earnings'—earnings between the LEL and the UEL—on which an employed earner has paid contributions). Long before the introduction of the state scheme, however, many employers were already operating occupational pension schemes which provided their employees with just such an 'additional component'. It was provided, therefore, that, so long as certain specific and stringent conditions laid down by SSPA 1975, ss. 33 to 41 are fulfilled (essentially that the rules of the employer's scheme provide for, and safeguard, guaranteed minimum pension rights equal to or greater than those which may be enjoyed under the state scheme), an employer may contract-out of the state scheme. The overseeing of these provisions is the responsibility of the Occupational Pension Board (which was established under the Social Security Act 1973) and employment under an employer whose scheme meets with the Board's approval becomes a contracted-out employment. As the arrangement under most occupational pension schemes is that the employed earner will receive the basic component of his pension from the state and only the additional component of his pension from the scheme, it is equitable that he and his employer should pay the standard rate of contributions on earnings which are not reckonable for additional component purposes, but that a reduction in the standard rate of contribution should be made on any earnings which are so reckonable. Accordingly, there results a two-tier contribution arrangement as regards earnings in contracted-out employments.

5.18 Rates of contribution

Clearly, contribution rates cannot remain static if the Fund which they finance is subject to changing demands. Accordingly, the Secretary of State is, at any time, empowered to make an order altering the percentage rates for primary and secondary Class 1 contributions if he thinks it expedient to do so with a view to adjusting the level at which the National Insurance Fund stands in relation to sums which may be expected to be paid from the Fund in any future period (SSA 1975, s. 122(1)(a)). This power is, however, limited in various ways. Firstly, it is, by Treasury direction, exercisable only in conjunction with the Treasury (SSA 1975, s. 166(5)). Secondly, no order can be made which would increase for any tax year the percentage rate for primary or secondary Class 1 contributions to a percentage rate more than 0.25% higher than the percentage rate applicable for the preceding tax year (SSA 1975, s. 122(6) as amended by SSA 1980, Sch. 1, para. 13). Thirdly, an order to alter primary or secondary Class 1 contribution rates must first be laid before each House of Parliament, accompanied by the Government Actuary's report on the likely effect of the order on the National Insurance Fund (SSA 1975, s. 123(2)), and must be approved by resolution of each House (SSA 1975, s. 123(1)). Any such order takes effect from the beginning of the tax year following that in which it receives the approval of the House of Lords (SSA 1975, s. 123(3)).

The Secretary of State has identical powers to those described above to alter the percentage rate for secondary Class 1 contributions only, if he thinks it expedient to do so with a view to adjusting the level at which the Redundancy Fund or the Maternity Pay Fund stands in relation to likely future calls upon either or both of those funds (SSA 1975, s. 122(4)). The same strictures apply to an order under s. 122(4) as to an order under s. 122(1) except that no actuarial report need be laid before Parliament (SSA 1975, s. 123(2)).

Any alteration in the primary or secondary contribution rates which would go beyond the powers of the Secretary of State as described above must be made by statute.

From 6 April 1982, the standard percentage rate for primary Class 1 contributions has been set at 8.75 (SSA 1975, s. 4(6)(a) as amended by the Social Security (Contributions) Act (SS(C)A) 1982, ss. 1(2)), but the percentage rate of secondary Class 1 contributions has remained unchanged since 6 April 1980 at 10.2 (SSA 1975, s. 4(6)(b) as amended by the Social Security (Contributions, Re-rating) (No. 2) Order 1979, No. 1736, art. 2).

In the case of certain married women and widows who have an election in force (see **3.20** ante), the standard percentage rate for primary (but not secondary) Class 1 contributions is, from 6 April 1982, reduced to 3.2 (SI 1979, No. 591, reg. 104 as amended by SS(C)A 1982, s. 1(3)). This rate is termed 'reduced rate' and is thus distinguished from 'standard rate' (SI 1979, No. 591, reg. 1(2)).

In the case of certain mariners (see **7.33** post) and registered dock workers who have no general entitlement to redundancy payments under EP(C)A 1978, s. 81, the percentage rates of primary and secondary Class 1 contributions are, from 6 April 1982, reduced by 0.35 and 0.15 respectively (ie currently to 8.4 and 10.05) (SI 1979, No. 591, reg. 89(1)(a) as amended by SI 1980, No. 13, reg. 2, and SS(C)A 1982, Sch. 1, para. 3(2) and SI 1979, No. 591, reg. 133(1) as amended by SI 1980, No. 13, reg. 5 and SS(C)A 1982, Sch. 1, para. 3(4)); and, in the case of serving members of the forces (see **7.52** post) the standard percentage rate for primary contributions is reduced by 1.05, the reduced percentage rate of primary Class 1 contributions is reduced by 0.5 and the percentage rate for secondary Class 1 contributions is reduced by 1.25 (SI 1979, No. 591, reg. 115(1)(a) and (b) as amended by SI 1980, No. 13, reg. 4 and SS(C)A 1982, Sch. 1, para. 3(3)).

In the case of a contracted-out employment (see **5.17** ante) the contracted-out percentage rate for primary Class 1 contributions on upper band earnings has, from 5 April 1978, been set at 2.5 less than the normal percentage rate (ie the contracted-out primary rate is currently 6.25%), and the contracted-out percentage rate for secondary contributions on upper band earnings has been set at 4.5 less than the normal percentage rate (ie the contracted-out secondary rate is currently 5.7%) (SSPA 1975, s. 27(2)). The 'normal' percentage rate is the rate which would have been payable if the employment were not a contracted-out employment (SSPA 1975, s. 27(2)), except that the reduced rate cannot be further reduced even if the employment is contracted-out (SSPA 1975, s. 27(5)).

EXAMPLE 5(P)

Gordon is a registered dock worker who does not fall within the redundancy provisions of EP(C)A 1978, s. 81, and his wife, Helen, has a reduced rate election in force. Both are in contracted-out employments.

In the week ended 5 June 1982, Gordon's gross pay is £120 and Helen's gross pay is £60. Contributions are calculated as follows:

Gordon:

Lower band earnings £29.50 × 8.4% (ie registered dock workers' normal rate = 8.75% normal rate, less 0.35% redundancy allocation reduction)	2.48
Upper band earnings £9.50 × 5.9% (ie registered dock workers' contracted-out rate = 8.75% normal rate, less 0.35% redundancy allocation reduction, less 2.5%)	5.34
	7.82

Gordon's employer:

Lower band earnings £29.50 × 13.55% (ie registered dock workers' normal rate = 10.2% normal rate, less 0.15% redundancy allocation reduction, plus 3.5% national insurance surcharge (see **5.19** post))	4.00
Upper band earnings £90.50 × 9.05% (ie dock workers' contracted-out rate = 10.2% normal rate, less 0.15% redundancy allocation reduction, less 4.5%, plus 3.5% national insurance surcharge)	8.19
	12.19

Helen:

Lower band earnings £29.50 × 3.2% (ie reduced rate)	.94
Upper band earnings £30.50 × 3.2% (ie no further reduction even though contracted-out)	.98
	1.92

Helen's employer:

Lower band earnings £29.50 × 13.7% (ie 10.2% normal rate, plus 3.5% national insurance surcharge (see **5.19** post))	4.04
Upper band earnings £30.50 × 9.2% (ie contracted-out rate = 10.2% normal rate, less 4.5%, plus 3.5% national insurance surcharge)	2.81
	6.85

The Secretary of State has power to make orders altering the contracted-out percentage rate of primary and secondary Class 1 contributions, provided such orders are laid before, and approved by resolution of, each House of Parliament (SSPA 1975, s. 28(4)). The draft order must be supported by a report by the Government Actuary on any changes in the factors affecting the cost to occupational pension schemes of providing guaranteed minimum pensions and by a report by the Secretary of State himself as to the alterations he considers such changes necessitate (SSPA 1975, s. 28(1)). The first such reports were completed in August 1981 and the contracted-out rates are, as a result, to be adjusted from 6 April 1983.

5.19　National insurance surcharge

Anyone who pays, or is liable to pay, a secondary Class 1 contribution on earnings is liable to pay with that secondary contribution a surcharge (NISA 1976, s. 1(1)) with the exception of charities within the meaning of ICTA 1970, s. 360 (FA 1977, s. 57(1)). As regards earnings paid on or after 2 October 1978 the surcharge is 3.5% of the amount of the earnings in respect of which the secondary contribution is paid or payable (FA 1978, s. 75(1) and (2)). The surcharge as regards earnings paid prior to that date but on or after 6 April 1977 was 2% (NISA 1976, s. 1(1)).

It can be seen that, though the surcharge is, in law, distinguishable from the secondary contributions to which it is related and has, in fact, a different destination in state funds, the surcharge is effectively an increase in the secondary contribution and is commonly treated as such. Accordingly, the current rate of secondary Class 1 contributions is often (wrongly) stated as 13.7% rather than (correctly) 10.2% plus 3.5% surcharge.

5.20　Calculation of contributions

By regulations made under SSA 1975, Sch. 1, para. 4(a) it is provided that, to avoid fractional amounts and to facilitate computation, primary and secondary Class 1 contributions at standard rate and primary and secondary Class 1 contributions at the normal percentage rate and at the contracted-out percentage rate are each to be calculated separately and each such calculation is to be to the nearest penny with any amount of a half-penny or less being disregarded (SI 1979, No. 591, reg. 9(1)(a) and (b)). This method is primarily used in payroll computer programs. It is known as the exact percentage method (DHSS Leaflet NP15, paras. 59 to 61) and is illustrated in Example 5(P) above. Alternatively (and more commonly) contributions may be calculated in accordance with appropriate scales prepared by the Secretary of State (SI 1979, No. 591, reg. 9(2)) which take the form of tables obtainable from the DHSS. Form CF391 (obtainable from local DHSS offices) contains tables for use where the employment is a non-contracted-out employment; form CF392 (obtainable from the Contracted-Out Employment Group at Newcastle-upon-Tyne) contains tables for use where the employment is a contracted-out employment; and form CF398 (obtainable from any collector of taxes) contains tables for employers such as churches and charities who are exempt from the national insurance surcharge.

Each of the tables is divided into sections appropriate to standard rate contributions, reduced rate contributions and secondary-contributor-only contributions. (This latter section is of relevance where, for example, the employed earner is age-exempt or has paid contributions in advance or has arranged to defer contributions.) The tables cater only for earnings periods of one week or one month. Accordingly, where an earnings period is a multiple of a week or a month, the earnings in question must be divided so as to obtain equivalent earnings for a week or a month (as appropriate). The contributions shown by the tables for those equivalent earnings are then to be multiplied by the factor by which the earnings were divided (SI 1979, No. 591, reg. 9(4)). In the case of weekly earnings periods the tables are banded in earnings steps of fifty pence, and, in the case of monthly earnings periods, in steps of two pounds. Except at the lower and upper earnings limits, the contributions stated in the tables have been calculated on the mid-point of the band. Where the amount of earnings on which contributions are to be calculated does not appear on the scale, contributions are to be calculated by reference to the next smaller amount of earnings on the scale (SI 1979, No. 591, reg. 9(3)).

EXAMPLE 5(Q)

Ian's earnings for the quarter ended 5 February 1982 are £1,295. Class 1 contributions are calculated using tables CF391 as follows:

£1,295/3 = £431.66. No band entry for £431.66, therefore next smaller band entry applied, ie £431. Employee's contribution = £33.48; employer's contribution = £59.18. Contributions for the quarter to 5 February 1982 = primary: £100.44 (£33.48 × 3); secondary: £177.54 (£59.18 × 3).

While both the exact percentage method and the official table method are equally acceptable, all the contributions payable in a particular tax year as regards the earnings paid to or for the benefit of an employed earner in respect of his employed earner's employment (or employments, if he has more than one and they fall to be aggregated) are, unless the Secretary of State agrees to the contrary, to be calculated wholly in accordance with either one method or the other (SI 1979, No. 591, reg. 9(5)). Permission to change from one method to the other is not required, however, where the change is due to the employed earner being transferred to a payroll where contributions are calculated by the other method, or where the change is due to a change in payroll procedure (eg from manual to computer payroll preparation) (DHSS Leaflet NP15, para. 59). It is, of course, permissible for an employer to use one method for some of his employees and the alternative method for others.

There are special rules for the calculation of contributions where earnings in respect of different employments are to be aggregated (see **5.13** ante) and those employments include both contracted-out and non-contracted-out employment. If the aggregated earnings are less than the lower earnings limit there is, of course, no problem. If the aggregated earnings exceed the lower earnings limit, however, contributions are first to be calculated on the earnings attributable to any contracted-out employments in so far as such earnings do not exceed the upper earnings limit. If those earnings alone reach the upper earnings limit, no contributions fall to be calculated on earnings from any non-contracted-out employments. If the earnings attributable to the contracted-out employments do not reach the upper earnings limit, however, contributions at the non-contracted-out rate are to be calculated on the balance of earnings up to and including the upper earnings limit (SSA 1975, Sch. 1, para. 1A as inserted by SSA 1980, Sch. 1, para. 16). Where the balance of earnings last referred to is less than the lower earnings limit it will be necessary to use the exact percentage method of calculation as no contribution table figure is available. In these circumstances, DHSS permission for change of method is not required (DHSS Leaflet NP15, paras. 59 and 92).

EXAMPLE 5(R)

From 5 April 1982, Jeremy is employed in a contracted-out employment with K Ltd from which he derives earnings of £40 per week. He is also employed in a contracted-out employment with L Ltd at a salary of £400 per month, and in a non-contracted-out employment with M Ltd at a wage of £85 per week. K, L and M are all associated.

The common earnings period must be one week (see **5.10** ante) and the aggregated earnings are £225 (£40+£400/4+£85) of which £125 relate to contracted-out employment. Contributions are calculated on these as follows:

		£
Primary Class 1:	£29.50 (LEL) × 8.75%	2.58
	£95.50 (Balance of contracted-out earnings) × 6.25%	5.97
		8.55
Secondary Class 1:	£29.50 (LEL) × 13.7%	4.04
	£95.50 (Balance of contracted-out earnings) × 9.2%	8.79
		12.83

The balance of earnings (£100) related to non-contracted-out employment and contributions are calculated on it viz:

Primary Class 1:	£95 (UEL £220 less earnings of £125 on which contributions calculated above) × 8.75%	8.31
Secondary Class 1:	£95 (as for primary contributions) × 13.7%	13.01
		21.32

Total primary contributions are, therefore, £16.86 and total secondary contributions are £25.84. £5 of the earnings from the non-contracted-out employment is free of contributions as, to that extent, total aggregated earnings exceed the UEL.

CLASS 2 CONTRIBUTIONS

5.21 Class 2 contributions defined

Class 2 contributions are payable weekly by self-employed earners at a flat-rate (SSA 1975, s. 1(2)). Accordingly, there are no rules of calculation and, except for the purpose stated at **5.22** post, no ascertainment of earnings is required. Reference should be made to **7.12** post, which describes the provisions relating to persons who are exceptionally self-employed.

Where a contribution week falls partly in one tax year and partly in another, it is to be treated for Class 2 purposes as falling wholly within the year in which it begins (SSA 1975, Sch. 1, para. 6(e) and SI 1979, No. 591, reg. 131).

5.22 Small earnings exception

Regulations made under SSA 1975, s. 7(5) (as amended by SS(C)A 1982, s. 1(4)(b)) provide for an earner who would otherwise be liable for Class 2 contributions in respect of an employment as a self-employed earner to be excepted from that liability in respect of any period in which his earnings from such employment are (or are treated as being) less than (from 5 April 1982) £1,600. The corresponding amount for 1981–82 was £1,475 and amounts for earlier years are set out in Appendix 7. It must be emphasised that exception will not be granted to a self-employed earner

'. . . otherwise than on his own application . . .' (SSA 1975, s. 7(6))

and that, if granted, will not be retrospective in its effect for more than thirteen weeks (SSA 1975, s. 7(6)); possibly less as any retrospective effect is given entirely at the Secretary of State's discretion (SI 1979, No. 591, reg. 24(5)(b)).

Before exception will be granted it must be shown to the Secretary of State's satisfaction that

'. . . in the year preceding the particular year . . . earnings . . . were less than the amount so specified for the preceding year and that there has since been no material change of circumstances . . .' (SI 1979, No. 591, reg. 25(1)(a))

or that

'. . . in the particular year . . . earnings are expected to be less than the specified amount' (SI 1979, No. 591, reg. 25(1)(b)).

The ascertainment of earnings for this purpose has been described at **4.27** ante.

EXAMPLE 5(S)
Nigel is a grocer. His net profit for the year ended 5 April 1982 was only £1,450 and, on 1 September 1982, as trade has become even worse he applies for Class 2 exception. As his earnings for 1981–82 (the year preceding the year of application) were below the exception limit for that

year (£1,475) and circumstances have changed only for the worse, exception will be granted, but only from (at the earliest) 2 June 1982.

EXAMPLE 5(T)

Olive is a milliner. Her net profit for the year ended 5 April 1982 was £1,480 but, between 6 April 1982 and 6 June 1982, her takings have been insufficient to cover even her fixed overhead expenses. Accordingly, she applies for Class 2 exception. Her application will be granted provided she has good grounds for believing that her trading position is unlikely to improve, but (at best) her exception will be effective only from 5 April 1982 even though that date is only eight weeks prior to her application. The reason for this is that, in the year ended 5 April 1982, her earnings exceeded the exception limit.

Application for exception from Class 2 liability on the grounds of small income is to be made to the Secretary of State (SI 1979, No. 591, reg. 24(1)) in a form approved by him (SI 1979, No. 591, reg. 24(2)). In practical terms this involves completing and signing a form CF10 and lodging it with a DHSS office (DHSS Leaflet NI27A). The application is to be supported by such information and evidence of earnings as the Secretary of State may require (SI 1979, No. 591, reg. 24(3)) and this will usually take the form of accounts, tax assessments or records of receipts and payments (DHSS Leaflet NI27A).

If the application is approved, the Secretary of State will issue to the applicant a certificate of exception (CF17) which will state the period for which exception is to apply (SI 1979, No. 591, reg. 24(4)). This will normally be from the date of application to the following 5 April, but, as has been explained earlier, may extend retrospectively to a date up to thirteen weeks prior to application or to 5 April prior to application, whichever is the later (DHSS Leaflet NI27A).

If the conditions attaching to a certificate of exception cease to be fulfilled, the certificate ceases to have force and the Secretary of State is to be notified (SI 1979, No. 591, reg. 24(5)(a)). This requirement is met by completing and signing declaration B on the certificate of exception itself and returning it to the DHSS office (DHSS Leaflet NI27A).

A certificate of exception may be cancelled at any time the holder so wishes (SI 1979, No. 591, reg. 24(6)(b)) and the necessary notice in writing is given to the Secretary of State by returning the certificate to a DHSS office with declaration C completed and signed (DHSS Leaflet NI27A).

Anyone holding a certificate of exception must produce it for inspection if required to do so (SI 1979, No. 591, reg. 24(6)(a)).

Although a certificate of exception excepts the holder from liability to pay Class 2 contributions for any whole contribution week for which it is in force (SI 1979, No. 591, reg. 26(a)), that holder may nevertheless pay contributions if he so wishes (SI 1979, No. 591, reg. 26(b)).

5.23 Excepting circumstances

Apart from exception on the grounds of small income as described in the preceding section, a self-employed earner will be excepted from liability to pay a Class 2 contribution for any whole contribution week in which he or she is either in receipt of sickness benefit, invalidity benefit or injury benefit (SI 1979, No. 591, reg. 23(1)); incapable of work as evidenced by doctor's statements (SI 1979, No. 591, reg. 23(2) and DHSS Leaflet NI41); in receipt of maternity allowance (SI 1979, No. 591, reg. 23(3)); undergoing imprisonment or detention in legal custody (SI 1979, No. 591, reg. 23(4)); or in receipt of unemployability supplement or invalid care allowance (SI 1979, No. 591, reg. 23(5)). A whole contribution week for these purposes excludes Sunday or some religiously-acceptable alternative day (SI 1979, No. 591, reg. 23(2)(a) and (b)).

Anyone excepted from liability to pay Class 2 contributions in the circumstances described is, nevertheless, entitled to pay contributions if he or she so wishes (SI 1979, No. 591, reg. 23(3)).

5.24 Contribution rates

From 6 April 1982, the weekly rate at which Class 2 contributions are payable is £3.75 (SSA 1975, s. 7(1) as amended by SS(C)A 1982, s. 1(4)(a)), except for share fishermen (see **7.43** post) who are liable to contribute at the specially increased weekly rate of £5.85 (SI 1979, No. 591, reg. 98(c) as amended by SS(C)A 1982, s. 1(5)).

The weekly rate at which Class 2 contributions are payable may, under SSA 1975, s. 122, be altered at any time by the Secretary of State in the same manner and under the same circumstances as he may alter the percentage rates for primary and secondary Class 1 contributions (see **5.18** ante). In the case of Class 2 contributions, however, there are no fixed boundaries within which any alteration must be confined, though the other controls remain the same. If the Secretary of State thinks it expedient, he may, at the same time as he makes an order altering the rate of Class 2 contributions, also alter the small earnings exception limit (SSA 1975, s. 122(3)(a)).

CLASS 3 CONTRIBUTIONS

5.25 Class 3 contributions defined

No liability to pay Class 3 contributions can ever arise as Class 3 contributions are simply a means whereby earners and others are enabled, on a voluntary basis, to satisfy contribution conditions of entitlement to basic Category A or Category B retirement pension, widow's allowance, basic widowed mother's allowance, basic widow's pension, child's special allowance and death grant (SSA 1975, ss. 8(2) and 13(1)). Questions of calculation do not arise, therefore, except for the purpose of determining whether conditions of entitlement have already been satisfied and, should they not have been, the extent of the deficiency which may be made good. Such calculations will always centre on a person's 'earnings factor'.

5.26   Earnings factors

Entitlement to pay a Class 3 contribution in any tax year depends on the level at which a person's earnings factor already stands in that particular year. The earnings factor may be thought of as the link between the contribution and the benefit sides of the social security scheme. Accordingly, an employed earner whose earnings factor has fallen below a qualifying level for a particular year is notified of the deficiency by the DHSS on a form RD20(NP) and is advised of the number of Class 3 contributions which may be paid to rectify matters. Such notification is given to Class 1 contributors because of the complexity of the calculations necessary to the ascertainment of the earnings factor where Class 1 contributions are involved. As will be seen, Class 2 contributions give rise to no such difficulties.

An earnings factor is a figure derived from the amount of contributions paid or credited in a tax year, by reference to which the satisfaction of contribution conditions of entitlement to contributory benefits is judged (SSA 1975, s. 13(2)). Separate earnings factors are derived from contributions of different classes actually paid and from contributions of different classes merely credited in the same tax year (SSA 1975, s. 13(5)) and these separate earnings factors are aggregated to give a person's overall earnings factor for the year.

The earnings factor deriving from Class 1 contributions actually paid in a year (including Class 1 contributions overpaid even if subsequently refunded, and Class 1 contributions which would have been overpaid if they had not been deferred (SI 1979, No. 676, reg. 4)) is approximately equal (in round pounds) to the minimum actual earnings sufficient to yield contributions of that amount (SSA 1975, s. 13(5)(a)). The formula to be applied is:

$$100 \times \left[\left(\frac{(P-Q)+S}{R} \right) + \left(\frac{Q+S1}{R1} \right) \right]$$

where P is the amount of Class 1 contributions actually paid in respect of the year, S or S1 is the smallest sum required to make the factor $((P-Q)+S)$ or $(Q+S1)$ a multiple of 10p (treating 0p for this purpose as a sum), Q is the amount of contracted-out contributions paid in respect of the year, R is the figure appropriate for expressing the percentage rate at which non-contracted-out contributions were payable for the year (eg 8.75 is the figure appropriate to express 8.75%), and R1 is the correspondingly appropriate figure for expressing the percentage rate for contracted-out contributions (SI 1979, No. 676, Sch. 1, Pt. I, paras. 1(1)(a)(b)(e) and 2). The result is rounded to the nearest whole penny (SI 1979, No. 676, Sch. 1, Pt. I, paras. 1(1)(f) and 2).

It should be noted that the resultant earnings factor is not necessarily the amount of gross earnings for the year: there may have been weeks where earnings were below the lower earnings limit with no contributions whatsoever payable, or weeks where the earnings were above the upper earnings limit with no contributions payable on the excess.

The earnings factor derived from Class 1 contributions credited in respect of a year is ascertained by applying the formula 100C/R where C is the amount of Class 1 contributions credited and R is the figure appropriate for expressing the standard percentage rate at which Class 1 contributions were payable for the year (SI 1979, No. 676, Sch. 1, Pt. I, para. 4(b)). The result, aggregated with the earnings factor derived from Class 1 contributions paid, and rounded to the nearest whole pound, gives an earnings factor for Class 1 contributions paid or credited (SI 1979, No. 676, Sch. 1, Pt. I, paras. 4 and 5).

The earnings factor deriving from Class 2 or Class 3 contributions paid or credited in respect of a tax year is equal (in round pounds) to that year's lower earnings limit for Class 1 contributions (expressed as a weekly amount) multiplied by the number of contributions paid or credited (SSA 1975, s. 13(5)(b) and SI 1979, No. 676, Sch. 1, Pt. II, paras. 8 and 9), eg number of Class 2 contributions paid for the year ended 5 April 1982, 28: earnings factor, $28 \times £29.50 = £826$.

No earnings factor is derived from primary Class 1 contributions paid at the reduced rate, or from secondary Class 1 contributions (SSA 1975, s. 13(3)), or from Class 4 contributions (SSA 1975, s. 13(2)).

Having arrived at a person's aggregate earnings factor for a tax year, this must then be compared with both the 'qualifying earnings factor' for the year and the 'standard level' for the year (SI 1979, No. 676, Sch. 1, Pt. I, para. 6). The qualifying earnings factor is an earnings factor equal to the weekly lower earnings limit for a year multiplied by 52 (SSPA 1975, s. 5(3)) and the standard level is an amount equivalent to the weekly lower earnings limit multiplied by 50 (SI 1979, No. 676, Sch. 1, Pt. I, para. 1(1)(d)). Where a person has actually paid Class 1 contributions in respect of a year and the aggregate earnings factor falls short of either the qualifying earnings factor by £14 or less, or the standard level by £14 or less, or three-quarters of the standard level by £11 or less or a half of the standard level by £7 or less, the aggregate earnings factor is increased by the shortfall and the result is rounded up to the next whole pound (SI 1979, No. 676, Sch. 1, Pt. I, para. 6). Only where the adjusted aggregate earnings factor for a year then neither equals nor exceeds the qualifying earnings factor will a person be entitled to pay Class 3 contributions for that year (SSPA 1975, s. 5(1)).

EXAMPLE 5(U)

Philip was self-employed until his business ceased on 31 July 1981. For each of those 17 weeks in 1981–82 he paid a Class 2 contribution. Between 1 August 1981 and 5 April 1982 he found occasional employment and paid primary Class 1 contributions of £42.55. In May 1982 he obtains a permanent position and decides to make good any deficiency in his contribution record. The extent to which he may do this calculated as follows:

£

Data
Qalifying earnings factor 1981–82:

	£
52 × £27 =	1,404.00
Standard level: 50 × £27	1,350.00
3/4 standard level: 3/4 × £1,350.00	1,012.50
1/2 standard level: 1/2 × £1,350.00	675.00
1/4 standard level: 1/4 × £1,350.00	337.50

£

Computation

	£	£
Class 2 earnings factor: 17 × £27 =	459.00	
Class 1 earnings factor:		
100 × ((£42.55 + £0.05)/7.75) =	549.68	
		1,008.68
Addition of shortfall to bring earnings factor to 3/4 standard level		3.82
		1,012.50
Addition to round up to nearest whole pound		.50
Aggregate earnings factor		1,013.00
Qualifying earnings factor		1,404.00
Earnings factor deficiency		391.00

Number of Class 3 contributions permissible:

£391/£27 = 14.48 = 14

Before considering additional limitations which are placed on an entitlement to pay Class 3 contributions, it is necessary to be aware of the circumstances in which a person will be credited with contributions.

5.27 Credited contributions

Regulations made under SSA 1975, s. 13(4), provide for crediting a person with contributions for the purpose of bringing his earnings factor in a tax year to a figure which will enable him to satisfy contribution conditions of entitlement to certain benefits. As, however, the entitlement to most benefits depends on the satisfaction of two contributory conditions of which the first is that contributions have, in any one tax year after 5 April 1975, actually been paid at a specified minimum level (see **1.17** ante), credited contributions alone are unable to create a benefit entitlement. They are, therefore, credited only for the purpose of enabling a person to satisfy the second of the contributory conditions (SI 1975, No. 556, reg. 3(1)).

Apart from the termination of a woman's marriage (when, in certain circumstances, a miscellany of protective credits and substitute-contributions may be awarded under the Social Security (Benefit) (Married Women and Widows' Special Provisions) Regulations, SI 1974, No. 2010, regs. 2 to 7, as amended), there are five circumstances in which a person (other than a married woman with a reduced rate election (see **3.20** ante) in force (SI 1975, No. 556, regs. 5(2), 7(3), 8(2)(b) and 9(6)) may be credited with contributions which he has not actually paid, and the first of these arises when a person makes his initial entry into the contributory scheme. For the purpose of entitlement to a Category A or B retirement pension, a widowed mother's allowance or a widow's pension, a person is to be credited with sufficient Class 3 contributions in the tax year in which he attains the age of sixteen and for each of the two following tax years to bring his relevant earnings factor in each of those years to the required level for the second contribution condition to be satisfied (SI 1975, No. 556, reg. 4(1)). For the purpose of entitlement to unemployment benefit, sickness benefit and maternity allowance, starting credits are of primary Class 1 contributions calculated at the standard rate on a weekly earnings figure equivalent to the lower earnings limit (SI 1975, No. 556, reg. 3(2)(b)) and are given for the year in which a person attains the age of seventeen or any previous year (SI 1975, No. 556, reg. 5(1)(a)) or any later year up to and including the first year in which he pays (or is treated as paying) a Class 1 or Class 2 contribution (SI 1975, No. 556, reg. 5(1)(b)).

The second circumstance in which credits may be given arises where a person (other than an employed earner pursuing his employment) undergoes an approved course of full-time training which is not (unless it is a course for the disabled) intended to continue for more than twelve months (SI 1975, No. 556, regs. 7(1) and (2)(b)). An approved training credit is a primary Class 1 contribution (calculated in the manner described in the foregoing paragraph) and is given for any week in any part of which such training is being undergone, provided that, before the beginning of the tax year in which the week falls, the person has attained the age of eighteen (SI 1975, No. 556, reg. 7(2)(c)) and provided also that (unless there are reasonable grounds for waiving the requirement) for at least one of the last three tax years before the course began the person's earnings factor derived from Class 1 or Class 2 contributions paid or credited has amounted to at least fifty times the lower earnings limit for the year (SI 1975, No. 556, reg. 7(2)(a)).

The third circumstance in which credits may be given arises when an apprenticeship or a course of full-time education or approved training, begun by a person under the age of twenty-one, is terminated (SI 1975, No. 556, reg. 8(1)(a)(b)(c) and (2)(a)). Sufficient training termination credits of primary Class 1 contributions (calculated in the manner described in the foregoing paragraphs) are awarded for the year in which termination occurs to bring the earnings factor for that year to the level necessary for the second contributory condition of entitlement to unemployment benefit, sickness benefit or maternity allowance to be satisfied (SI 1975, No. 556, regs. 8(1) and 3(2)(a)).

The fourth circumstance in which credits may be given arises when a person becomes unemployed or incapacitated for work for any complete week. A week of unemployment or incapacity includes any week for which unemployability supplement or allowance is payable (SI 1975, No. 556, reg. 9(2)(b)) or throughout which a person is entitled to unemployment benefit, injury benefit, sickness benefit or maternity allowance (SI 1975, No. 556, reg. 9(3)(a) and (5)(a) and (c)) whether claimed or not (SI 1975, No. 556, reg. 9(3)(b) and (5)(b)(c)), provided that the person 'signs on' at an unemployment benefit office or furnishes alternative evidence of unemployment (SI 1975, No. 556, reg. 9(7)(a) and (b)) or gives notice of his grounds for credit in the case of sickness or maternity (SI 1975, No. 556, reg. 9(8)), supplying doctor's statements if required (DHSS Leaflet NI42), and provided that certain requirements have been met with regard to the tax year preceding the year of claim (SI 1975, No. 556, reg. 9(9) as inserted by SI 1977, No. 788, reg. 2). The credit given for each such week is a primary Class 1 contribution calculated in the manner described in foregoing paragraphs (SI 1975, No. 556, reg. 9(1)). Such a credit is similarly available to a person for any week or part of a week in which invalid care allowance is paid to him (SI 1975, No. 566, reg. 7A as inserted by SI 1976, No. 409).

The fifth circumstance in which a credit may be given arises where, for any year, a contributor's earnings factor derived from all contributions paid or credited falls short of a figure which is 52 times that year's weekly lower earnings limit by an amount equal to, or less than, half that year's weekly lower earnings limit. The credit given is one Class 3 contribution'(SI 1979, No. 591, reg. 36).

5.28   Precluded Class 3 contributions

The basic limitation on the payment of Class 3 contributions has already been stated at **5.26** ante. There are further prohibitions, however, which must now be described.

Firstly, no Class 3 contribution may be paid where, but for the payment of such a contribution, there would be an entitlement to a credited contribution (SI 1979, No. 591, reg. 28(1)(a)). A credited contribution means, throughout this section, a contribution credited for the purposes of retirement pension, widowed mother's allowance and widow's pension (SI 1979, No. 591, reg. 28(3)). It does *not*, therefore, include primary Class 1 starting credits or termination of training or education credits.

Secondly, even where neither the first nor the second contributory condition for benefit entitlement has been met in a particular year, no Class 3 contributions may be paid in respect of that year once the time limit for the payment of such contributions (see **6.24** post) has expired or once application for the return of Class 3 contributions paid in respect of that year (see **6.33** post) has been made (SI 1979, No. 591, reg. 28(1)(b) and (c)), unless the payment of such contributions would enable either the first contribution condition for retirement pension, widow's pension, widowed mother's allowance, widow's allowance or death grant to be met (SI 1979, No. 591, reg. 28(2)(a) and (b)) or the second contribution condition for unemployment or sickness benefit in transitional cases involving the termination of training or education begun before 5 April 1975 to be satisfied (SI 1979, No. 591, reg. 28(2)(d)).

Thirdly, no Class 3 contribution may be paid in respect of any year if it causes the earnings factor derived from contributions paid or credited in respect of that year to exceed the qualifying earnings factor by an amount which is half or more than half that year's lower earnings limit (SI 1979, No. 591, reg. 28(1)(d)).

EXAMPLE 5(V)

Quentin undergoes full-time training on an approved six-month course which ends on 5 October 1981. He immediately finds employment but pays only £46.50 in primary Class 1 contributions before 5 April 1982. He obtains an RD20(NP) contribution statement from the DHSS for 1981–82 and this informs him that he may pay only 4 Class 3 contributions for that year. The reason is explained by the following calculation:

	£
1981–82 Qualifying earnings factor: 52 × £27	1,404.00
1/2 weekly lower earnings limit for year	13.50
Amount below which earnings factor must fall for eligibility to pay Class 3 contributions to arise	1,417.50

	£	£
Maximum permitted earnings factor		1,417
Training credits: 26 weeks × £27 × 7.75% = £54.40 giving earnings factor of £54.40 × 100/7.75:	702	
Primary Class 1 contributions paid: £46.50 giving earnings factor of £46.50 × 100/7.75:	600	
Aggregate earnings factor		1,302
Earnings factor deficiency		115
Permitted Class 3 contributions: £115/£27 = 4.26 = 4 giving an earnings factor of		108

Four Class 3 contributions will bring Quentin's earnings factor to £1,410 (ie £1,302 + £108) which exceeds the qualifying earnings factor by £6. The maximum permitted excess is £13 (ie a rounded amount under 1/2 × £27). A fifth Class 3 contribution would obviously take the earnings factor over the limit.

The payment of Class 3 contributions is, fourthly, prohibited in respect of any year in which a person attains pensionable age or in respect of any subsequent year (SI 1979, No. 591, reg. 28(1)(e)), and in respect of years in which a person attains seventeen or eighteen years of age if, in an earlier year, he has satisfied the first contribution condition for retirement pension, widow's pension or widowed mother's allowance (SI 1979, No. 591, reg. 28(1)(f)).

Fifthly, a woman who has a reduced rate election in force (see **3.20** ante) is precluded from paying Class 3 contributions for any year throughout the whole of which the election is in force (SI 1979, No. 591, reg. 105).

5.29   Contribution rate

From 6 April 1982 the amount of a Class 3 contribution is £3.65 (SSA 1975, s. 8(1) as amended by SS(C)A 1982, s. 1(6)).

The specified amount of a Class 3 contribution may, under SSA 1975, s. 122, be altered at any time by the Secretary of State in the same manner and under the same circumstances as he may alter the percentage rate for primary and secondary Class 1 contributions (see **5.18** ante) and the weekly rate for Class 2 contributions (see **5.24** ante). As in the case of Class 2 contributions, however, there are no fixed boundaries within which any alteration in the amount of a Class 3 contribution must be confined, though the other controls described at **5.18** ante remain the same.

CLASS 4 CONTRIBUTIONS

5.30 Class 4 contributions defined

Class 4 contributions are payable in respect of profits or gains immediately derived from the carrying on or exercise of one or more trades, professions or vocations, being profits or gains chargeable to income tax under Case I or Case II of Schedule D for any year of assessment beginning on or after 6 April 1975 (SSA 1975, s. 9(1)). As has already been explained at **4.28** et seq ante, however, the profits or gains are subject to various deductions, additions and reliefs before they become earnings on which Class 4 contributions may be calculated. Class 4 contributions are earnings-related in so far as they are calculated at a percentage rate on so much of the adjusted profits or gains as falls between a lower and an upper annual limit (SSA 1975, s. 9(2)).

5.31   Limits of profits or gains

Because of a superficial similarity between Class 4 limits and the lower and upper earnings limits applicable to earnings on which Class 1 contributions are payable, it is necessary to emphasise the one fundamental difference between them. Once the lower earnings limit for Class 1 purposes has been reached, all earnings, including those below the lower earnings limit, are subject to Class 1 contributions, in so far as those earnings do not exceed the upper earnings limit. The lower annual limit for Class 4 purposes operates differently, however. Even when profits or gains exceed it, Class 4 contributions are payable only on the excess, up to and including the upper annual Class 4 profit limit. In effect, Class 2 contributions (although not related to earnings) have been levied in place of

Class 4 contributions on profits below the lower annual limit and there is, in fact, a fairly complex actuarial link between the two and between Class 2, Class 4 and Class 1 (see the DHSS discussion document: *The Self Employed and National Insurance*, 1980, paras. 27 to 31).

The Class 4 lower annual limit for 1982–83 is £3,450 and the upper annual limit for that year is £11,000 (SSA 1975, s. 9(3) as amended by SS(C)A 1982, s. 1(7)(b) and (c)). These limits may be altered by order of the Secretary of State as a result of the review of contributions and general level of earnings which, in the absence of statutory direction to the contrary, he is obliged to carry out annually under SSA 1975, s. 120 (SSA 1975, s. 120(5)(e)).

5.32   Rate of contribution

For the tax year beginning 6 April 1982, Class 4 contributions are payable at a percentage rate of 6.00 of so much of the profits or gains (calculated in accordance with the rules described at **4.28** et seq ante) as exceeds the lower annual limit of £3,450 and does not exceed the upper annual limit of £11,000 (SSA 1975, s. 9(3) as amended by SS(C)A 1982, s. 1(7)(a)).

EXAMPLE 5(W)

Robert, Stephen and Timothy are in partnership sharing profits in the ratio 4:2:1. The assessable profits (adjusted for Class 4 purposes) are £21,000 for 1982–83. Class 4 contributions are payable as follows:

	£
Robert: 4/7 × £21,000	12,000.00
Less: Lower annual limit	3,450.00
	8,550.00
Less: Excess of profit-share over upper annual limit:	
£12,000 − £11,000	1,000.00
	7,550.00
Class 4 contribution: £7,550 × 6%	453.00
Stephen: 2/7 × £21,000	6,000.00
Less: Lower annual limit	3,450.00
	2,550.00
Less: Excess profit-share over upper annual limit:	Nil
	2,550.00
Class 4 contribution: £2,550 × 6%	153.00
Timothy: 1/7 × £21,000	3,000.00
Less: Lower annual limit	3,450.00
	Nil
Class 4 contribution:	Nil

The percentage rate at which Class 4 contributions are payable may, under SSA 1975, s. 122, be altered at any time by the Secretary of State in the same manner and in the same circumstances as he may alter the percentage rate for primary and secondary Class 1 contributions (see **5.18** ante). The limitations and controls relating to his powers in this respect are the same, but the maximum possible rate to which he may order an increase in Class 4 contributions is 8.25% (SSA 1975, s. 122(1)(d) and (6) as amended by SSA 1980, Sch. 1, para. 13). The rate may, of course, be altered to any extent by statute.

5.33   Special Class 4 contributions

By regulation made under SSA 1975, s. 10(1), special Class 4 contributions are payable by any earner who is, by regulation (see **2.16** ante), treated as self-employed and who has, in any tax year, earnings (which would otherwise be Class 1 earnings) chargeable to tax under Schedule E in excess of the Class 4 lower profits limit (SI 1979, No. 591, reg. 71(a)(b)(c) and (d)). Earnings are to be calculated (see **4.02** et seq ante) as if they were employed earner's earnings and the total is to be rounded down to the nearest pound (SI 1979, No. 591, reg. 73(a) and (b)).

The earnings so arrived at are subjected to the same Class 4 contribution calculation rules as have been described above (SI 1979, No. 591, reg. 71) but the assessment of contributions and the notification of the amount payable will be made by the Secretary of State rather than by the Inland Revenue (SI 1979, No. 591, reg. 74). The person paying the earnings in question will make no Class 1 adjustment to pay but will merely mark the person's deductions workings sheet as directed by the Secretary of State and note the national insurance number (SI 1979, No. 591, reg. 72). It should be noted that the only group of earners to which these provisions currently relate are certain examiners, moderators and invigilators (see **7.09** post).

5.34   Exception from liability

It has already been noted (at **3.18** and at **3.10** ante) that anyone who, at the beginning of a year of assessment, is over pensionable age or who, during a year of assessment, is not resident for income tax purposes, is excepted from liability for Class 4 contributions. It has also been noted (at **3.17** ante) that anyone who is under the age of sixteen at the beginning of a year of assessment may be so excepted. The first two types of exception are automatic, but application must be made for the third (SI 1979, No. 591, reg. 60(2)), preferably before the beginning of the year of assessment for which the exception is sought and, in any event, before contributions become due and payable for that year (SI 1979, No. 591, reg. 60(3) and (4)). An application form (RD901) is obtainable from the

DHSS Class 4 Group at Newcastle-upon-Tyne and once that has been submitted and approved the Secretary of State will issue a certificate of exception authorising the Inland Revenue not to collect any Class 4 contributions for that year (SI 1979, No. 591, reg. 60(3)(4) and (5)).

There are other grounds for exception besides age and non-residence. A sleeping partner (ie someone who invests capital in a business and takes a share of the profits but takes no active part in the running of the business) is excepted from liability to pay Class 4 contributions on his share of profits. This exception arises not from regulation but by a strict construction of the words 'immediately derived' in SSA 1975, s. 9(1) quoted at **4.28** ante (DHSS Leaflet NP18).

A trustee, guardian, tutor, curator, or committee of an incapacitated person who would otherwise be assessable and chargeable to Class 4 contributions under the Taxes Management Act 1970, s. 72, is excepted from such contributions by SSA 1975, Sch. 2, para. 6(a), as is any trustee who would be liable for Class 4 contributions under ICTA 1970, s. 114 (SSA 1975, Sch. 2, para. 6(b)).

The Class 4 exception relating to divers or diving supervisors who work as employees in the North Sea or some other designated area but are assessed to tax under Schedule D is described at **7.58** post.

A final circumstance in which exception from payment of Class 4 contributions may be sought is where an earner has paid Class 1 contributions on earnings chargeable to tax under Schedule D (SI 1979, No. 591, reg. 61(1)). An example of the circumstances in which this kind of situation may arise is where a person in practice as an accountant or a solicitor has director's remuneration or fees (on which Class 1 contributions are payable) which he brings into his practice accounts. It also frequently occurs in the case of actors, musicians, film techniques and sub-postmasters. The exception extends to an amount of profits or gains otherwise liable for Class 4 contributions and equal to an earnings figure derived from contributions paid or payable by application of the appropriate contribution rate, be it standard rate, reduced rate or contracted-out rate (SI 1979, No. 591, reg. 61(1)(a)(b) and (c)).

EXAMPLE 5(X)

Uriah is a practicing solicitor and also a director of Vee Ltd. His accounting year ends on 31 May and his assessable profits adjusted for Class 4 purposes (based on the accounts to 31 May 1981) are £15,000 for 1982–83. During 1982–83 he pays primary Class 1 standard rate contributions of £175 on director's fees voted at 31 December 1982. Although those fees will not fall to be assessed until 1984–85, Class 4 exception will be given in 1982–83 on an amount of profits arrived at as follows:

Contributions paid: £175
Rate at which paid: 8.75%
Equivalent earnings: £175 × 100/8.75 = £2,000

Profits on which Class 4 contributions are payable for 1982–83 will, therefore, be:

	£
Profits as adjusted for Class 4 purposes	15,000
Less: Lower annual limit	3,450
	11,550
Less: Excess of adjusted profits over the upper annual limit: £15,000–£11,000	4,000
	7,750
Less: Class 4 exception	2,000
	5,550

Had Uriah's profits been only, say, £4,000 for 1982–83, the Class 4 exception would, of course, have been limited to £550, ie the only amount on which, but for the exception, Class 4 contributions would have been payable.

Exception from liability in these circumstances is conditional upon application being made to the Secretary of State before the beginning of the year of assessment to which the exception is to relate, or before such later date as the Secretary of State (with Revenue agreement) allows (SI 1979, No. 591, reg. 61(2)). The application must be in such form, and must be supported by such evidence, as the Secretary of State requires (SI 1979, No. 591, reg. 61(3)).

Where a certificate of exception has been issued by the Secretary of State as a result of erroneous or misleading or inadequate information having been supplied to him, he may revoke the certificate (SI 1979, No. 591, reg. 64(5)(a)). Thereupon, the applicant becomes liable to pay all contributions which would have been due but for the issue of the certificate (SI 1979, No. 591, reg. 64(5)(b)) and these will be calculated by the Secretary of State and not by the Inland Revenue (SI 1979, No. 591, reg. 65(a)). The applicant must furnish such information and evidence as the Secretary of State may require for this purpose (SI 1979, No. 591, reg. 65(b)(i)).

Chapter 6

Collection, deferment and repayment

6.01 Introduction

Having considered the principles of assessment and the rules of calculation whereby amounts of contributions due are ascertained, it is now necessary to examine the procedures for payment and collection whereby it is ensured that all such contributions find their way into the National Insurance Fund. As not all contributions reaching the Fund belong there, however, this chapter will also consider such provisions as have been made to prevent overpayment taking place and those which enable repayment to be obtained where overpayment has, in fact, occurred.

6.02 National insurance numbers

Under arrangements authorised by the Secretary of State, a national insurance number is generally allocated to a person within the year preceding his sixteenth birthday (SI 1979, No. 591, reg. 44(3)) and notified to him on a NI number card which is given to him shortly before his school-leaving date is reached. A national insurance number consists of two prefix letters, six figures and a suffix letter (eg AB123456C) and is of great importance as it is by reference to this number (as it appears on returns, claims, elections and PAYE documentation) that a person's contribution record (against which claims to benefit are checked) is maintained and updated in the DHSS central computer.

Anyone who has not been allocated a national insurance number but who is resident or present in Great Britain and over the age of sixteen must, therefore, if he is an employed or self-employed earner or wishes to pay a Class 3 contribution, apply to the Secretary of State for such a number forthwith (SSA 1975, Sch. 1, para. 6(1) and SI 1979, No. 591, reg. 44(1) and (2)). In practical terms, such application will be made to a person's local DHSS office on form CF8 or, if the person is under eighteen, to his local Careers Office.

Anyone who has a national insurance number must supply it to any person who is liable to pay an earnings-related contribution in his respect (SI 1979, No. 591, reg. 45).

COLLECTION OF CLASS 1 CONTRIBUTIONS

6.03   Liability for payment

Where earnings are paid to an employed earner and a liability for primary and secondary Class 1 contributions arises in respect of that payment, the secondary contributor is (except in the circumstances described below)

> '. . . as well as being liable for his own secondary contribution . . . liable in the first instance to pay also the earner's primary contribution, on behalf of and to the exclusion of the earner . . .' (SSA 1975, Sch. 1, para. 3(1)).

Primary contributions so paid by the secondary contributor are deemed to have been paid by the earner (SSA 1975, Sch. 1, para. 3(1)) and the secondary contributor is entitled to recover such primary contributions by deduction from the earner's earnings but in no other way (SSA 1975, Sch. 1, para. 3(3) and SI 1979, No. 591, Sch. 1, regs. 6(2) and 13(1)). Where two or more payments of earnings fall to be aggregated (see **5.13** ante) the secondary contributor may deduct the primary contributions based on those earnings wholly from one payment or partly from each or any of them (SI 1979, No. 591, Sch. 1, reg. 13(1A)). If, because of an error made in good faith or for certain other reasons, a secondary contributor fails to recover the full amount of primary contributions which he is entitled to recover, he may recover the amount so under-deducted by additional deductions from subsequent payments to the earner during the same tax year (SI 1979, No. 591, Sch. 1, reg. 13(2A)). He may not, however, deduct from any payment an additional amount which is greater than the amount of the earner's ordinary contribution on that payment (SI 1979, No. 591, Sch. 1, reg. 13(3A)(a)(ii)). Under no circumstances may a secondary contributor make any deduction from earnings in respect of secondary contributions or recover such contributions from the earner in any other way, even if he has contracted with the earner to do so; and any such action or attempted action carries a fine of up to £50 on summary conviction (SSA 1975, Sch. 1, para. 3(2)).

If a secondary contributor dies, his liabilities pass to his personal representatives or, if he merely paid earnings as an agent, to his successor or, if no one succeeds him, to his principal (SI 1979, No. 591, Sch. 1, reg. 33). Similarly, but to a more restricted degree, a successor to a trade or business is liable to carry out the former owner's obligations under the social security acts and regulations except that he is not liable for contributions which were deductible from earnings paid to an employed earner before the change-over but are no longer so deductible (SI 1979, No. 591, Sch. 1, reg. 34).

The only circumstances in which the foregoing rules do not, or cannot, apply, are those which arise where there has been a failure to pay primary contributions due to an act or default on the part of an employed earner and not to any negligence on the part of the secondary contributor (SI 1979, No. 591, reg. 50(1)(a)); where the secondary contributor is a person against whom the provisions of the social security acts cannot be enforced and who is not willing to pay on behalf of an employed earner primary contributions due in respect of earnings paid to or for the benefit of that earner (see **6.06** post); or where an earner has, under an arrangement authorised by the Secretary of State (see **6.04** post), agreed that he himself will pay any primary contribution payable in respect of his earnings from an employed earner's employment. In the latter circumstance, the Secretary of State will notify the secondary contributor in writing of the arrangement and of the period to which it relates (SI 1979, No. 591, reg. 48(1) and (2)). An arrangement of the kind described is often made in connection with the deferment of primary Class 1 contributions in respect of earnings from one or more employed earner's employments where an employed earner has two or more such employments and expects to pay Class 1 contributions on earnings from one or more of them at the upper earnings limit throughout a tax year. The question of deferment is covered at **6.35** post.

6.04 PAYE-linked arrangements

The Secretary of State is empowered to authorise any arrangement for the payment of earnings-related contributions, subject to such terms and conditions as he may impose (SI 1979, No. 591, reg. 47). The direct collection and recovery of primary contributions from an earner as described in the preceding paragraph is an example of such an arrangement. Except for such special arrangements, however, earnings-related contributions are (by regulations made with the concurrence of the Inland Revenue under SSA 1975, Sch. 1, para. 5(1)(a) and (b)) to be paid, accounted for and recovered in the same way as income tax deducted from the emoluments of an office or employment by virtue of the PAYE regulations made under ICTA 1970, s. 204 (SSA 1975, Sch. 1, para. 5(1)(a) and SI 1979, No. 591, reg. 46). To this end, the Income Tax (Employments) Regulations 1973, No. 334, have been extended and modified and, in so far as they apply to earnings-related contributions, appear as SI 1979, No. 591, Sch. 1 (SSA 1975, Sch. 1, para. 5(1)(b) and SI 1979, No. 591, reg. 46). These provide, inter alia, that a secondary contributor must record on the deductions working sheet (P11(New)) for each employed earner the year to which the deductions working sheet relates, the name and national insurance number of the employed earner, the category letter indicating which contribution tables are appropriate to that employed earner (A: standard rate; B: reduced rate; C: no primary liability; D: contracted-out standard rate; E: contracted-out reduced rate) and, as regards each payment of earnings made, the amount of the earnings, the total Class 1 contributions payable, the primary Class 1 contributions included in those total contributions and, where the employment is a contracted-out employment, the part of those primary Class 1 contributions payable at contracted-out rate on earnings above the lower earnings limit (SI 1979, No. 591, Sch. 1, reg. 13(6) as amended by SI 1981, No. 82, reg. 5). Within fourteen days of the end of a tax year, end of year returns (P14 or such other form as the Secretary of State may approve) summarising each employed earner's deduction working sheet must be supplied to the collector of taxes accompanied by an employer's annual statement, declaration and certificate (P35 or such other form as the Secretary of State may approve) summarising those summaries and a remittance in respect of any Class 1 contributions remaining due (SI 1979, No. 591, Sch. 1, reg. 30(1)(2) and (5)). In the case of a body corporate, the declaration and certificate must be signed by a director or the company secretary (SI 1979, No. 591, Sch. 1, reg. 30(3)). Where returns are made in some special form approved by the Secretary of State, they are subject to such conditions as he may impose and are to be sent to him and not to the collector of taxes (SI 1979, No. 591, Sch. 1, reg. 30(6A)).

6.05   Collection from secondary contributors

A secondary contributor must, within fourteen days of the end of every income tax month, pay to the Collector of Taxes all amounts of Class 1 contributions due in respect of earnings paid by him during that month, other than primary Class 1 contributions which, in error etc (see **6.03** ante), he has failed to deduct from earnings paid (SI 1979, No. 591, Sch. 1, reg. 26(1)). A single remittance may cover both contributions and tax but the payslip (P30B(Z) or P30(Z)) must distinguish between the two (DHSS Leaflet NP15, para. 129). Receipts will be issued if requested (SI 1979, No. 591, Sch. 1, reg. 26(2)). Any genuinely erroneous overpayment of contributions to the collector may be deducted in arriving at a subsequent payment to the collector, provided that, in so far as the overpayment relates to an over-deduction of primary contributions from an employed earner's earnings, the employed earner has been reimbursed (SI 1979, No. 591, Sch. 1, reg. 26(3) as amended by SI 1980, No. 1975, reg. 5).

Amounts paid to the collector of taxes are, of course, initially paid into the Inland Revenue account but, as and when directed to do so by the Treasury, the Inland Revenue accounts for and pays to the Secretary of State sums which it estimates have been paid to it as contributions (SSA 1975, Sch. 1, para. 5(3)).

6.06   Direct collection

Where, in respect of an employed earner's employment, the secondary contributor does not fufil the prescribed conditions of residence or presence (see **3.14** ante) or is a person who, by reason of any international treaty or convention which is binding on the United Kingdom, is exempt from the provisions of the social security acts or is a person against whom such provisions are not enforceable, the provisions described above are to apply to the employed earner himself if the secondary contributor will not submit to them on a voluntary basis (SI 1979, No. 591, reg. 50(1)(b) and (2) and Sch. 1, reg. 50(1)). The practical application of this is that the employed earner will be issued with, or must obtain, a deduction working sheet, enter all appropriate data upon it and, when earnings are received, record on it the amount of such earnings and the primary Class 1 contributions payable thereon (SI 1979, No. 591, Sch. 1, reg. 51(1) and (2)). On the due dates, he must pay the contributions to the Collector of Taxes (SI 1979, No. 591, Sch. 1, reg. 51(3)) and failure to do this will result in recovery procedures being applied in the manner described at **6.07** post (SI 1979, No. 591, Sch. 1, reg. 51(4)). An end of year (or, if such earnings cease before the tax year ends, earlier) return of total earnings and contributions due will be required by the collector in the normal way (SI 1979, No. 591, Sch. 1, reg. 51(5) and (6)). Deduction working sheets must be retained for at least three years after the end of the year to which they relate (SI 1979, No. 591, Sch. 1, reg. 51(9) as inserted by SI 1981, No. 82, reg. 9(d)).

6.07 Recovery of unpaid contributions

If a person fails, within the time allowed, to pay any contribution for which he is liable, he is guilty of an offence and is liable, on summary conviction and without proof of his failure to pay any particular contribution (SSA 1975, Sch. 1, para. 5(2)), to a fine of up to fifty pounds, and a further fine of up to ten pounds for each day on which the offence continues after conviction (SSA 1975, s. 146(1) and (5)). In order, therefore, to establish whether an offence has been committed by the non-payment of Class 1 contributions due, a collector of taxes may, where within fourteen days of the end of any income tax month a secondary contributor has either paid no Class 1 contributions to the collector or has paid an amount of contributions which the collector considers to be less than the full amount due, give the secondary contributor notice requiring him to supply details of all payments of earnings made by him since the beginning of the tax year and details of the Class 1 contributions due (SI 1979, No. 591, Sch. 1, reg. 27(1) and (5)). The collector will then ascertain and certify the amount of Class 1 contributions which the secondary contributor is liable to pay (SI 1979, No. 591, Sch. 1, reg. 27(2)) and such a certificate of non-payment will, until the contrary is proved, be sufficient evidence in any proceedings before any court that the sum stated in the certificate is unpaid and due (SSA 1975, s. 149(1) and (2) and SI 1979, No. 591, Sch. 1, reg. 27(3)). Any document purporting to be such a certificate will be deemed to be such a certificate until the contrary is proved (SSA 1975, s. 149(3) and SI 1979, No. 591, Sch. 1, reg. 27(3)).

If communications from the collector of taxes are ignored or the response is inadequate, the collector will usually visit the secondary contributor's premises to make an inspection (see **1.10** ante). If under- or non-payment of contributions is discovered a certificate of non-payment will be prepared in the manner described in the preceding paragraph (SI 1979, No. 591, Sch. 1, reg. 32).

The social security acts and regulations impose no limits on the period to which the certificate of non-payment may relate. It will be

> '. . for the years or income tax months covered by the inspection . . .' (SI 1979, No. 591, Sch. 1, reg. 32(2)(a)).

It may be that a secondary contributor will claim that the Class 1 contributions in question, or some of them, have, in fact, been paid. If, however, a search for the record of the alleged payment is unsuccessful, a statutory declaration by an officer of the Secretary of State to the effect that no record of payment has been found is, in any proceedings for an offence, admissible (to the extent to which oral evidence to like effect would have been admissible) as evidence of the fact that payment has not been made (SSA 1975,

s. 149(4)). A copy of any statutory declaration must, not less than seven days before a hearing or trial, be served on the person charged with the offence in the same way in which a summons (in Scotland, a citation) in a summary prosecution may be served (SSA 1975, s. 149(6)(a)). If, however, not later than three days before the hearing or trial or within such further time as the court may allow, the person charged with the offence to which the statutory declaration relates gives notice to the prosecutor requiring the person by whom the declaration was made to attend the trial, the statutory declaration will not be admissible as evidence (SSA 1975, s. 149(6)(b)).

It is usually the case that, where contributions are unpaid, tax is unpaid also. For this reason it is provided that proceedings may be brought for the recovery of the total amount of both Class 1 contributions and tax which is outstanding without distinguishing between the two or between the amounts due in respect of each employed earner, though such differentiation may be made and separate proceedings for the recovery of separate amounts may be brought if required (SI 1979, No. 591, Sch. 1, reg. 28(2)).

Proceedings for the offence of failure to pay contributions due within the prescribed time may be commenced within the period of three months from the date on which evidence, sufficient in the opinion of the Secretary of State to justify a prosecution for the offence (or, in Scotland, to justify a report to the Lord Advocate with a view to considering the question of prosecution), comes to his knowledge, or within a period of twelve months after the commission of the offence, whichever period last expires (SSA 1975, s. 147(3) and (4)). A certificate purporting to be signed by or on behalf of the Secretary of State as to the date on which the evidence in question came to his knowledge is conclusive evidence of the date on which it did so (SSA 1975, s. 147(5)).

Only the Secretary of State or someone acting with his consent or an inspector or other officer authorised by special or general directions of the Secretary of State may, in England and Wales, institute proceedings for the offence of non-payment of contributions due (SSA 1975, s. 147(1)) but an inspector or other officer so authorised may, although not of counsel or a solicitor, prosecute or conduct proceedings before a magistrates' court for such an offence (SSA 1975, s. 147(2)).

In any proceedings for an offence such as that described, the wife or husband of the person accused is competent to give evidence for or against the accused but may neither be compelled to do so nor, in giving evidence, to disclose any communication made to her or him by the accused during the marriage (SSA 1975, s. 147(6)).

It is important to note that, where an offence of failure to pay contributions has been committed by a body corporate and

> '. . . is proved to have been committed with the consent or connivance of, or to be attributable to any neglect on the part of, a director, manager, secretary or other similar officer of the body corporate, or any person who was purporting to act in any such capacity, he, as well as the body corporate, shall be guilty of that offence and be liable to be proceeded against accordingly' (SSA 1975, s. 147(7)).

Where the affairs of a body corporate are managed by its members, guilt extends to members acting managerially under the same circumstances and in the same way as it extends to directors (SSA 1975, s. 147(7)).

In the event of the body corporate having been dissolved by the time proceedings are brought the company may be restored to the register for the special purpose of prosecution (Companies Act 1948, s. 353(6)).

If, in any proceedings involving payment, non-payment or recovery of contributions, a categorisation question arises the court dealing with the case is to adjourn the proceedings until a final decision on the question is obtained (SSA 1975, s. 148). The categorisation decision procedure been described at **2.14** ante.

Upon conviction, a person guilty of the offence of failing to pay contributions is, if the contributions are still unpaid, liable to pay to the Secretary of State a sum equal to the amount which he failed to pay, in addition to the penalties described earlier (SSA 1975, s. 150(1)). Furthermore, evidence may be given of any failure to pay contributions during the two years preceding the date of the offence of which he is convicted (provided notice of intention to give such evidence is served with the summons or warrant or, in Scotland, the complaint on which the person appeared before the court which convicted him) and, on proof, the person convicted will be liable to pay a sum equal to the amount of those contributions also (SSA 1975, s. 151(1)(2)(3) and (5)).

It should be noted that where the person convicted of the offence of failing to pay contributions is a body corporate, the contribution-equivalent monetary sum remaining due, which the company is then ordered to pay, is

'. . . a debt due to the Secretary of State jointly and severally from any directors of the body corporate who knew, or could reasonably be expected to have known, of the failure to pay the contributions . . . in question' (SSA 1975, s. 152(4)).

and civil proceedings may be taken against any or all of such directors.

At the time of prosecution under SSA 1975, s. 146, all the directors of the body corporate are interviewed by a DHSS inspector and informed of such possible action against them personally under SSA 1975, s. 152(4); and, if civil proceedings then ensue, it will be no defence for a person to show that he is no longer a director of the body corporate as SSA 1975, s. 152(4) imposes a liability on anyone who was a director at the time the contributions ought to have been paid (*DHSS v Wayte* [1972] 1 WLR 19, CA). The four necessary conditions under which a personal liability will arise were set out by the Divisional Court in the unreported case of *DHSS v Baxter* (1974) as being that, following conviction of the offence of failing to pay contributions due within the prescribed time, the body corporate has been ordered to pay a sum equal to the amount of the unpaid contributions; that the body corporate has then failed to pay the sum directed by the order; that the person now proceeded against was a director at the time the contribution liability was incurred; and that during the period when the contributions were unpaid that director knew or could reasonably have been expected to have known that the contributions had not been paid.

This clearly draws aside the veil of incorporation and the provision is of great (and increasing) use to the Secretary of State in small company situations where contributions have not been paid over to the Collector of Taxes as a result of a company being placed in liquidation. Although unpaid contributions are accorded priority in such cases (see **6.09** post), the company may nevertheless be unable to pay but, if it appears to the Secretary of State that this is not true of one or more of the directors, he may well bring an action against the company which, if successful, will, by reason of the provision quoted above, open the way for recovery of the unpaid contributions from one or more of those directors. In small companies, a defence by a director that he could 'not reasonably be expected to have known' of the company's failure to pay would be exceedingly difficult to sustain.

In England and Wales, a person charged with an offence of failing to pay contributions due may be convicted of that offence in his absence (SSA 1975, s. 152(1) and Magistrates' Courts Act 1980, s. 12(2)). If it is proved to the satisfaction of the court that notice of intention to give evidence of other earlier offences has been duly served to a person so convicted and the clerk of the court has received a statement in writing purporting to be made by the accused or by a solicitor acting on his behalf to the effect that, if convicted in his absence of the offence charged, he wishes to admit the earlier offences, the court will proceed as if those earlier offences have been proved (SSA 1975, s. 152).

A conviction resulting in a probation order or an absolute discharge is to be treated as a conviction of both present and previous offences (SSA 1975, s. 152(2) and (3)).

Sums recoverable by the Secretary of State upon a conviction of failure to pay contributions are, in England and Wales, recoverable as a penalty (SSA 1975, s. 152(5)) but, in so far as they represent contributions which should have been paid, are treated for all purposes of the social security acts as contributions received of the appropriate class or classes and as paid in respect of the persons in respect of whom they were originally payable (SSA 1975, s. 152(6) and (7)).

6.08 Waiver of arrears

It is clear that the Secretary of State does not always take the proceedings open to him where there are unpaid contributions. The circumstances in which he will not do so are, however, unspecified. In answer to a parliamentary question it has been said that

> 'Standing instructions provide for officials of the Department to waive proceedings for arrears . . . in various circumstances. The most common cases are those where the person concerned would have been entitled to exception from liability for contributions if he had claimed it, or where it would not be practicable to recover arrears because of his financial circumstances. Separate statistics are not kept of the numbers of cases where proceedings are waived, but they run into many thousands each year' (Hansard, 24 February 1978, Vol. 944, No. 67, col. 836).

6.09 Priority of contribution debts

Sums owed on account of contributions payable in the period of twelve months immediately preceding the date of the 'relevant event' are included among those accorded priority under the various enactments relating to personal insolvency, companies' winding-up and the remedies of debenture holders and chargees (SSA 1975, s. 153). A relevant event in connection with personal insolvency is the receiving order or death (or, in Scotland, the award of sequestration or death or the concourse of diligence for distribution of the estate of a party being notour bankrupt) (SSA 1975, Sch. 18, para. 1(2)). In connection with a company's winding-up the relevant event is, if the company is wound-up compulsorily, the appointment of a provisional liquidator or, in the absence of such an appointment, the making of the winding-up order, or, if the company had previously commenced to be wound-up voluntarily or is being wound-up voluntarily, the passing of the winding-up resolution (SSA 1975, Sch. 18, para. 2(2)). In connection with the remedies of debenture holders and chargees, the relevant event is the appointment of a receiver or the taking of possession of property (SSA 1975, Sch. 18, para. 3(2)).

The comments made at **6.07** ante in connection with the liability of a company's directors where the company cannot meet its contribution debts should be referred to.

COLLECTION OF CLASS 2 CONTRIBUTIONS

6.10 Contribution cards

Anyone who is liable to pay a Class 2 contribution or who, being entitled though not liable to pay a Class 2 contribution, wishes to do so, must (unless Class 2 contributions are deferred—see **6.37** post) apply to the Secretary of State for a contribution card at such times and in such manner as he directs (SI 1979, No. 591, reg. 51(1)(a) and (3)). In practical terms this involves completing a form CF11 and sending it to a local DHSS office whereupon a CF1 contribution card will be issued. The card remains the property of the Secretary of State (SI 1979, No. 591, reg. 52(1)) though the contributor is responsible for its custody (SI 1979, No. 591, reg. 51(1)(b)) and commits an offence punishable upon summary conviction with a fine of up to £400 and/or a term of up to three months imprisonment if he sells it, offers it for sale, gives it in exchange or pawns it (SSA 1975, s. 146(3)(a)). It is an equal offence to buy, take in exchange or take in pawn a contribution card (SSA 1975, s. 146(3)(a)). A contribution card may not be assigned or charged and any sale, transfer, assignment of, or charge on, a contribution card is void and of no effect (SI 1979, No. 591, reg. 56(1)).

A contribution card must be produced for inspection at the request of an inspector who may, if he thinks fit, retain it but must, if he does retain it, give a receipt (SI 1979, No. 591, reg. 51(1)(c) and (2)). A contribution card generally covers a tax year but may be current for such period as the Secretary of State provides and, within six days (or such longer period as may be allowed) of the card ceasing to be current, it must be returned to the local DHSS office, bearing the contributor's current address; thereupon a fresh card will be issued if appropriate (SI 1979, No. 591, reg. 52(2)).

It is forbidden to deface or destroy a contribution card or to alter, amend or erase any of the figures or particulars except to the extent authorised by the Secretary of State (SI 1979, No. 591, reg. 56(2)). If a contribution card is destroyed, lost or defaced, application must be made to the Secretary of State for a new card (SI 1979, No. 591, reg. 51(1)(e)) and if a person is directed to return his card, ceases to be self-employed, or dies, his card must be returned immediately to the local DHSS office (SI 1979, No. 591, reg. 53).

6.11   Payment of contributions

A Class 2 contribution liability may be discharged by one of two methods: a stamp of the appropriate value may be affixed to the contribution card in the space indicated on the card for the purpose (SSA 1975, Sch. 1, para. 6(2)(a) and SI 1979, No. 591, reg. 54(1)(a)) not later than the last day in the contribution week for which the contribution is due (SI 1979, No. 591, reg. 54(2)) and immediately cancelled by writing or over-stamping in ink across the face of it the date on which it is affixed (SI 1979, No. 591, reg. 54(4)); or, under an arrangement authorised by the Secretary of State, a payment may be made by direct debit of a bank or National Girobank account (SSA 1975, Sch. 1, para. 6(2)(b) and SI 1979, No. 591, reg. 54(3)(a) and (c)). The second of these methods is instituted by completing and sending to a local DHSS office a form CF351(Bank) or CF351(NG) accompanied by the contribution card. The form will be sent by the DHSS to the appropriate bank which will normally make contribution payments from the contributor's account on the second Friday in each month. Each payment will cover four or five contributions depending on the number of Sundays in the preceding tax month but contributions will not be collected for any complete weeks for which the contributor proves incapacity for work because of illness (DHSS Leaflet NI41). It is a condition of a direct debit arrangement that any payment made to the DHSS after the authority of the bank or Post Office to make such a payment has ceased will not be accepted as a payment of contributions (SI 1979, No. 591, reg. 54(3)(c)).

The provisions of the Stamp Duties Management Act 1891 and the Post Office Act 1953, s. 63 apply (with adaptations) to contribution stamps (SSA 1975, Sch. 1, para. 6(3) and SI 1979, No. 591, reg. 57). These empower the Secretary of State to grant licences to deal in stamps and impose penalties for offences of unauthorised dealing in stamps, forgery etc. It should be noted that, just as it is an offence to buy, sell, offer for sale, take or give in exchange, pawn or take in pawn a contribution card (see **6.10** ante), so it is an offence to commit such acts with respect to a used (ie cancelled) contribution stamp, or to affix a used contribution stamp to a contribution card (SSA 1975, s. 146(3)(a) and (b)). To remove or erase a contribution stamp from a contribution card amounts to defacing the card (SI 1979, No. 591, reg. 56(3)).

Where a person is in receipt of a war disablement pension or a pension or allowance specified in the Supplementary Benefits Act 1976, Sch. 1, para. 23(5) and (6), the Secretary of State may, with that person's consent, pay any Class 2 contribution due and deduct the amount paid from the pension or allowance (SSA 1975, Sch. 1, para. 8(1) and SI 1979, No. 591, reg. 55).

6.12 Recovery of unpaid contributions

Failure to pay a Class 2 contribution within the time allowed is an offence punishable upon summary conviction by a fine of up to fifty pounds and a further fine of up to ten pounds for each day on which the offence continues after conviction (SSA 1975, s. 146(1) and (5)). To this end, a statutory declaration by an officer of the Secretary of State that a particular contribution card or a particular contribution has been searched for but not found, is admissible in proceedings for the offence of non-payment as evidence of the facts stated in the declaration (SSA 1975, s. 149(4)). The provisions relating to such statutory declarations and to the institution and conduct of proceedings have been described at **6.07** ante. If, upon conviction, contributions still remain unpaid, there is, in addition to any fine imposed, a liability to pay to the Secretary of State an amount equal to the amount of those unpaid contributions (SSA 1975, s. 150(1)). Any such sum is, in England and Wales, recoverable as a penalty but will, nevertheless, in so far as it represents Class 2 contributions, be treated as Class 2 contributions paid in respect of the offender (SSA 1975, s. 152(5)(6) and (7)).

6.13 Waiver of arrears

Reference should be made to **6.08** ante where a parliamentary reply of particular relevance to Class 2 contributors is quoted.

6.14 Priority of contribution debts

Reference should be made to **6.09** ante in so far as that section is concerned with matters of personal insolvency.

COLLECTION OF CLASS 3 CONTRIBUTIONS

6.15 Contribution cards

Anyone who is entitled to pay a Class 3 contribution and wishes to do so must apply to the Secretary of State for a contribution card in the same way as anyone liable or wishing to pay a Class 2 contribution (SI 1979, No. 591, reg. 51(3)). An identical card (CF1) is utilised in either case and the provisions described at **6.10** ante are of equal application.

6.16   Payment of contributions

Either of the methods of payment which may be adopted for the payment of Class 2 contributions (see **6.11** ante) may be adopted for the payment of Class 3 contributions also and, if the direct debit method is chosen, the same application forms (CF351(Bank) or CF351(NG)) are appropriate. Alternatively (in the case of Class 3 contributions only) payment may be made in cash or by cheque at (or after) the end of the tax year by taking or sending the appropriate amount with the contribution card to the local DHSS office (DHSS leaflet NI42). If no contribution card has been obtained, a note of the contributor's full name, address and national insurance number should accompany the remittance.

Whereas, in the case of Class 2 contributions, payment is regarded as taking place as soon as a contribution stamp is affixed to a contribution card (SI 1979, No. 591, reg. 54(1)(a)), payment of Class 3 contributions is not regarded as taking place until either a contribution card with stamps affixed to it is surrendered to a local DHSS office or a DHSS inspector (SI 1979, No. 591, reg. 54(1)(b)) or a remittance in respect of Class 3 contributions is received. The reason for this is that Class 3 contributions are a 'topping-up' measure and have no due dates but merely relate to the tax year in respect of which they are paid or to which they are allocated.

COLLECTION OF CLASS 4 CONTRIBUTIONS

6.17   Inland Revenue collection

As has been explained at **5.30** et seq ante, Class 4 contributions are calculated by reference to adjusted annual profits or gains chargeable to income tax under Case I or II of Schedule D. Such contributions are payable

> '... in the same manner as any income tax which is, or would be, chargeable in respect of those profits or gains (whether or not income tax in fact falls to be paid) ... by the person on whom the income tax is (or would be) charged, in accordance with assessments made from time to time under the Income Tax Acts' (SSA 1975, s. 9(1)).

Accordingly, all the provisions of the Income Tax Acts (including provisions as to assessment, collection, repayment and recovery) apply with necessary modifications to Class 4 contributions (SSA 1975, s. 9(3)) and the interest and penalty provisions of the Taxes Management Act 1970 (TMA) also apply except for the s. 86 provisions relating to interest on amounts overdue (SSA 1975, Sch. 2, para. 7). One consequence of this is that, under TMA 1970, s. 88, significant charges to interest on unpaid Class 4 contributions can arise as a result of back-duty investigations made under the Taxes Act.

As the income tax assessment and collection procedures apply to Class 4 contributions, it follows that the due dates for payment of such contributions arising on assessment are the same as the due dates for any income tax arising under the same assessment. Normally these dates will be 1 January and 1 July or, where the assessment is not raised until after one or both of the due dates has elapsed, thirty days after the date of the assessment.

EXAMPLE 6(A)

Andrew started up in business on 1 January 1981. In May 1982 his first year's accounts are agreed by the Inland Revenue and he receives assessments dated 22 May 1982 which include Class 4 contributions as follows:

	£
1980–81	17.50
1981–82	393.87

The due dates for 1980–81 (1 January 1981 and 1 July 1981) have been passed as has the first of the due dates for 1981–82 (1 January 1982). Accordingly £214.44 (£17.50 + 1/2 × £393.87) is due for payment on 21 June 1982. The second instalment of the 1981–82 Class 4 contributions (£196.93) will, however, not become payable until its normal due date, 1 July 1982.

A single payslip for each instalment incorporates the amounts due in respect of both income tax and Class 4 contributions, and remittance is made in a single sum to the collector of taxes. The destination of payment remains the same even where no income tax is collectable.

Class 4 contributions which have been collected by the Collector of Taxes along with income tax due under Case I or II of Schedule D are, of course, initially paid into the Inland Revenue account, but provision is made for the Inland Revenue to account for, and pay over to the Secretary of State, at Treasury direction, sums estimated to have been collected in respect of such contributions (SSA 1975, s. 9(5)).

6.18 Finality of assessment

Where an assessment has become final and conclusive for income tax purposes, it is also final and conclusive for Class 4 contribution purposes and no subsequent adjustment is permissible except by reference to relief for interest, annuities or other annual payments (see **4.32** ante) made in the year of assessment (SSA 1975, Sch. 2, para. 8).

6.19 Husband and wife

Where there is separate assessment of husband and wife for income tax purposes, there will be separate assessment for Class 4 contribution purposes also and the wife will be liable to pay her own contributions (SSA 1975, Sch. 2, para. 4(1)). In all other cases, a wife's Class 4 contributions (though calculated on her own profits or gains) are assessed and recoverable from her husband (SSA 1975, Sch. 2, para. 4(3)).

6.20   Partnership

Where a trade or profession is carried on in partnership, Class 4 contributions may be either be charged on each partner separately or be the subject of a joint assessment to contributions made in the partnership name (SSA 1975, Sch. 2, para. 5(2)).

6.21   Special Class 4 contributions

Where a person is, by regulations, treated as a self-employed earner and has earnings on which he is liable to pay Class 4 contributions (see **5.33** ante), it is for the Secretary of State and not the Inland Revenue to recover such contributions (SSA 1975, s. 10(2)). Non-payment of Class 4 contributions is not an offence under the social security acts, however (SSA 1975, s. 146(2)), and recovery proceedings are instituted under the provisions of the Income Tax Acts.

6.22   Recovery of deferred contributions

Even if a certificate of deferment is issued in respect of an earner who would otherwise be liable to pay Class 4 contributions (see **6.37** post), a Class 4 assessment must nonetheless be made by the Inland Revenue, though no figure representing contributions payable is to appear on the assessment (SI 1979, No. 591, reg. 66(1)(a)). The person named on the assessment has his normal right of appeal and this should, of course, be exercised if the amount of the assessment is disputed. Responsibility for calculation, administration, collection and recovery of any deferred Class 4 contributions ultimately found to be payable is, however, passed from the Inland Revenue to the Secretary of State (SI 1979, No. 591, reg. 66(1)(b)).

For the purpose of enabling the Secretary of State to make his calculations, the Inland Revenue is, at his request and if the assessment has become final and conclusive, to certify to him and to the earner the amount of the earner's profits or gains as adjusted for Class 4 purposes or, if the adjusted profits or gains exceed the upper annual limit (see **5.31** ante), merely to certify that they do so (SSA 1975, s. 9(9)(b) and SI 1979, No. 591, reg. 66(3)). A certificate may be given even where the assessment is under appeal provided the Inland Revenue and the earner have reached agreement or it appears to the General or Special Commissioners that the amount not in dispute is higher than the upper annual limit (SI 1979, No. 591, reg. 66(4)). Any exception from Class 4 liability by reference to Class 1 contributions paid on earnings chargeable to income tax under Schedule D (see **5.34** ante) is to be recognised by the Secretary of State in making his calculation of an earner's Class 4 liability (SI 1979, No. 591, reg. 66(2)).

Once the calculation has been made, notice of the amount of contributions due must be given to the earner (SI 1979, No. 591, reg. 66(5)) who must then, within twenty-eight days of receipt of the notice, pay those contributions to the Secretary of State, unless, before that period expires, he has raised a categorisation question (see **2.14** ante) or has made some claim or late appeal which affects the certified profits or gains and has notified the Secretary of State that he has done so (SI 1979, No. 591, reg. 66(6)).

If the Inland Revenue make any amendment to an assessment the original amount of which has already been certified to the Secretary of State and that amendment affects the amount of profits or gains for Class 4 purposes, a further certificate stating the altered amount must be supplied to the Secretary of State (SI 1979, No. 591, reg. 66(7)).

6.23 Priority of contribution debts

Insofar as **6.09** ante relates to personal insolvency, that section applies to unpaid Class 4 contributions which rank in the same manner as income tax assessed and unpaid (SSA 1975, s. 153(3)).

LATE PAID AND UNPAID CONTRIBUTIONS

6.24 Reckonability for benefit purposes

As has been explained in earlier sections of this chapter, failure to pay contributions by their due date is an offence for which proceedings may be instituted by the Secretary of State. Nevertheless, by regulations made under SSA 1975, Sch. 1, para. 6(1)(b) and (c), late paid and unpaid contributions are, in certain circumstances, to be taken into account for the purposes of entitlement to contributory benefits.

The basic rules are that a contribution must be paid before the end of the second tax year following that in which liability or entitlement to pay the contribution arose, otherwise it will be permanently disregarded for the purpose of entitlement to contributory benefits (SI 1979, No. 591, reg. 38(2)); and that, under no circumstances, may a contribution be taken into account for the purpose of entitlement to benefit in respect of any period before the date on which it is actually paid (SI 1979, No. 591, reg. 38(5)(a)).

For the purpose of determining whether the second contribution condition (see **1.17** ante) of entitlement to unemployment benefit, sickness benefit or maternity allowance has been satisfied, there is an additional rule: the late-paid contribution must be paid before the beginning of the benefit year in which the period of interruption of employment which gives rise to the claim for benefit falls (SI 1979, No. 591, reg. 6(1)(a)). A late-paid contribution which is not paid until after the beginning of the relevant benefit year will be taken into account only as regards days of claim falling forty-two days or more after the actual date of payment (SI 1979, No. 591, reg. 38(6)(b)).

EXAMPLE 6(B)

Bernard has not yet paid a Class 2 contribution which he was liable to pay by 19 December 1981. If he wishes that contribution, when paid, to be recognisable in connection with benefit entitlement, it must be paid before 6 April 1984.

Bernard does, in fact, pay the contributions on 3 March 1983 and, on 10 April 1983 begins to claim sickness benefit. The benefit year is that beginning 2 January 1983 and the relative tax year is that ended 5 April 1982. As the late-paid contribution belongs to that tax year but is not paid until after the benefit year has begun, it cannot be taken into account in determining whether the second contribution condition of entitlement to sickness benefit has been met for any day of claim prior to 14 April 1983.

The rules stated above are modified in the case of Class 3 contributions so that, where a person was entitled to pay a Class 3 contribution in respect of a year during which, for at least six months, he underwent full-time education, apprenticeship or training (with earnings less than the lower earnings limit) or imprisonment or detention in legal custody, such a contribution will be recognised for the purpose of benefit entitlement if it is paid before the end of the sixth tax year following that in which the entitlement to pay the contribution arose (SI 1979, No. 591, regs. 27(3)(b)(ii) and 38(3)) and, where a person was entitled to pay a Class 3 contribution in respect of a year during any part of which a temporary allowance under a scheme implemented on or after 1 May 1979 and made by virtue of the Job Release Act 1977 was payable, such a contribution will be so recognised if paid before the end of the sixth year following the year in which the allowance ceased to be payable (SI 1979, No. 591, regs. 27(4) and 38A as inserted by SI 1980, No. 1975, regs. 3(b) and 4). This Class 3 extention of the late-payment rules is shortened by the occurrence of an event such as the attainment of pensionable age or death, when the contribution in question must be paid before the end of the tax year following the one in which the event occurs (SI 1979, No. 591, reg. 38(4)).

Class 4 contributions carry no benefit entitlement and are, accordingly, not subject to any special rules concerning late payment.

6.25 Failure through ignorance or error

Where a person has failed to pay a Class 3 contribution which he was entitled to pay or a Class 2 contribution which he was entitled (but not liable) to pay and the Secretary of State is satisfied that his failure is attributable to ignorance or error not resulting from failure to exercise due care and diligence, the contribution may be paid within such further period as the Secretary of State directs (SI 1979, No. 591, regs. 29 and 40). The Secretary of State may further direct that any such contribution, and any other contribution paid late for the same reasons, may, if it is paid after the latest date when it would have been recognised as paid for benefit entitlement purposes, be treated as paid on such earlier date as he considers appropriate in the circumstances (SI 1979, No. 591, reg. 41).

6.26 Failure by the secondary contributor

Where a primary Class 1 contribution which is payable by a secondary contributor on a primary contributor's behalf is paid after the dute date or is not paid and

'. . . the delay or failure . . . is shown to the satisfaction of the Secretary of State not to have been with the consent or connivance of, or attributable to any negligence on the part of, the primary contributor, the primary contribution shall be treated . . . as paid on the due date' (SI 1979, No. 591, reg. 39).

Where, in these circumstances, payment has not been made relative to and before a day in respect of which unemployment benefit, sickness benefit or maternity allowance is claimed, the primary contribution is, for the purpose of the first contribution condition of entitlement (see **1.17** ante), treated as paid on the day on which the earnings relative to that primary contribution were paid (SI 1979, No. 591, reg. 39).

6.27 Deferred contributions

Where the payment of a contribution has been postponed or deferred under an arrangement authorised by the Secretary of State (see **6.35** et seq post), the due date for the payment of that contribution remains the same as it would have been had the arrangement not been made (SI 1979, No. 591, reg. 42(a)) but any payment of (or on account of) such a contribution made subsequent to that due date will be treated as if it had been made on the due date (SI 1979, No. 591, reg. 42(b)).

6.28 Death of a contributor

Any contributions which a person was entitled (though not liable) to pay immmediately before his death may be paid after his death, subject to the rules described in the foregoing paragraphs (SI 1979, No. 591, reg. 43). This provision may be of use to a man's widow in enabling her to benefit from an otherwise deficient contribution record on the part of her husband.

REPAYMENT AND RE-ALLOCATION OF CONTRIBUTIONS

6.29 Annual maximum

The maximum amount of contributions payable by an employed earner who is engaged in only one employment throughout a tax year is, because of the application of the calculation rules described in Chapter 5, limited to (at most) an amount equal to 53 primary contributions payable at the standard rate in respect of weekly earnings of an amount equal to the weekly upper earnings limit for the year in question. Where, however, an earner is employed in more than one employment, there is no such automatic limitation to his overall liability. By regulations made under SSA 1975, s. 11(1) and (2), therefore, it is provided that, in such circumstances,

'. . . liability in any year for primary Class 1 contributions, or, where both Class 1 and Class 2 contributions are payable by an earner in any year, for both primary Class 1 contributions and Class 2 contributions shall not exceed an amount equal to 53 primary Class 1 contributions at the maximum standard rate' (SI 1979, No. 591, reg. 17(1)).

For the purpose of determining liability in the way described, the amount of any primary Class 1 contributions paid at a rate less than the standard rate is to be treated as equal the amount of any primary Class 1 contributions payable at the standard rate on the same amount of earnings (SI 1979, No. 591, reg. 17(2)) and 'contributions at the maximum standard rate' means primary Class 1 contributions payable at the standard rate in respect of weekly earnings of an amount equal to the upper earnings limit for the year in question (SI 1979, No. 591, reg. 17(3)).

EXAMPLE 6(C)

Cedric was self-employed until 30 June 1981 when he became employed in a contracted-out employment with Dea Ltd at a monthly salary of £650 and a non-contracted-out employment with Ee Ltd at a weekly salary of £200. No Class 4 contributions were payable for 1981–82 but Class 1 and Class 2 contributions paid in respect of that tax year were:

	£	£
Class 2: 12 × £3.40		40.80
Primary Class 1:		
Dea Ltd: £117 × 7.75% =	9.07	
£533 × 5.25% =	27.98	
	37.05 × 9 =	333.45
Ee Ltd: £200 × 7.75% =	15.50 × 39 =	604.50
Total contributions:		978.75

For the purpose of ascertaining whether the annual maximum has been exceeded, however, it is necessary to include the contributions paid at contracted-out rate as if they had been paid at standard rate, ie the total contributions are

£978.75 − £333.45 + (9 × (£650 × 7.75%))   £1,098.63

As the maximum liability for 1981–82 is not to exceed:

53 × £200 = £10,600 × 7.75%   £821.50

a return of contributions amounting to £277.13 (ie £1,098.63 − £821.50) will be due. Note, however, that had an amount less than £277.13 actually been paid in Class 2 or non-contracted-out standard rate Class 1 contributions, the return of contributions would have been restricted (see **6.34** post).

If, in the above example, Class 4 contributions had been payable for the year as well as Class 1 and/or Class 2 contributions, further regulations would come into effect. In such a case

'. . . the liability . . . for . . . Class 4 contributions for that year shall . . . not exceed such amount as, when added to the amount of such other . . . contributions as are ultimately payable . . . for that year, equals in value the sum of the amount which . . . would be payable . . . on profits or gains equal to . . .'

the upper annual Class 4 limit

'. . . and 53 times the amount of a Class 2 contribution payable for that year' (SI 1979, No. 591, reg. 67(1)).

In determining liability under this regulation, the rule stated earlier whereby the amount of any primary Class 1 contributions paid at a rate less than standard rate is to be grossed-up to the equivalent standard rate is still to apply (SI 1979, No. 591, reg. 67(2)).

EXAMPLE 6(D)
The facts are as in Example 6(C) except that Class 4 contributions of £230.00 have also been paid for the tax year 1981–82.

The Class 4 contributions are not to exceed:

	£
$5.75\% \times (£10,000 - £3,150)$	393.87
$53 \times £3.40$	180.20
	574.07
Less: other contributions payable	821.50
	Nil

Accordingly, a return of the £230.00 Class 4 contributions paid would fall to be made in addition to the £277.13 already calculated as returnable.

Where, in addition to any primary Class 1 and/or Class 2 and/or ordinary Class 4 contributions, a special Class 4 contribution (see **5.33** ante) is payable for any year, the maximum amount of that special Class 4 contribution is not to exceed the difference between the ordinary Class 4 annual maximum and the amount of primary Class 1, Class 2 and Class 4 contributions ultimately payable for the year (SI 1979, No. 591, reg. 76(b)). Where there are no Class 1 or Class 2 contributions payable for the year, the special Class 4 annual maximum is not to exceed the difference between the maximum contributions payable on the special Class 4 annual upper limit (presently the same as the ordinary Class 4 annual upper limit) and the amount of ordinary Class 4 contributions ultimately payable for the year (SI 1979, No. 591, reg. 76(a)).

The ordinary annual maxima for 1982–83 are calculated as follows:

	£
Class 1 and Class 2 contributions only: $8.75\% \times (53 \times £220)$	1,020.25
Class 2 and Class 4 contributions only: $6.00\% \times (£11,000 - £3,450)$	453.00
$53 \times £3.75$	198.75
	651.75

The maxima for earlier years are set out in Appendix 7.

6.30 Incorrectly paid contributions

Where contributions are paid which are of the wrong class, or at the wrong rate, or of the wrong amount, the Secretary of State may treat them as paid on account of contributions properly payable under the social security acts (SSA 1975, Sch. 1, para. 6(f) and SI 1979, No. 591, regs. 31, 68 and 77). Such adjustments will be made before, and will be reflected in, any calculation relating to the return of contributions (SI 1979, No. 591, regs. 35(1)(a) and 69(1)).

6.31 Return of contributions paid in error

By virtue of regulations made under SSA 1975, Sch. 1, para. 6(1)(h) contributions paid in error are to be returned by the Secretary of State to the person or secondary contributor who paid them (SSA 1975, Sch. 1, para. 6(h) and SI 1979, No. 591, regs. 32(1), 69(1) and 78(1)) provided, however, that, in the case of Class 1 or Class 2 contributions, the error was made at the time of payment and related to some then present or past matter (SI 1979, No. 591, reg. 32(6)). This proviso should be carefully noted as it would, for instance, preclude a secondary contributor from reclaiming secondary contributions for past years after a categorisation decision to the effect that a person who has been treated as an employed earner in his employment is, in fact, self-employed.

Where contributions have been paid in error by a secondary contributor on behalf of some other person (eg primary contributions on behalf of an employee) and have not been recovered (eg out of earnings paid), they will normally be repaid to the secondary contributor (SI 1979, No. 591, reg. 32(4)). Where such contributions have been recovered from the person on whose behalf they were paid, however, they will be returned to that person unless he consents in writing to their return to the secondary contributor (SI 1979, No. 591, reg. 32(4)).

No amount will be returnable unless, in the case of Class 1 or Class 4 contributions, it exceeds fifty pence or, in the case of Class 2 contributions, is not less than half a Class 2 contribution (SI 1979, No. 591, regs. 32(1), 69(1) and 78(1)); and, in calculating an amount to be returned, any amount of contributory benefit paid because of, and attributable to, the contributions paid in error is to be deducted (SI 1979, No. 591, reg. 35(1)(b)).

Application for the return of contributions paid in error must be made in such form and manner as the Secretary of State directs within six years from the end of the year in which the contributions were paid or, if the Secretary of State is satisfied that there has been good reason for delay, within such longer period as he may allow (SI 1979, No. 591, reg. 32(5)).

6.32   Return of non-contracted-out element in contributions

Where a secondary contributor has paid an amount on account of Class 1 contributions at the non-contracted-out rate but the employment concerned is, or has become, a contracted-out employment, the Secretary of State will, on the secondary contributor's application, return the amount so paid after deducting the amount of Class 1 contributions payable at the contracted-out rate (SI 1979, No. 591, reg. 33(1)). Any such amount which has been paid on behalf of the earner (ie the primary contribution) will be returned to the earner unless he consents in writing to its return to the secondary contributor (SI 1979, No. 591, reg. 33(2)).

Application for the return of contributions in these circumstances must be made in such form and manner as the Secretary of State approves and within six years from the end of the year in which the contracting-out certificate in respect of the employment was issued or, if the Secretary of State is satisfied that there has been good reason for the delay, within such longer period as he may allow (SI 1979, No. 591, reg. 33(3)).

6.33   Return of precluded Class 3 contributions

Where a contributor has paid a Class 3 contribution which he was not entitled to pay, the Secretary of State will, on written application being made to him in an approved manner, return such contribution to the contributor (SI 1979, No. 591, reg. 34). Alternatively, the contribution may, with the consent of the contributor, be appropriated to the earnings factor of another year if there is an entitlement to pay Class 3 contributions in that other year (SI 1979, No. 591, reg. 30).

6.34   Return of excess contributions

By virtue of regulations made under SSA 1975, s. 11(2)(b) and Sch. 1, para. 6(1)(h) contributions paid in excess of the annual maximum (see **6.29** ante) are to be returned provided written application is made to the Secretary of State within, in the case of Class 1, Class 2 and *special* Class 4 contributions, six years of the end of the year in which they were paid (SI 1979, No. 591, regs. 32(1) and (5) and 78(3)) and, in the case of ordinary Class 4 contributions, six years of the end of the year of assessment in respect of which the payment was made or two years of the end of the year in which the payment was made (SI 1979, No. 591, reg. 69(2)). A longer period may be allowed in the case of Class 1, Class 2 and special Class 4 contributions if the Secretary of State is satisfied that there has been good reason for the delay (SI 1979, No. 591, regs. 32(5) and 78(3)). For an amount to be returnable it must, in the case of Class 1 or ordinary or special Class 4 contributions, exceed fifty pence or, in the case of Class 2 contributions, be not less than half a Class 2 contribution (SI 1979, No. 591, regs. 32(1), 69(1) and 78(1)).

Contributions are returned in a prescribed order of priority: first, ordinary and special Class 4 contributions (SI 1979, No. 591, regs. 67(1) and 78(1)), then primary Class 1 contributions at the special forces rates (SI 1979, No. 591, reg. 32(3)), then primary Class 1 contributions at the reduced rate, then Class 2 contributions, then primary Class 1 contributions at the standard rate in respect of non-contracted-out employments and, finally, primary Class 1 contributions in respect of contracted-out employments (SI 1979, No. 591, reg. 32(2)). The amount to be returned in respect of this final item is dependent on the amount of contributions paid at the contracted-out rate (see **5.18** ante). If the amount paid at that rate is not less than 53 times the amount payable at that rate on maximum upper band earnings for the year, any amount paid at the contracted-out rate plus the excess of the amount paid at the normal rate over 53 times the amount payable at that normal rate on earnings at the weekly lower earnings limit will (to the extent any overpayment remains unreturned) be returned (SI 1979, No. 591, reg. 32(2)(d)(i)). If the amount paid at the contracted-out rate is less than 53 times the amount payable at that rate on maximum upper band earnings for the year, or if no amount has been paid at contracted-out rate, the amount paid at the normal rate is returned to the extent that a repayment remains due (SI 1979, No. 591, reg. 32(2)(d)(ii) and (iii)).

These somewhat abstruse provisions are designed to ensure the retention of benefit-yielding contributions and, in particular, to ensure that where contracted-out employment is involved, the annual maximum amount of contributions which remains unreturned contains the annual maximum amount of contributions at normal rate with only the balance at contracted-out rate.

EXAMPLE 6(E)

Throughout 1981–82, Frank was employed by G Ltd, H Ltd and I Ltd at an annual salary of £2,000, £6,500 and £7,000 respectively. Until 5 October 1981, he was also self-employed. His employments by H and I were contracted-out. He paid contributions as follows:

	Class 2	Class 4	Class 1 S. Rate	Class 1 N. Rate	Class 1 C/o. Rate
	£	£	£	£	£
S/employment	88.40	287.50			
G Ltd			155.00		
H Ltd				108.81	267.54
I Ltd				108.81	293.79
	88.40	287.50	155.00	217.62	561.33

His payments have exceeded his maximum contribution liability for 1981–82 by £755.65 of which £717.62 is returnable, viz:

	£	£	£
Class 2		88.40	
Class 4		287.50	
Class 1: SR		155.00	
Class 1: NR		217.62	
Class 1:			
COR £561.33			
× 7.75/5.25		828.63	
		1,577.15	
Class 1 and 2 maximum		821.50	
Excess contributions		755.65	
Returnable:			
Class 4		287.50	287.50
		468.15	
Class 2		88.40	88.40
		379.75	
Class 1: SR		155.00	155.00
		224.75	
Class 1: NR	217.62		
NR maximum (53			
× (£27 × 7.75%))	110.77		
		106.85	106.85
		117.90	
Class 1: COR		117.90 × 5.25/7.75	79.87
Contributions returned			717.62

A form suitable for executing calculations such as that exemplified above is included in Appendix 6.

A contributor who over-contributes as regards Class 1 contributions (by reason, for example, of being concurrently employed in two or more employments) will eventually be informed of the fact by the DHSS and will be invited to apply for the return of the amount overpaid. The long delays inherent in this process can, however, be avoided by applying directly, without awaiting notification of overpayment, to the DHSS Refunds Group, Records Division, Newcastle-upon-Tyne, NE98 1YX on a form CF28F which may be obtained for this purpose from any local DHSS office. Repayment will be expedited if the application is supported by evidence of contribution payments, ie P60s or detailed statements from the secondary contributors concerned.

Where over-contribution extends beyond Class 1 into other classes of contribution, positive action becomes not only desirable but essential. There is no automatic correlation of contributions paid of classes other than Class 1 and, in consequence, any over-contribution will remain unreturned unless and until it is claimed. As has been stated earlier, the time limit for such a claim is six years, though this may be extended at the Secretary of State's discretion. The claim procedure is to obtain a form CF28E from the DHSS Class 4 Group at Newcastle-upon-Tyne and to complete and return it with evidence of contributions paid.

DEFERMENT AND PAYMENT IN ADVANCE

6.35 Class 1 deferment

Where in any year an earner has earnings from two or more employed earner's employments, an arrangement may be authorised by the Secretary of State under which the normal collection procedures (ie collection of Class 1 contributions through the PAYE system) are not to apply to earnings paid in respect of one or more of those employments but are to apply to earnings paid in respect of one or more others (SI 1979, No. 591, regs. 47 and 49(1)). For this to be so, the earner must have reason to believe that during the year he will pay by way of contributions in respect of the earnings to which the normal collection procedures are to apply a sum equal to at least 52 primary Class 1 contributions at the rate applicable to him on earnings at the weekly upper earnings limit or twelve such contributions on earnings at the monthly upper earnings limit (SI 1979, No. 591, reg. 49(2) and (3)) and the arrangement will consist of the deferment of payment of contributions on the earnings to which the normal collection procedures are not to apply (DHSS Leaflet NP28). If, once the year has ended, the earner's expectations have been fulfilled and the Secretary of State finds that maximum contributions have in fact been paid, exception from liability is granted in respect of the contributions deferred (SI 1979, No. 591, reg. 49(2)). If, however, there is found to have been a shortfall in contributions, direct collection procedures will apply as regards the amount underpaid (SI 1979, No. 591, reg. 47) and arrears will be payable within twenty-eight days of demand.

EXAMPLE 6(F)

Julian has three employments in which he earns £150, £75 and £35 per week respectively. He expects those earnings to remain constant throughout 1982–83. On application, an arrangement for deferment of contributions on the £35 per week employment will be granted as the earnings from the other two employments together exceed the upper earnings limit of £220 per week. A return of contributions paid on the excess of £5 per week will then be obtainable once the year has ended. If, however, earnings in those two employments fall below £220 per week before the year ends, any resultant underpayment will, of course, become payable to the DHSS.

Application for deferment is made by completing and sending to the DHSS Class 4 Group at Newcastle-upon-Tyne a form CF379 which is obtainable from any local DHSS office. It is advisable to support the application by payslips or other evidence where possible and, if the arrangement is to apply from the first pay day in the year, to ensure that the application reaches the Class 4 Group as soon before 6 April as possible. If the application is not approved until after 6 April, deferment may not begin to operate until after one or more pay days have passed. The secondary contributor will, however, be instructed to repay primary contributions already deducted from earnings paid in the year and these may then be recouped from subsequent payments of contributions to the collector of taxes. No deferment arrangement may be made for a year in which application has not been received by 15 February, or a year in which the earner will attain pensionable age (DHSS Leaflet NP28).

An earner has no choice as to which of his employments are to be subjected to a deferment arrangement. That decision is made by the Class 4 Group, which will ensure that non-contracted-out contributions are deferred rather than contracted-out contributions (DHSS Leaflet NP28). An earner is notified of the Class 4 Group's decision on form RD951 and deferment certificates (RD950) are sent to the secondary contributors concerned instructing them to no longer deduct primary Class 1 contributions from the employed earner's earnings. Secondary contributions are unaffected by deferment arrangements and secondary contributors are given no information about an earner's other employments.

Once a deferment arrangement is in operation, there is an obligation on the earner to inform the DHSS of the termination of any employment in which contributions have continued to be payable or of the change to contracted-out of any non-contracted-out employment in respect of which a deferment arrangement is in operation (DHSS Leaflet NP28). Where a new employment is begun during a year for which a deferment arrangement has been made, a further form CF379 should be sent to the DHSS Class 4 Group in order that an additional deferment certificate may be issued if appropriate.

6.36   Class 1 advance payment

As an alternative to a deferment arrangement of the kind described at **6.35** ante, deferment of contributions in respect of earnings from all employments may be authorised if an advance payment of an amount equal to the earner's maximum contribution liability for the year is made. The maximum contribution liability is calculated on the basis of 53 weeks of contributions at the appropriate rate on earnings at the upper earnings limit, and the appropriate rate will be either reduced rate (if the earner holds a reduced rate certificate), standard rate (if all the earner's employments are non-contracted-out or if earnings from any contracted-out employments amount to less than the upper earnings limit), or contracted-out rates (if all the earner's employments are contracted-out or if earnings from those which are amount to or exceed the upper earnings limit). The respective maxima for 1982–83 are £373.12, £1,020.25 and £767.97.

Application for a full deferment and payment in advance arrangement is made on the same form and in the same manner as application for partial deferment described at **6.35** ante. Payment of the appropriate advance amount must, however, accompany the application. Other aspects of the deferment arrangement—notification of secondary contributors, reporting of changes, return of excess contributions and direct collection of underpaid contributions—remain the same.

6.37   Class 2 and 4 deferment

Where, during a year, a person is both an employed earner and a self-employed earner and the Secretary of State is satisfied that the total amount of Class 1 contributions which are likely to be paid by that person will exceed an amount equal to 53 primary Class 1 contributions at the standard rate on the weekly upper earnings limit for the year, the Secretary of State may make an arrangement with that person with a view to avoiding excess payments of contributions (SI 1979, No. 591, reg. 54(3)(a)). Such an arrangement will usually involve the deferment of the earner's liability for Class 2 contributions until after the year has ended. Similarly, where it appears to the Secretary of State that there is doubt as to the extent, if any, of an earner's liability to pay Class 4 contributions for a year of assessment or that it is not possible to determine whether or not a liability to pay such contributions for that year will arise, the Secretary of State may defer the earner's liability for such contributions until a later date (SSA 1975, ss. 9(7)(b) and 9(8)(c); SI 1979, No. 591, reg. 62).

Application for deferment of Class 2 and/or Class 4 contributions is made to the DHSS Class 4 Group at Newcastle-upon-Tyne on a form CF359 which may be obtained from any local DHSS office (SI 1979, No. 591, regs. 63(1) and 64(1); DHSS Leaflet NP18). It should be made before the beginning of the year to which it relates, though late applications are considered and may be allowed (SI 1979, No. 591, reg. 63(2)(a)).

Deferment will be granted in respect of Class 4 contributions if the application shows that Class 1, Class 2 and Class 4 contributions are, in total, likely to exceed the Class 2 and Class 4 contribution maximum for the year by more than ten pounds (DHSS Leaflet NP18). The contribution maximum is an amount equivalent to 53 Class 2 contributions plus contributions at the specified Class 4 rate on profits or gains at the Class 4 upper annual limit. In effect, therefore, Class 4 deferment may be obtained wherever there is a Class 1 involvement and a potential Class 4 liability in excess of ten pounds is in question.

Class 2 contributions will be deferred in addition to Class 4 contributions if it can be shown that Class 1 and Class 2 contributions are, in total, likely to exceed the Class 1 maximum described above.

Notification of deferment decisions are made to applicants on form RD904A and, where the decision is favourable, a certificate of Class 4 deferment is issued to the Inland Revenue and responsibility for the assessment and collection of Class 4 contributions then passes from the Inland Revenue to the Secretary of State (SI 1979, No. 591, reg. 66(1)(b)). The Inland Revenue continues to assess profits or gains for Class 4 purposes, however, and certifies these (or the fact that they exceed the Class 4 annual upper limit) to the Secretary of State for each deferment year (SI 1979, No. 591, reg. 66(3)). The relevant provisions have been described at **6.22** ante. Any deferred contributions which are subsequently found to be due are payable within twenty-eight days of demand (SI 1979, No. 591, reg. 66(6)).

Chapter 7

Special classes of earner

7.01 Introduction

The preceding chapters have been devoted to a detailed examination of the social security contribution scheme so far as it operates in relation to the vast majority of earners, employers and others who fall within its scope. There are, however, certain earners who, for one reason or another, cannot be adequately accommodated by the scheme without some modification of the normal framework of rules and these special classes of earner now fall to be considered in this penultimate chapter. Each class is singled out for separate treatment either by statute or by regulation or by both.

EMPLOYED EARNERS BY REGULATION

7.02 General

It has already been noted (**2.16** ante) that the Act provides

'. . . for a person in employment of any prescribed description to be treated . . . as falling within one or other categories of earner . . . notwithstanding that he would not fall within that category apart from . . . regulations' (SSA 1975, s. 2(2)(b)).

and, accordingly, SI 1978, No. 1689, reg. 2(2) directs that, in respect of the various employments described in the following paragraphs,

'. . . every earner shall . . . be treated as falling within the category of an employed earner in so far as he is gainfully employed in such employment . . . notwithstanding that the employment is not under a contract of service, or in an office . . . with emoluments chargeable to income tax under Schedule E'.

In other words, certain persons who would otherwise fall to be categorised as self-employed earners under the normal categorisation rules described in Chapter 2 are, by regulation, to be categorised as employed earners.

7.03 Office cleaners

In accordance with the modified rule stated above, anyone entering employment

'. . . as an office cleaner or in any similar capacity in any premises other than those used as a private dwelling house' (SI 1978, No. 1689, Sch. 1, Pt. I, para. 1).

on or after 6 April 1975 is to be treated as falling within the category of employed earner whether employed under a contract of service or not. To this rule there are no exceptions. Even if the employment is through an agency (see **7.04** post) in circumstances which would admit of self-employment, categorisation as an employed earner will still ensue (SI 1978, No. 1689, Sch. 1, Pt. I, para. 2).

The limitation as to the area of operation built into the description of the prescribed employment should be noted, however. Because of it, the modified categorisation rule is confined to cleaners of office, industrial and commercial premises only. A domestic cleaner is unaffected and will fall to be categorised in the normal way (see Chapter 2 and DHSS Leaflet NI11).

In most cases, the person with whom the office cleaner contracts to do the work will be treated as the secondary Class 1 contributor (SI 1978, No. 1689, Sch. 3, para. 1(b)), unless that person is a limited company which has been placed in voluntary liquidation in which case the person holding the office of liquidator for the time being will be treated as the secondary contributor (SI 1978, No. 1689, Sch. 3, para. 4). Where an office cleaner is supplied by or through the agency of some third person, however, and receives remuneration by or through that agency, the agency will fall to be treated as the secondary contributor (SI 1978, No. 1689, Sch. 3, para. 1(a)).

7.04 Persons employed through agencies

Even though (as has been explained in the introduction to this section) a person's employment may not be under a contract of service, a person who, on or after 6 April 1975, obtains employment

'. . . by or through some third person . . .' (SI 1978, No. 1689, Sch. 1, Pt. I, para. 2)

will (unless he belongs to one of the excepted groups described below) fall to be categorised as an employed earner, provided he

'. . . renders, or is under an obligation to render, personal service and is subject to supervision, direction or control, or to the right of supervision, direction or control, as to the manner of the rendering of such service . . .' (SI 1978, No. 1689, Sch. 1, Pt. I, para. 2)

and there is a continuing financial relationship between him and the third person (ie the agency) (DHSS Leaflet NI192).

There is a continuing financial relationship between a person and the third person through whom he obtains employment when earnings for services such as have been described above

> '. . . are paid by or through, or on the basis of accounts submitted by, that third person or in accordance with arrangements made with that third person . . .' (SI 1978, No. 1689, Sch. 1, Pt. I, para. 2(a))

or where

> '. . . payments, other than to the person employed, are made by way of fees, commission or other payments of like nature which relate to the continued employment in that employment of the person employed' (SI 1978, No. 1689, Sch. 1, Pt. I, para. 2(b));

but not where the only payment to the agency is an introductory fee (DHSS Leaflet NI192) and the only continuing financial relationship is one which arises between the person employed and the person to whom the agency has introduced him on the basis of a contract of service entered into as a result of that introduction (SI 1978, No. 1689, Sch. 1, Pt. I, para. 2(c)).

The person falling to be treated as the secondary contributor as regards any employment to which the above provisions relate will, in most cases, be the third person by whom or through whose agency the person employed has been supplied (SI 1978, No. 1689, Sch. 3, para. 2(a)). In England and Wales only, however, where the agency is an unincorporated body of persons and the person employed is himself a member of that body, the secondary contributor will be the other members of that body (SI 1978, No. 1689, Sch. 3, para. 2(a)) (see Example 7(A) below). If the person who should, according to these regulations, fall to be treated as the secondary contributor cannot be so treated because he does not fulfil the residence requirements of SI 1979, No. 591, reg. 119(b) (see **3.14** ante), the person to whom the person employed is supplied will fall to be treated as the secondary contributor (SI 1978, No. 1689, Sch. 3, para. 2(c)).

It is sometimes the case that a partnership or a company will, in slack periods of trading or during the time when the business is being established and there is insufficient work to fully occupy the key personnel, put forward one of their number to an agency for temporary employment. In the case of a member of a partnership becoming so employed, the above rules apply in their entirety; in the case of an employee or director of a limited company, however, the limited company and not the agency will be treated as the secondary contributor (DHSS Leaflet NI192).

There are three groups of persons to whom the modified rule of categorisation described in the foregoing paragraphs does not apply. The first is comprised of those who, although falling to be categorised according to a modified rule, do so under another part of the regulations, ie office cleaners (see **7.02** ante), persons employed by their spouses for the purpose of their spouse's employment (see **7.05** post) and ministers of religion (see **7.07** post). The second group consists of those who, though fulfilling all the requirements noted above, render their services in their own homes or on other premises not under the control or management of the person to whom they are supplied (SI 1978, No. 1689, Sch. 1, Pt. I, para. 2(a)). This second group is not to include, however, persons who, because of the nature of the service rendered, are obliged to render it on premises not under the control and management of the person to whom they are supplied (eg audit work performed in the premises of an accountant's client by a clerk supplied to that accountant through an agency; building work performed on a building site by a brick-layer supplied to a construction firm through an agency) (SI 1978, No. 1689, Sch. 1, Pt. I, para. 2(a)). The third group includes anyone employed as an actor, singer, musician or other entertainer or as a fashion, photographic or artist's model (SI 1978, No. 1689, Sch. 1, Pt. I, para. 2(b)).

The effect of this modified rule of categorisation is to bring within the category of employed earner all persons such as secretaries, clerks, teachers and non-NHS nurses and midwives who, obtaining through agencies temporary non-contract-of-service employment in offices, schools, hospitals and nursing homes, would otherwise fall to be treated as self-employed earners for social security purposes and would be uninsured against unemployment. Parallel provisions in the Finance (No. 2) Act 1975, s. 38 ensure that such persons are treated as employees for income tax purposes also.

A point to note is that the term 'third person' used in the regulation cited above is specifically to include, in the case of an unincorporated body, a body of which the person employed is a member. This may have unforeseen consequences:

EXAMPLE 7(A)

Three secretaries, Alice, Brenda and Connie, form a partnership which trades as The ABC Secretarial Agency. Temporary work is found for various secretaries who register with the agency, and also for Alice and Brenda. Connie manages the business. Alice and Brenda each render personal service to their temporary employers and are subject to supervision. Payment for their work is on the basis of accounts rendered by the agency.

Though all three partners fall to be categorised as self-employed earners by reason of the partnership being an independent contractor supplying staff to various clients, Alice and Brenda also fall to be categorised as employed earners by reason of their temporary engagements through the agency of which they are members. Moreover, regardless of whether the payments for their services are actually passed on to them personally or simply added to partnership income, they will each be liable, individually, to pay primary Class 1 contributions on those payments and the two remaining partners (ie Connie and Brenda with regard to Alice and Connie and Alice with regard to Brenda) will be liable to pay secondary Class 1 contributions on the same amounts.

DHSS Leaflet NI192 deals in general terms with the position of persons employed through agencies and DHSS Leaflet NI46 deals specifically with the position of non-NHS nurses and midwives.

7.05   Employment of a person by his/her spouse

Any person who, on or after 6 April 1975, becomes employed

> '. . . by his or her spouse for the purposes of the spouse's employment' (SI 1978, No. 1689, Sch. 1, Pt. I, para. 3)

is to be treated as falling within the category of employed earner even though the employment may not be under a contract of service. There are no exceptions to this rule, though it should be noted that

> '. . . employment (whether or not under a contract of service) of a person by his or her spouse otherwise than for the purposes of the spouse's employment' (SI 1978, No. 1689, Sch. 1, Pt. III, para. 8)

is an employment which is to be disregarded for social security purposes (see **7.10** post).

In cases where a person is employed by his or her spouse for the purposes of the spouse's employment, the spouse falls to be treated as the secondary contributor (SI 1978, No. 1689, Sch. 3, para. 3).

The expression 'spouse's employment' is frequently interpretated as meaning merely 'spouse's self-employment', that being the kind of employment under which the employment of a wife by her husband most commonly arises (eg a general medical practitioner or dentist employing his wife as secretary/receptionist). The expression must be accorded its full meaning, however (see **2.02** ante), which extends it to employed earner's employment also.

EXAMPLE 7(B)

David, a sales representative for a clothing manufacturer, was disqualified from driving in April 1980 and, in order not to lose his job, employed Enid, his wife, as his chauffeuse. In what he thought was a smart move, David paid Enid £50.00 per week from his net earnings and anticipated tax relief of £15.00 per week on this amount. Enid, however, fell by the modified categorisation rule described above to be categorised as an employed earner for social security purposes and became liable to pay primary Class 1 contributions of £3.37 per week as well as income tax under Schedule E of £7.07 per week. Furthermore, David fell to be categorised as the secondary contributor and thus became liable to pay secondary Class 1 contributions of £6.85 per week in respect of Enid's earnings. Although he managed to obtain tax relief of £2.06 per week on those secondary contributions, it can be seen that he and Enid between them were 23p worse off as a result of David's little tax saving scheme!

In certain circumstances, contributions may be saved by the employment of a spouse and this topic is explored in Chapter 8.

7.06   Lecturers, teachers and instructors

Even though his employment may not be under a contract of service, anyone who, on or after 6 April 1978, obtains employment

> '. . . as a lecturer, teacher, instructor or in any similar capacity in an educational establishment by any person providing education . . .' (SI 1978, No. 1689, Sch. 1, Pt. I, para. 4)

will (for the reasons stated at the outset of this section) be treated as falling within the category of employed earner, provided that the employment is not through an agency in circumstances such that the categorisation rules described at **7.04** ante apply, the instruction is not given as public lectures, and the employment is one in which

> '. . . the person employed has agreed, prior to giving the instruction, to give it on at least four days in three consecutive months; and . . . gives the instruction in the presence of the person to whom the instruction is given except where the employment is in the Open University; and . . . the earnings in respect of the employment are paid by, or on behalf of, the person providing the education' (SI 1978, No. 1689, Sch. 1, Pt. I, para. 4).

'Educational establishment' includes

> '. . . a place where instruction is provided in any course or part of a course designed to lead to a certificate, diploma, degree or professional qualification . . .' (SI 1978, No. 1689, reg. 1(2))

or any like place where the courses are 'substantially similar' but do not lead to a certificate, etc (SI 1978, No. 1689, reg. 1(2)). The term accordingly covers universities, colleges and schools of all kinds including 'schools of arts and crafts and languages' (DHSS Leaflet NI222).

The clause 'on at least four days in three consecutive months' is capable of supporting two possible but opposing meanings, and the DHSS guidance note, though paraphrasing the words as 'on four or more days over a period of three consecutive months' (DHSS Leaflet NI222) does not finally resolve the matter. (Such leaflets do not, in any case, purport to give an authoritative statement of the law.) Does 'in three months' mean 'in each of three months' or 'in an overall period of three months'? The DHSS paraphrase would seem to endorse the latter meaning which, if it is correct, reveals that the rule is more stringent than might be supposed for it brings within the category of employed earner anyone who, in fact, on a regular basis, works more than one day per month as well as anyone who works for four or more days in any one month. It is difficult to believe that this was ever the intention of the regulation, but the wording of the rule does not strictly favour the alternative which would only bring into the category of employed earner those who work for at least four days per month on a regular basis.

Finally, it should be noted that the clause 'in the presence of the person to whom instruction is given' precludes instruction by correspondence and videotape (except where the educational establishment is the Open University); and the qualification concerning pay precludes the payment of fees directly to the instructor by individual students (DHSS Leaflet NI222).

The person falling to be treated as the secondary contributor as regards any employment within the scope of this regulation is the person providing the education (SI 1978, No. 1689, Sch. 3, para. 6).

7.07   Ministers of religion

Even though a minister of religion may (particularly as regards pastoral or ecclesiastical work) have no employer in the general sense of the word and may be neither under a contract of service, nor in an office with emoluments chargeable to tax under Schedule E, he is, nevertheless, from 6 April 1975, to be treated as falling within the category of employed earner for social security contribution purposes unless his

'. . . remuneration in respect of that employment (disregarding any payment in kind) does not consist wholly or mainly of stipend or salary' (SI 1978, No. 1689, Sch. 1, Pt. I, para. 5)

For the rule to operate as stated, stipend or salary (including any regular payment of like kind, however described) must be payable as of right (DHSS Leaflet NP21) and must form the major part of the minister's remuneration, disregarding such benefits as free housing, provision of a motor car, etc.

Because of this regulation most ministers of religion, whether employed in a parish, circuit etc or by a public or local authority or in a school or as a chaplain, will fall to be treated as employed earners. Only in instances where the major part of a minister's remuneration consists of offerings, gifts and occasional fees (for weddings, baptisms, funerals etc) will a minister fall into the category of earner indicated by the application of the normal rules of categorisation (see Chapter 2); normally that of a self-employed earner.

In the case of an employment as a minister in the Church of England, the Church Commissioners for England fall to be treated as the secondary contributor (SI 1978, No. 1689, Sch. 3, para. 7).

The secondary contributor as regards any other employment as a minister of religion is, however, to be identified by examining the source of his remuneration and, in this connection, remuneration includes any payment in respect of stipend or salary, excludes any payment to be disregarded under SI 1979, No. 591, reg. 19 (see Chapter 4) and any specific and distinct payment made towards the maintenance or education of a dependent of the person receiving the payment (SI 1978, No. 1689, reg. 1(2)).

Where the whole of a such remuneration is paid from one fund, the person responsible for the administration of that fund is to be treated as the secondary contributor (SI 1978, No. 1689, Sch. 3, para. 8(a)). This will be so even if the fund is assisted by another fund in order to be enabled to make the payment (DHSS Leaflet NP21). Where, however, the minister is remunerated directly from one fund but receives regular additional payments from one or more other funds, the person reponsible for the administration of the fund out of which such payments are made to the greater, or greatest, number of ministers will fall to be treated as the secondary contributor (SI 1978, No. 1689, Sch. 3, para. 8(b)(i) and (ii)). In practice, this generally means that where some payments are made from a local fund and others from a central fund, the person responsible for the central fund falls to be treated as the secondary contributor, irrespective of the comparative values of the local and central payments (DHSS Leaflet NP21). Where a minister is remunerated from more than one fund but each fund makes payments to an equal number of ministers, the person responsible for administering the fund from which the minister first receives a payment of remuneration in the tax year will fall to be treated as the secondary contributor (SI 1978, No. 1689, Sch. 3, para. 8(b)(iii)).

In situations where a minister is engaged in separate employments for each of which he is separately remunerated, there will be separate secondary contributors (eg the Church Commissioners with regard to stipend and a local authority with regard to salary for teaching work undertaken). Where, however, a minister has but one employment there will be but one secondary contributor as indicated above and it will be the responsibility of that secondary contributor to account for contributions as regards all payments made to the minister (DHSS Leaflet NP21).

SELF-EMPLOYED EARNER BY REGULATION

7.08 General

Just as the Act provides for certain persons to be categorised by regulation as employed earners even though they are neither employed under contracts of service nor in offices with emoluments chargeable to income tax under Schedule E, so it provides for certain other persons to be categorised by regulation as self-employed earners even if their employment is under such a contract or in such an office (SSA 1975, s. 2(2)(b); SI 1978, No. 1689, reg. 2(3)). At the present time there is only one such class of earners.

7.09 Examiners, moderators or invigilators

Even where his employment is under a contract of service, or in an office with emoluments chargeable to tax under Schedule E, any person becoming employed on or after 6 April 1975

'. . . by any person responsible for the conduct or administration of any examination leading to any certificate, diploma, degree or professional qualification . . . as an examiner, moderator or invigilator or in any similar capacity; or . . . to set questions or tests for any such examination' (SI 1978, No. 1689, Sch. 1, Pt. II, para. 6)

is to be treated as falling into the category of self-employed earner, provided he is employed under a contract which relates exclusively to the kind of duties described (DHSS Leaflet NI222) and under which

'. . . the whole of the work to be performed is to be performed in less than twelve months' (SI 1978, No. 1689, Sch. 1, Pt. II, para. 6)

but not through an agency in circumstances such as would cause the person to fall into the category of employed earner (see **7.04** ante). To this rule there are no exceptions.

NON-EMPLOYED BY REGULATION

7.10 General

While certain persons are, as has been explained at **7.01** and **7.08** ante, to be placed by regulation in a category of earner to which they would not otherwise belong, certain other persons are, by reason of their employment, to be excluded by regulation from categorisation as either employed or self-employed earners with regard to that employment (SI 1978, No. 1689, reg. 2(4)).

7.11 Persons employed by close relatives

Employment of a person by his or her

'. . . father, mother, grandfather, grandmother, stepfather, stepmother, son, daughter, grandson, granddaughter, stepson, stepdaughter, brother, sister, half-brother, half-sister . . .' (SI 1978, No. 1689, Sch. 1, Pt. III, para. 7)

is to be entirely disregarded for social security contribution purposes, provided such employment is

'. . . employment in a private dwelling house in which both the person employed and the employer reside; and . . . is not employment for the purposes of any trade or business carried on there by the employer' (SI 1978, No. 1689, Sch. 1, Pt. III, para. 7).

This rule covers the situation which exists where a person resides with and works for a close relative in a private household, either indoors (as, for example, a cook, cleaner, secretary or housekeeper) or outdoors (as, for example, a gardener, chauffeur or handyman) and the work is not in any way connected with any business carried on by that close relative.

It will be observed that husband and wife are not included in the list of close relatives, the rules relating to employment by a person of his or her spouse being dealt with under separate regulations as described in **7.05** ante.

7.12   Persons exceptionally self-employed

SI 1978, No. 1689, Sch. 1, Pt. III, para. 9 provides that

> '. . . any employment . . . as a self-employed earner . . . where the earner is not ordinarily employed in such employment . . .'

is to be entirely disregarded for social security purposes and this includes any employment which is by regulation (see **7.08** ante) to be treated as self-employment (SI 1978, No. 1689, Sch. 1, Pt. III, para. 9).

The practical application of this rule depends entirely on the meaning of the term 'ordinarily employed' but, unfortunately, this is nowhere defined. It is DHSS practice, however, to regard a person as coming within the scope of this rule so long as he is employed in employed earner's employment on a regular basis with spare-time self-employed earnings not in excess of (for 1981–82) £800 per annum (DHSS Leaflet NI27A). The figure for 1982–83 has not yet been announced. Thus a person who is, for example, employed as an engineer but keeps poultry as a spare-time occupation, may sell surplus eggs without becoming a self-employed earner for social security purposes, provided his total sales in a year do not exceed the figure stated. (Even where they do, he may, of course, be excepted from liability to pay contributions (see **5.22** ante) but this will be on the grounds of small income, not on the grounds of being excluded by regulation from the category of self-employed earner.)

7.13   Returning and counting officers

Employment on or after 6 April 1978 for the purposes of any election or referendum authorised by Act of Parliament

> '. . . as a returning officer or acting returning officer; or . . . as Chief Counting Officer or counting officer . . .' (SI 1978, No. 1689, Sch. 1, Pt. III, para. 10(a) and (b))

is to be disregarded for social security contribution purposes, as is any employment by any of the officers described for any of the purposes stated (SI 1978, No. 1689, Sch. 1, Pt. III, para. 10(c)).

The elections referred to include local government as well as parliamentary elections.

7.14   Persons employed in or by visiting forces

Employment

> '. . . as a member of the naval, military or air forces of a country to which a provision of the Visiting Forces Act 1952 applies . . .' (SI 1978, No. 1689, Sch. 1, Pt. III, para. 11 as inserted by SI 1980, No. 1713, reg. 2)

or

> '. . . as a civilian by any such force' (SI 1978, No. 1689, Sch. 1, Pt. III, para. 11)

is, from 1 December 1980, to be disregarded for social security contribution purposes, provided that, in the case of a civilian, he or she is not ordinarily resident in the United Kingdom. The meaning of that term has been discussed at **3.05** ante.

7.15   Members of defence organisations

Employment

'. . . as a member of any international headquarters or defence organisation designated under section 1 of the International Headquarters and Defence Organisations Act 1964' (SI 1978, No. 1689, Sch. 1, Pt. III, para. 12 as inserted by SI 1980, No. 1713, reg. 2)

is, from 1 December 1980, to be disregarded for social security contribution purposes unless the person so employed is serving in Her Majesty's regular forces, or is a civilian ordinarily resident (see **3.05** ante) in the United Kingdom who is not a member of the pension scheme of the headquarters or organisation (SI 1978, No. 1689, Sch. 1, Pt. III, para. 12 as inserted by SI 1980, No. 1713, reg. 2).

AIRMEN

7.16   General

By regulations made under SSA 1975, s. 129(1), airmen fall to be treated as a special class of earners for social security contribution purposes.

7.17   An 'airman' defined

An airman is

'. . . a person who is, or has been, employed under a contract of service either as a pilot, commander, navigator or other member of the crew of any aircraft . . .' (SI 1979, No. 591, reg. 81)

and the term also covers a supernumerary, ie a person employed on board in some other capacity (eg as a film projectionist or shop assistant) provided the employment is

'. . . for the purposes of the aircraft or its crew or of any passengers or cargo or mails carried thereby . . .' (SI 1979, No. 591, reg. 81(a))

and

'. . . the contract is entered into in the United Kingdom with a view to its performance (in whole or in part) while the aircraft is in flight . . .' (SI 1979, No. 591, reg. 81(b)).

Ther term does not, however, include members of the forces (SI 1979, No. 591, reg. 81).

7.18 Modification of categorisation rules

Under the normal rules of categorisation (see Chapter 2) a person must be gainfully employed 'in Great Britain' if he is to be categorised as an employed earner. He must, furthermore, fulfil certain conditions of residence and presence (see Chapter 3) if he is then to be actually liable to pay Class 1 contributions. An airman, however, does not, because of the very nature of his employment, meet these requirements, but is, nevertheless, to be treated as

> '. . . employed in employed earner's employment and . . . as present in Great Britain' (SI 1979, No. 591, reg. 82(1))

provided that he is employed as an airman on board an aircraft and his employer or the person paying his earning (whether acting as the employer's agent or not) or the person determining the terms of his employment and the amount of his earnings has a place of business in Great Britain (SI 1979, No. 591, reg. 82(1)(a)) which, if the aircraft is not a British aircraft, is his principal place of business (SI 1979, No. 591, reg. 82(1)(b)).

The DHSS interprets 'a place of business' as meaning a place from which a person can, as of right, conduct his business, or from which his agent has power to conduct business on his behalf. It does not accept that a registered office is necessarily a place of business in this context (DHSS Leaflet NI132).

A 'British aircraft' is one which is either in the service of the Crown or is registered in the UK and has an owner, manager or hirer who resides or has a principal place of business in Great Britain (SI 1979, No. 591, reg. 81).

7.19 Non-liability of non-domiciled airmen

By overriding the conditions of residence and presence whereby the scope of the contribution scheme is normally limited to persons 'attached' in some degree to Great Britain, SI 1979, No. 591, reg. 82 brings within the scheme many airmen who do not properly belong there. Accordingly, the regulation contains a proviso that, subject to any EEC regulation or reciprocal agreement to the contrary (SI 1979, No. 591, reg. 82(3)), any airman who is neither domiciled nor has a place of residence in Great Britain shall not be liable to pay contributions in respect of his earnings as an airman even though he has technically become an employed earner under the British scheme (SI 1979, No. 591, reg. 82(2)).

Domicile is a legal concept beyond the scope of this book, but it must not be confused with residence which is a matter of degree and fact (see Chapter 3). It can, however, be stated here, briefly, that every person acquires at birth a 'domicile of origin' which, regardless of the country of birth, is that of the father if the father is alive and married to the mother at the time, or that of the mother if the father is dead, the parents are divorced, or the child is illegitimate. Once a child has come of age, he may set aside his domicile of origin by acquiring a 'domicile of choice' (but only by positive, unambiguous action and intent) though, if that domicile of choice is then abandoned, the domicile of origin will revive. It is quite possible, therefore, that a person may have a country of domicile in which he has never set foot and is never likely to do so.

7.20 Modification of compliance rules

Where an airman (because of his employment in that capacity and by reason of being outside Great Britain) is unable to comply with time-limits imposed on any acts which he is required to perform under the rules of the social security scheme

> '. . . he shall be deemed to have complied . . . if he performs the act as soon as is reasonably practicable . . .' (SI 1979, No. 591, reg. 83).

PERSONS EMPLOYED ON THE CONTINENTAL SHELF

7.21 General

Under SSA 1975, s. 132 regulations have been made which modify the contribution scheme in relation to prescribed employment in connection with continental shelf operations.

7.22 Prescribed employment

The modifications extend to any employment (whether under a contract of service or not) in connection with the exploitation of resources or the exploration of the sea bed and subsoil in any area designated under the Continental Shelf Act 1964, s. 1(7) (SI 1979, No. 591, reg. 85(1)).

7.23 Modification of the scheme

Although areas designated under the Continental Shelft Act 1964, s. 1(7) are not in Great Britain, the social security scheme is to apply to anyone in employment as described at **7.22** ante as if those areas are in Great Britain and compliance with conditions of residence and presence (see Chapter 3) is to be judged accordingly (SI 1979, No. 591, reg. 85(2)).

7.24 Modification of compliance rules

Where a person in prescribed employment on the continental shelf (see **7.22** ante) is (because of his employment in that capacity and by reason of being outside Great Britain) unable to comply with any time-limit imposed on acts which he is required to perform under the social security scheme, he shall be deemed to have complied if he performs the act as soon as is reasonably practicable (SI 1979, No. 591, reg. 85(3)).

MARINERS

7.25   General

Regulations made under SSA 1975, s. 129 provide for the modification of the social security contribution scheme so far as it relates to

> '. . . persons who are or have been, or are to be, employed on board any ship, vessel, hovercraft . . .' (SSA 1975, s. 129(1)).

SI 1979, No. 591, regs. 86–97 are concerned with mariners; regs. 86 and 98 relate to share fishermen and are considered in the next section (see **7.40** et seq post).

7.26   A 'mariner' defined

A mariner is

> '. . . a person who is or has been in employment under a contract of service either as a master or member of the crew of any ship or vessel . . .' (SI 1979, No. 591, reg. 86)

and the term also covers a supernumerary, ie a person employed on board in some other capacity (eg as a cattleman, shop assistant, hairdresser) provided the employment is

> '. . . for the purposes of that ship or vessel or her crew or any passengers or cargo or mails carried thereby . . .' (SI 1979, No. 591, reg. 86)

and

> '. . . the contract is entered into in the United Kingdom with a view to its performance (in whole or in part) while the ship or vessel is on her voyage . . .' (SI 1979, No. 591, reg. 86).

The term does include a radio officer but does not include a member of the forces (SI 1979, No. 591, reg. 86).

7.27   Modification of categorisation rules

Under the normal rules of categorisation (see Chapter 2) a person must be gainfully employed 'in Great Britain' if he is to fall within the category of employed earner. By the very nature of his employment, however, a mariner does not fulfil this requirement but is, nevertheless, to be treated as an employed earner, provided that he is employed either as a mariner on board a British ship (SI 1979, No. 591, reg. 88(a)(i)), or as a mariner on board a non-British ship under a contract of employment entered into in the UK with a view to its performance (in whole or in part) while the ship or vessel is on her voyage and the person paying his earnings (or, if the mariner is the ship's master or a crew member, the ship's owner or managing owner) has a place of business in Great Britain (SI 1979, No. 591, reg. 88(a)(ii) and (iii)).

A mariner who does not fulfil these requirements will nevertheless still fall to be treated as an employed earner if he is employed as a master, crew member or radio officer (but not merely as a supernumerary) on board any ship or vessel (including a hovercraft) and (if the contract of service was not entered into in the UK) his employer or the person paying his earnings has his principal place of business in Great Britain (SI 1979, No. 591, reg. 88(b)(ii)). If the employment is as a radio officer and the contract of employment is entered into in the UK, the mariner's treatment as an employed earner is conditional upon his employer or the person paying his earnings having a place of business in Great Britain (SI 1979, No. 591, reg. 88(b)(i)).

A British ship is any ship or vessel in the service of the Crown; any ship or vessel registered at a port in Great Britain; or any hovercraft registered in Great Britain (SI 1979, No. 591, reg. 86).

As to the meaning of 'place of business' see **7.18** ante.

7.28 Non-liability of non-domiciled mariners

Because, by the nature of his employment, a mariner is unable to fulfil the conditions of residence and presence antecedent to a liability to pay Class 1 contributions (see Chapter 3), SI 1979, No. 591, reg. 87(1)(a) directs that those conditions are to be waived. That regulation thereby brings within the contribution scheme, however, many mariners who do not properly belong there and, accordingly, SI 1979, No. 591, reg. 87(1)(b) provides that, subject to any EEC regulations or reciprocal agreements to the contrary (SI 1979, No. 591, reg. 87(2))

> 'it shall be a condition of liability to pay a contribution . . . that the mariner is domiciled or resident in Great Britain . . .'

Residence is discussed at **3.04** ante and domicile is briefly considered at **7.19** ante. It should be noted, however, that mariners who sign crew agreements in Great Britain under National Maritime Board conditions are treated as having a place of residence in Great Britain whether they have such a place or not (DHSS Leaflet NI25, para. 2) and that, by virtue of 'joint arrangements' made for the purpose of co-ordinating the social security schemes of Great Britain and Northern Ireland (SSA 1975, s. 142) and similar arrangements made with the Isle of Man, a mariner who is domiciled or resident in either of those countries will, if he becomes employed on a British ship, be regarded as domiciled or resident in Great Britain, and vice versa (DHSS Leaflet NI25, para. 56).

The arrangements made between Great Britain and other member states of the EEC as described at **3.12** ante apply equally to mariners as to other employed earners, as do the reciprocal agreements described at **3.13** ante (DHSS Leaflet NI25, paras. 53, 54 and 58).

A mariner who is not liable to pay contributions by reason of the regulations described should apply for a certificate of mariner's non-liability on form RD79 (RD79A if the mariner was born in Great Britain) obtainable from the DHSS Maritime Section, Records Division, Newcastle-upon-Tyne, NE98 1YU or from any Mercantile Marine office.

7.29 Earnings

A mariner's earnings are to be calculated according to the normal rules described in Chapter 4 though the provisions specifically relating to mariner's pay should be especially noted (**4.22** ante). It is also worth drawing attention (as the regulations themselves do) to the fact that interim payments of a seaman's earnings by way of an advance, or a payment of part of his earnings to some other person at his behest, are to be disregarded until the earnings they represent are actually due (SI 1979, No. 591, reg. 94(1)(a)(i) amd (ii)). This accords with the normal treatment of amounts paid in advance or on account of earnings (see **4.03** ante). Likewise, in accordance with the normal principle that sums set aside for future payments are earnings once an entitlement to them has arisen, amounts retained by an employer (or the person who pays a mariner's earnings) to cover repatriation expenses in relation to a mariner left abroad are to be included in gross pay (DHSS Leaflet NI25, para. 30).

7.30 Earnings periods

Where a mariner is paid at regular intervals (eg a week or month), the length of the earnings period by reference to which contributions are to be assessed will be ascertained in the normal way (see Chapter 5). Where, however, a mariner receives a general settlement of his earnings at the end of a voyage, the voyage period is to be the earnings period (SI 1979, No. 591, reg. 90(1)).

A voyage period is a pay period comprising an entire voyage or series of voyages and it includes any period of paid leave which immediately follows the day on which termination of the voyage or series of voyages occurs (SI 1979, No. 591, reg. 86). It is measured in weeks which, for these purposes, are periods of seven consecutive days (SI 1979, No. 591, reg. 86).

Where a voyage period is less than a week, the earnings period will be a week (SI 1979, No. 591, reg. 90(2)(a)) and where the voyage period exceeds a week (or a number of weeks) by more than three days, those days are to be treated as an additional week (SI 1979, No. 591, reg. 90(2)(b)(i)). Where a voyage period exceeds a week (or number of weeks) by three days or less, those days are to be disregarded but the earnings relative to them are to be aggregated with the earnings in the immediately preceding week (SI 1979, No. 591, reg. 90(2)(b)(ii)).

A voyage period should exclude any period of leave in respect of which leave is liquidated and a payment in lieu is made (DHSS Leaflet NI25, para. 22).

7.31 Apportionment of contributions paid

Although voyage periods often fall partly in one contribution year and partly in one or more others, the contributions due in respect of voyage earnings normally all fall to be paid only in the last of the contribution years concerned. As this would otherwise create a defective contribution record for benefit entitlement purposes, it is provided that the total contributions paid as regards a voyage shall be apportioned on a time-basis over the voyage period and treated as paid accordingly (SI 1979, No. 591, reg. 90(3)).

EXAMPLE 7(C)

On 5 July 1981, R. Shaftoe, a storeman on a cargo ship, completed a voyage which began on 6 October 1980 and received £4,500 less deductions which included £348.75 in respect of primary Class 1 contributions. Although these were all paid in 1981–82, they will be apportioned as follows:

		£
1980–81	6/9 × £348.75	232.50
1981–82	3/9 × £348.75	116.25
		348.75

and treated as paid in the years indicated.

7.32   Identification of the secondary contributor

The shipowner will, as a mariner's employer, normally fall to be treated as the secondary contributor with respect to Class 1 contributions payable on a mariner's earnings (though, in practice, the task of assessing and collecting those contributions will generally fall to the ship's master). It is, however, a condition of liability to pay secondary contributions that the secondary contributor is resident, or has a place of business in, Great Britain (SI 1979, No. 591, reg. 87(1)(c)). If, therefore, the employer of a mariner does not satisfy either of these conditions, but the person who actually pays the mariner does, that person (even if he is merely acting as agent for the employer) will be treated as the secondary contributor in the employer's stead (SI 1979, No. 591, reg. 93; DHSS Leaflet NI25, para. 27).

A radio officer is usually employed by a marine radio company rather than by a shipowner. Where that is the case, the marine radio company will be treated as the secondary contributor and will be liable to pay contributions accordingly. Otherwise the secondary contributor will be identified according to the rules described above (DHSS Leaflet NI25, para. 28).

7.33   Contribution rates

Primary and secondary Class 1 contributions in respect of a mariner's earnings are normally payable at the same rate as would be applicable were the mariner a normal employed earner. There are two circumstances, however, under which contributions (at either contracted-out or not-contracted-out rate) are reduced for both mariners and their employers (or payers). The first is where a mariner is covered by the provisions of article 3 of the Redundancy Payments (Merchant Seamen Exclusion) Order 1973, No. 1281, and the second is where a mariner is master or a crew member on a foreign-going ship.

Article 3 of SI 1973, No. 1281 excludes from the provisions of the Employment Protection (Consolidation) Act 1978, s. 81 (which confers a right to redundancy payments under that Act) any mariner who is domiciled or resident in Great Britain and covered by the National Maritime Board Redundancy Payments Agreement. Mariners affected are those whose employers are represented by an organisation affiliated to the National Maritime Board or whose employer is a marine radio company incorporated in Great Britain (DHSS Leaflet NI25, para. 8). The provision does not, therefore, apply to mariners employed either in the fishing industry or as share fishermen, as supernumaries, on pleasure craft, salvage vessels, tug boats and the like. The rate of primary and secondary Class 1 contributions payable on the earnings of those mariners who are affected is reduced by the amount of the redundancy allocation, ie 0.35% and 0.15% respectively (SI 1979, No. 591, reg. 89(1)(a) as amended by SI 1980, No. 13, reg. 1(1) and (2) and SS(C)A 1982, Sch. 1, para. 3(2)).

Where a mariner is a master or crew member of a foreign-going ship, the rate of *secondary* Class 1 contributions payable by the secondary contributor is to be reduced by a rebate of 0.6% as agreed with the Shipping Industry (SI 1979, No. 591, reg. 89(1)(b)). A foreign-going ship is (in contradistinction to a 'home-trade ship') a ship or vessel which is employed in trading or going beyond the United Kingdom (including for this purpose the Republic of Ireland), the Channel Islands, the Isle of Man, and the continent of Europe between the rivers Elbe and Brest inclusive; and any fishing vessel proceeding beyond the limits of, on the south, latitude 48° 30' N; on the west, longitude 12° W; on the north, latitude 61° N (SI 1979, No. 591, reg. 86). If the employment is partly on a foreign-going ship but also partly on a home-trade ship, the rate of contributions payable (standard or rebated) will be determined by the nature of the voyage at the time the payment of earnings is made (SI 1979, No. 591, reg. 89(1)(b)(ii)).

Some employers make a practice of opening home-trade agreements between successive foreign-going voyages and, where this is the case, contributions at the rebated rate may be made on the earnings arising from the home-trade agreements as well as from the foreign-going voyages, provided those agreements are merely incidental to the distribution and collection of foreign cargo at ports within the home-trade limits and that the ship is not actually engaged in trade between those ports (DHSS Leaflet NI25, para. 11). Where, in circumstances other than these, a mariner is paid earnings for periods between foreign-going voyages, the standard rate of secondary contributions must, however, be paid, unless the mariner is on paid leave immediately following such a voyage or is employed in or about a ship in port 'off the crew agreement' which has just completed (or is about to begin) a foreign-going voyage on which the mariner has been (or will be) 'on the crew agreement' (DHSS Leaflet NI25, paras. 12 and 13).

The employment as a mariner to which the rebated contribution rules described above apply includes periods of leave other than study leave accruing from the employment (SI 1979, No. 591, reg. 89(2)).

Once the rate of contributions has been reduced as appropriate by either the redundancy allocation or the foreign-going rebate or by both, the normal rules for calculating contributions (see Chapter 5) apply without modification (SI 1979, No. 591, reg. 91).

7.34   The marine tax deduction scheme

Contributions payable on the earnings of mariners who fall within the definition of seamen in SI 1979, No. 591, Sch. 1, Pt. V, para. 35 are, until 5 April 1982, to be·assessed and collected through the marine tax deduction scheme (MTDS) instead of through the PAYE scheme. A seaman is anyone who has signed a crew agreement to which any determination of the National Maritime Board relating to remuneration applies or (if the agreement is signed outside the UK) is adopted; or who, being employed on a ship, holds a valid British seaman's card. The term does not include members of the forces, members of services administered by the Defence Council or anyone employed by the British Railways Board.

Three volumes of contribution tables are provided for the use of masters and employers of mariners. Volume 1 relates to home-trade voyages with contributions at either standard or redundancy rebated rates. Volume 2 relates to foreign-going voyages with contributions at a rate adjusted for foreign-going and redundancy allocation rebates. Volume 3 relates to foreign-going voyages at a rate adjusted for foreign-going rebate only.

The MTD scheme operates in much the same way as the PAYE scheme of which it is an adaptation, though there are certain circumstances and pay situations in which procedures differ from those laid down under the PAYE scheme. These are described in the remaining paragraphs of this section but it should be noted that, when the draft Social Security (Contributions) (Mariners) Amendment Regulations 1982, which are currently before Parliament, acquire the force of law, the various matters dealt with will be related to the normal PAYE scheme instead of to the MTDS which is to be abolished from 5 April 1982 (Income Tax (Employments) (No. 12) Regulations, SI 1982, No. 1), and new rules relating to earnings periods and the apportionment of earnings will become operative.

7.35   Overtime earnings

Overtime earnings due to a mariner will normally be included in the terminal payment made in general settlement of earnings at the end of a voyage. Where, however, overtime earnings are paid separately for the last six days (or less) of a voyage (or of the last in a series of voyages which make up one voyage period), the primary and secondary Class 1 contributions payable are, under the MTDS to be the difference between the contributions which would have been payable had the overtime earnings been included in the terminal payment and the contributions which were, in fact, payable on the general settlement excluding the overtime earnings (SI 1979, No. 591, reg. 95(2)(a) and (b)).

A terminal payment is a payment of earnings to a mariner in respect of his employment as such at (or following) the end of a voyage by way of general settlement of the mariner's earnings for that voyage (or, where the voyage includes more than one pay period, for the last of those pay periods) (SI 1979, No. 591, reg. 95(1)(a)).

Where overtime is paid separately for more than the last six days of a voyage, the payment is classed as an 'employer's payment' to which special rules apply (see **7.36** post).

7.36 Employers' payments

An 'employer's payment' is, under the MTDS, any payment of earnings (other than a six-day or less overtime payment such as has been described at **7.35** ante) made to a mariner either after the terminal payment or, if made through someone other than the person from whom the mariner will receive the terminal payment, before that payment (SI 1979, No. 591, reg. 3(1)(a) and (b)). Any such payment which is made at the same time as any normal payment of earnings is not to be treated as an employer's payment, however, but is to be treated as additional earnings for the pay period in respect of which the normal payment of earnings is made (SI 1979, No. 591, reg. 95(4)). Subject to these strictures, an employer's payment will include any payment in respect of bonus, commission, special qualifications allowance, belated overtime pay, belated leave pay and any special payment (other than one of the kind described at **4.22** ante) which is not included in a terminal payment (DHSS Leaflet NI25, para. 19).

The amount of contributions payable in respect of an employer's payment depends on whether or not the mariner is still in the service of the same employer when the employer's payment is made and whether, under the terms of his engagement to his employer, the mariner's earnings are expressed as weekly, monthly or quarterly calculated amounts. If the mariner is still in the employment of the person making the employer's payment at the time when the payment is made, the employer is to treat the payment as being for a pay period of either a week, a month or three calendar months (depending on whether the terminal payment was a weekly, monthly or quarterly calculated amount) and to calculate contributions as if the mariner had been paid his basic wage for the pay period and had suffered the contributions due thereon (SI 1979, No. 591, reg. 95(6)(a)).

EXAMPLE 7(D)

A. Ross's agreement with Ancient Shipping Lines provides for a basic wage of £60.00 per week payable at the end of each voyage. A six-week home-trade voyage ends on 26 June 1982 and Albert receives his terminal payment. Seven weeks later, while still in the employment of Ancient Shipping Lines, Albert receives an employer's payment of £210 being belated overtime earnings due for the whole voyage. The contributions payable on this are to be calculated as follows under the MTDS:

			Class 1	
			Primary	S'dary
		£	£	£
(i)	Employer's payment on 14.8.82	210.00		
	Hypothetical pay for week ended 14.8.82	60.00		
		270.00		

| Primary Class 1: £220 (UEL) × 8.75% | | 19.25 | |
| Secondary Class 1: £220 (UEL) × 13.7% | | | 30.14 |

(ii)	Hypothetical pay for week ended 14.8.82	60.00		
	Primary Class 1: £60 × 8.75%		5.25	
	Secondary Class 1: £60 × 13.7%			8.22
Contributions payable on £210.00			14.00	21.92

It will be observed that this result is not the same as that which would have been obtained by merely applying the appropriate contribution rates to the amount of the employer's payment, viz:

	£	£	£
Employer's payment on 14.8.82	210.00		
Primary Class 1: £210 × 8.75%		18.37	
Secondary Class 1: £210 × 13.7%			28.77
		18.37	28.77

Where a mariner is not still employed by the employer making an employer's payment at the time the payment is made, contributions are still to be calculated on the basis of a weekly, monthly or quarterly pay period, as appropriate, but as though no other earnings have been paid for that pay period (SI 1979, No. 591, reg. 95(6)(b)) so that, in Example 7(D) above, the 'incorrect' calculation at the end would, in fact, be correct.

7.37   Annual maximum

The limitation of total contributions paid to a prescribed annual maximum applies to mariners whose earnings-related contributions are assessed and collected under the MTDS just as it applies to other employed earners, subject to the condition that any payment of earnings for any voyage period falling partly into two or more years is to be apportioned between those years according to the length of the part of the voyage period which falls in each year (SI 1979, No. 591, reg. 96(2)).

7.38   Changes during a voyage period

Where, under the MTDS, earnings are paid to or for the benefit of a mariner in respect of a voyage period which falls partly in one year and partly in one or more other years and, during that voyage period, any change occurs in either the contracted-out or not contracted-out primary or secondary Class 1 contribution rates (or the amount by which they may be rebated) or in the lower or upper earnings limits, the earnings are to be apportioned between the years in which the voyage period falls, proportionately to the length of the part of the voyage period which falls in each year (SI 1979, No. 591, reg. 97(1) and (2)(a)). Each amount of earnings so apportioned is then to be treated as if it were paid at the end of the year or of the part of the year to which it has been apportioned, and the earnings period for each amount is to be the length of the period to which it has been apportioned (SI 1979, No. 591, reg. 97(2)(b) and (c)).

Where a voyage begins within the month immediately preceding the start of a contribution year (ie between 5 March and 6 April) or ends within the month immediately succeeding the end of a contribution year (ie between 5 April and 6 May), or where a voyage period extends beyond the date on which earnings are paid, there are complex provisions which effectively take any earnings apportioned to such short periods, or to periods after the date when earnings are paid, into the succeeding or preceding period as the case may be (SI 1979, No. 591, reg. 97(3) and (4)).

Where, in consequence of apportioning a voyage period into two or more earnings periods in accordance with the provisions described, an earnings period is less than a week, it is to be treated as a week; and where an earnings period exceeds a week (or a number of weeks) by more than three days, those days are to be treated as an additional week (SI 1979, No. 591, reg. 97(5)(a) and (b)(i)). Where, however, an earnings period exceeds a week (or a number of weeks) by three days or less, those days are to be disregarded but the earnings relative to them are to be aggregated with the earnings in the immediately preceding week (SI 1979, No. 591, reg. 97(5)(b)(ii)). A week is a period of seven consecutive days (SI 1979, No. 591, reg. 86).

Contributions paid in respect of earnings apportioned between two or more years in accordance with the regulations described are to be treated as paid in respect of the year to which the amount has been apportioned (SI 1979, No. 591, reg. 97(6)) and this will override the general rule described at **7.31** ante.

Apportionment of earnings will also be necessary where, during a voyage period, there is a change in a mariner's circumstances (eg reaching the age of sixty-five). Such change is to be given effect to from the date from which it would have had effect had the mariner's earnings period been a week and not a voyage period (SI 1979, No. 591, reg. 92).

7.39   Modification of compliance rules

Where any mariner (regardless of the scheme under which his contributions are collected) is unable, because of his absence from Great Britain by reason of his employment as a mariner, to comply with time limits on any acts which he is required to perform under the rules of the social security scheme, he shall be deemed to have complied if he performs the act as soon as is reasonably practicable (SI 1979, No. 591, reg. 96(1)).

SHARE FISHERMEN

7.40   General

Regulations made under SSA 1975, s. 129 provide for the modification of the social security contribution scheme so far as it relates to share fishermen.

7.41   A 'share fisherman' defined

A 'sea-going' share fisherman is any person who

> 'is ordinarily employed in the fishing industry otherwise than under a contract of service as a master or member of the crew of any British fishing boat . . . manned by more than one person, and remunerated in respect of that employment in whole or in part by a share of the profits or gross earnings of the fishing boat . . .' (SI 1979, No. 591, reg. 86)

and an 'on-shore' share fisherman is any person who

> 'has ordinarily been so employed, but who by reason of age or infirmity permanently ceases to be so employed and becomes ordinarily engaged in employment ashore in Great Britain otherwise than under a contract of service making or mending any gear appurtenant to a British fishing boat or performing other services ancillary to or in connection with that boat and is remunerated in respect of that employment in whole or in part by a share of the profits or gross earnings of that boat . . .' (SI 1979, No. 591, reg. 86).

The terms 'sea-going' and 'on-shore' are not used in the regulations but are descriptions employed in DHSS Leaflet NI47.

7.42   Modification of categorisation rules

Under the normal rules of categorisation (see Chapter 2) a person must be gainfully employed 'in Great Britain' if he is to be categorised as either an employed or a self-employed earner. He must, moreover, fulfil certain conditions of residence and presence (see Chapter 3) if he is then to be actually liable to pay contributions. A share fisherman, however, may not, because of the very nature of his employment, meet these requirements, but his employment will nevertheless

> '. . . be employment as a self-employed earner notwithstanding that it is not employment in Great Britain' (SI 1979, No. 591, reg. 98(a))

and the conditions of domicile and residence imposed on mariners in substitution for the normal conditions of residence and presence are to apply to share fishermen also (SI 1979, No. 591, reg. 98(b)). Those conditions of domicile and residence have been fully described at **7.28** ante and reference should be made to that section.

7.43 Modification of contribution rules

As ordinary Class 2 contributions do not carry any entitlement to unemployment benefit, it is provided that share fishermen, in order to build up a contribution record for such entitlement, are to pay a special higher rate of Class 2 contributions (SI 1979, No. 591, reg. 98(c)). From 6 April 1982 this rate has been £5.85 per week compared with the normal rate of £3.75 per week (SS(C)A 1982, s. 1(5)). For 1981–82 the rate was £5.15 per week.

7.44 Annual maximum

The special rate of Class 2 contributions described in **7.43** ante above is to be used in place of the normal rate when any calculations are being made in connection with the annual maximum contributions of a share fisherman (SI 1979, No. 591, reg. 98(d)).

7.45 Exception from Class 2 liability

The circumstances under which a self-employed person may be excepted from liability to pay a Class 2 contribution (see **5.23** ante) are extended, in the case of any share fisherman, so as to include any week in which he is entitled to unemployment benefit or would be so entitled were his contribution record adequate (SI 1979, No. 591, reg. 98(e)).

7.46 Contribution cards

There are special contribution cards for the use of share fishermen (SI 1979, No. 591, reg. 98(f)) and these are only obtainable from eighty or so DHSS local offices in the British Isles. A list is given in DHSS Leaflet NI47. The regulations described at **6.10** ante apply without modification.

7.47 Collection of Class 4 contributions

In so far as Class 4 contributions in respect of the profits or gains of a share fisherman are not collected by the normal Inland Revenue channels, the special direct collection procedure described at **6.22** ante is to apply (SI 1979, No. 591, reg. 98(g)).

MEMBERS OF THE FORCES

7.48   General

Regulations made under SSA 1975, s. 128(2) introduce modifications into the social security scheme in so far as it relates to members of Her Majesty's forces.

7.49   Establishments and organisations included

For the purposes of SSA 1975, s. 128(3), Her Majesty's forces are to be taken to consist of any of the regular naval, military or air forces of the Crown; Retired and Emergency Lists of Officers of the Royal Navy; Royal Naval Reserves (including Women's Royal Naval Reserve and Queen Alexandra's Royal Naval Nursing Service Reserve); Royal Marines Reserve; Army Reserves (including Regular Army Reserve of Officers, Regular Reserves, Long Term Reserve and Army Pensioners); Territorial and Army Volunteer Reserve; Royal Air Force Reserves (including Royal Air Force Reserve of Officers, Women's Royal Air Force Reserve of Officers, Royal Air Force Volunteer Reserve, Women's Royal Air Force Volunteer Reserve, Class E Reserve of Airmen, Princess Mary's Royal Air Force Nursing Service Reserve, Officers on the Retired List of the Royal Air Force and Royal Air Force Pensioners); Royal Auxiliary Air Force (including Women's Royal Auxiliary Air Force); and the Ulster Defence Regiment (SI 1979, No. 591, reg. 113 and Sch. 3, Pt. I as amended by SI 1980, No. 1975, reg. 6). A person whose employment in and membership of any such force originated outside of the United Kingdom and is confined to areas of the world and bases outside of the United Kingdom is not, however, a member of the forces for the purposes of the Act (SI 1979, No. 591, reg. 113 and Sch. 3, Pt. II).

7.50   Categorisation

Any member of the forces is, while he is serving as such, to be

'. . . treated . . . as an employed earner in respect of his membership of those forces' (SSA 1975, s. 128(1)).

so far as the contribution part of the social security scheme is concerned.

7.51   Residence and presence

In relation to the conditions of residence and presence under which a liability to pay contributions will arise (see **3.06** ante), a serving member of the forces

'. . . shall in respect of his employment as such be treated as present in Great Britain' (SI 1979, No. 591, reg. 114).

7.52 Rate of contributions

In the case of serving members of the forces, Class 1 contributions are payable at reduced rates. The primary Class 1 standard rate is reduced by 0.7%; the primary Class 1 reduced rate is further reduced by 0.15% and the secondary Class 1 rate is reduced by 1.25% (SI 1979, No. 591, reg. 115(1) as amended by SI 1980, No. 13, regs. 1(1) and 4). The normal methods of calculation apply (SI 1979, No. 591, reg. 115(2) and (3)).

7.53 Contributions paid late

For the purposes of entitlement to benefit, any late-paid contributions in respect of a person's employment as a member of the forces are to be treated as paid on the due date (SI 1979, No. 591, reg. 116).

7.54 Earnings

The earnings of a member of the forces are to be identified and calculated according to the normal rules described in Chapter 5 by the special items to be excluded (see **4.21** ante) should be particularly noted.

7.55 Earnings periods

In the case of a person serving in the regular naval, military or air forces, the earnings period to be applied in connection with earnings-related contributions is the accounting period from time to time applying under the Naval Pay Regulations, or, as the case may be, the Army Pay Warrant, Queen's Regulations for the Army or Queen's Regulations for the Royal Air Force (SI 1979, No. 591, reg. 117(2)(a)). In the case of a person undergoing training in any of the other establishments listed at **7.49** ante, the earnings period is one month (SI 1979, No. 591, reg. 117(2)(b)).

7.56 Modification of compliance rules

Where a member of the forces is (because of his employment in that capacity and by reason of being outside Great Britain or Northern Ireland) unable to comply with any time-limit imposed on acts which he is required to perform under the social security scheme, he shall be deemed to have complied if he performs the act as soon as is reaonably practicable (SI 1979, No. 591, reg. 118).

DIVERS AND DIVING SUPERVISORS

7.57 General

Although not designated as a special class of earners under the Act, divers and diving supervisors are accorded special treatment under the regulations and so fall to be discussed in this chapter.

7.58   Class 4 exception

For 1978–79 and future years a diver or a diving supervisor working as an employee in the North Sea or other designated area is to be treated as carrying on a trade for income tax purposes (Finance Act 1978, s. 29). In consequence, a liability to pay Class 4 contributions would normally arise, but, as such a person is an employed earner and therefore liable to Class 1 contributions, he is to be excepted from Class 4 contributions on so much of his profits or gains as are derived from that employment (SI 1979, No. 591, reg. 59).

CROWN EMPLOYEES

7.59   General

Although designated as a special class of earner for the purpose of industrial injury benefits, persons employed by, or under, the Crown are employed earners for social security contribution purposes and no special provisions apply to them (SSA 1975, s. 127).

Chapter 8

Contribution planning

8.01 Introduction

The point has been argued in Chapter 1 that social security contributions are, in fact, a thinly-disguised form of regressive direct taxation and, as such, are as legitimately open to avoidance as any other tax. Accordingly, this chapter will examine some of the ways in which reduction or elimination of contribution liability might be achieved without infringement of social security law.

8.02 Caveats

It must be stated at the outset of any discussion of contribution planning that social security contributions are unlike other taxes in one important respect: eligibility to certain state benefits does depend on the payment of contributions at a certain minimum level (see **1.17** ante). This being so, anyone who reduces his contributions to below that minimum level must be left in no doubt as to the likely consequences of his action should he, for example, become unemployed, fall sick or retire. A consideration of the benefits aspect of the social security scheme is beyond the scope of this book but sufficient information has been given at **1.17**, **5.26** and **5.27** ante for the extent to which a person needs to contribute in order to satisfy the contribution conditions for particular benefits to be ascertained. As a general rule, it may be stated that, provided 52 minimum Class 1 contributions or 52 Class 2 contributions are paid in each tax year, a right to all basic short and long term contributory benefits will be maintained; though Class 2 contributions do not, of course, carry any entitlement to unemployment benefit.

It must also be stated at this juncture that Parliament is (and has been since the inception of the scheme) at pains to minimise the extent to which avoidance of contribution liability might succeed: particularly in view of the fact that general taxation has to provide the 'safety-net' of non-contributory and supplementary benefits for those who are (or, by their own devices, become) ineligible for contributory benefits. This, combined with the fact that the working population is declining while the number of state dependants is increasing, makes it inevitable that the DHSS will grow ever more vigilant in the application of such anti-avoidance measures as are at its disposal so as to ensure that every possible contribution finds its way into the National Insurance Fund.

ANTI-AVOIDANCE MEASURES

8.03   The R.3(2) direction

This direction has already been described in some detail at **5.04** ante, for it specifically relates to the possible manipulation of the earnings period rules considered there. Such rules can operate to both a primary and secondary contributor's advantage as follows. Class 1 contributions are normally assessed on such total earnings paid in an earnings period as do not exceed an upper earnings limit relative to the length of that period. The shorter the earnings period and the greater the amount of earnings allocated to it, therefore, the greater will be the amount of earnings placed above the upper earnings limit and beyond the reach of contribution liability. Normally, however, earnings are paid at only one regular pay interval and, since the earnings period is equivalent to that pay interval, it is not possible to allocate more than a normal part of earnings to each earnings period. Where different parts of earnings are paid at different regular pay intervals, however, it is the rule that the earnings period to which all earnings paid are to be related is to be the shortest regular pay interval. By so arranging matters, therefore, that only minimal earnings are paid at the shortest pay interval while the balance of earnings is paid at the longest pay interval, it is possible to obtain exactly the desired effect.

EXAMPLE 8(A)

On 1 April 1982, Arnold is appointed general manager of Bee Ltd at a salary of £10,800 pa, payable monthly. As his wife's earnings are sufficient to cover their normal living expenses, however, he asks for his contract of service to provide for a monthly salary of only £128 with an annual bonus of £9,264. The earnings period rules then operate to produce a contribution saving to himself of £738.38 and a saving of £1,156.05 for the company, calculated as follows:

		£	£
Salary: £900 per month			
Primary Class 1:	£900 × 8.75% × 12	945.00	
Secondary Class 1:	£900 × 13.7% × 12		1,479.60
Salary: £128 per month. Bonus: £9264 per annum			
Primary Class 1:	£128 × 8.75% × 11	123.20	
	£9,392 (restricted to UEL		
	£953.33) × 8.75% × 1	83.42	
		206.62	

Secondary Class 1:	$£128 \times 13.7\% \times 11$	192.94
	$£9,392$ (restricted to UEL	
	$£953.33) \times 13.7\% \times 1$	130.61
		323.55
Class 1 savings:	738.38	1,156.05

Bee Ltd would, of course, lose any corporation tax relief which might have been available to it on the $£1,156.05$ saved.

It is worth emphasising that there is nothing unlawful about the arrangement illustrated above and that (in the absence of a direction by the Secretary of State to the contrary) any other method of calculating the contribution liability (ie the use of an annual earnings period for all earnings) would, in fact, be incorrect, even though it might result in extra contributions being paid into the National Insurance Fund! When the Secretary of State becomes aware of such an arrangement, however, he is empowered (and may be expected) to take steps to prevent the manoeuvre being repeated in future years and such action may take the form of a notification (commonly called a direction) to both the primary and secondary contributor that the length of the longer pay interval is in future to be the length of the earnings period (SI 1979, No. 591, reg. 3(2)). Such a notification precludes any saving in contributions in the kind of situation envisaged in Example 8(A) and is popular with the DHSS; over 15,000 such directions being made in the five years to March 1980!

The circumstances in which a reg. 3(2) direction may be made are, however, somewhat limited and, provided it is not carried to excess, the principle applied in Example 8(A) may be employed in such a way as to render reg. 3(2) inoperative. The regulation makes it plain that the Secretary of State must be satisfied that

'. . . the greatest part of the earnings . . . is normally paid at intervals of greater length than the shortest . . .' (SI 1979, No. 591, reg. 3(2)).

If in Example 8(A), therefore, Arnold's annual bonus were to be limited to $£5,400$ or less, the Secretary of State would be powerless to modify the earnings period rules by a reg. 3(2) direction and worthwhile savings would still be achieved.

EXAMPLE 8(B)

The facts are as in Example 8(A) but the contract of service is to provide for a monthly salary of $£450$ and an annual bonus of $£5,400$. Savings by Arnold and by Bee Ltd would then be $£428.51$ and $£670.84$ respectively and no reg. 3(2) direction could legitimately be made.

		£	£
Salary: £900 per month			
Primary Class 1:	£900 × 8.75% × 12	945.00	
Secondary Class 1:	£900 × 13.7% × 12		1,479.60
Salary: £450 per month. Bonus: £5,400 per annum			
Primary Class 1:	£450 × 8.75% × 11	433.07	
	£5,850 (restricted to UEL		
	£953.33) × 8.75% × 1	83.42	
		516.49	
Secondary Class 1:	£450 × 13.7% × 11		678.15
	£5,850 (restricted to UEL		
	£953.33) × 13.7% × 1		130.61
			808.76
Class 1 savings:		428.51	670.84

Furthermore, as the regulation refers not to the greater but to the 'greatest' part of earnings (see **5.04** ante), a third element with an intermediate pay interval (eg quarterly commission) could, just as effectively and almost as advantageously, be introduced into the remuneration structure to break down the 'greatest part of the earnings' into two separate parts, neither of which, viewed in isolation, would be greater than salary.

EXAMPLE 8(C)
The facts are as stated in Example 8(A) except that the contract of service is to provide for a monthly salary of £300, a quarterly incentive increment of £900 and an annual bonus of £3,600. Contribution savings would then be £401.32 and £628.36 by Arnold and Bee Ltd respectively and no one part of earnings would exceed another.

		£	£
Salary: £900 per month			
Primary Class 1:	£900 × 8.75% × 12	945.00	
Secondary Class 1:	£900 × 13.7% × 12		1,479.60

Salary: £300 per month. Incentive increment: £900 per quarter. Bonus £3,600 per annum

		£	£
Primary Class 1:	£300 × 8.75% × 8	210.00	
	£1,200 (restricted to UEL £953.33) × 8.75% × 3	250.26	
	£4,800 (restricted to UEL £953.33) × 8.75% × 1	83.42	
		543.68	
Secondary Class 1:	£300 × 13.7% × 8		328.80
	£1,200 (restricted to UEL £953.33) × 13.7% × 3		391.83
	£4,800 (restricted to UEL £953.33) × 13.7% × 1		130.61
			851.24
Class 1 savings:		401.32	628.36

Finally, it should be observed that, even if neither alternative were to be adopted and the bonus were to be left unrestricted at a level which exceeded salary, no reg. 3(2) direction could, it would seem, be justified until the arrangement had been repeated—in the following year at least—as not until then could the greatest part of earnings be said to be 'normally' paid at intervals of greater length than the shortest interval in the pay structure.

8.04 The R.21 direction

As has been pointed out, a reg. 3(2) direction is extremely limited in its application and, with forethought, may easily be rendered inoperative. Furthermore it cannot be applied retrospectively. This being so, the DHSS increasingly favour the use of reg. 21 or reg. 22 directions which are much wider in their scope and of less specific application.

By regulations made under SSA 1975, Sch. 1, para. 4(c) it is provided that

'with a view to securing that liability for the payment of earnings-related contributions is not avoided or reduced by a secondary contributor following in the payment of earnings any practice which is abnormal for the employment in respect of which the earnings are paid . . ., the Secretary of State may, if he thinks fit, determine any question relating to a person's earnings-related contributions where any such practice has been or is being followed, as if the secondary contributor concerned had not followed any abnormal pay practice, but had followed a practice or practices normal for the employment in question' (SI 1979, No. 591, reg. 21(2)).

A careful reading of this regulation will reveal that some 'question' for the Secretary of State's determination must arise in relation to contributions before an abnormal pay practice may be identified and reversed. Accordingly, it is provided that, where the Secretary of State has reason to believe that any abnormal pay practice has been or is being followed, he

> '. . . may determine any such question . . . as if application had been duly made to him for the determination thereof' (SI 1979, No. 591, reg. 21(3)).

A question 'relating to a person's contributions' is a question which must (in exactly the same manner as a categorisation question—see **2.14** ante) be determined under the provisions of SSA 1975, s. 93(1)(b). This entails the notification of all interested parties, the obtaining of information and particulars, the holding of an inquiry if appropriate, and the possibility of an appeal to the High Court if a question of law arises. It is doubtlessly in order to avoid such complications that, where possible, the Secretary of State takes anti-avoidance action under SI 1979, No. 591, reg. 3(2) or reg. 22 (which afford a contributor no right of appeal) rather than under reg. 21 (which does).

Where reg. 21 is invoked, however, it should be noted that it may be of limited retrospective effect. It is negatively provided that the regulation is not to apply in so far as the decision made by the Secretary of State

> '. . . relates to contributions based on payments made more than one year before the beginning of the year in which that decision is given' (SI 1979, No. 591, reg. 21(1)).

'Year' does, of course, mean tax year (SI 1979, No. 591, reg. 1(2)).

One unresolved difficulty which arises out of this regulation and which is central to its application is the problem of interpretation which attaches to the phrase 'normal for the employment in question'. Is 'employment' being used as a synonym for a particular category of trade or activity (eg engineering), or for the particular enterprise with which the secondary contributor in question may be identified (eg Cog Engineering Co Ltd)? If the former interpretation is correct, it would be no defence to argue, for instance, that 'we have always paid our weavers their overtime pay in one lump sum at Christmas' if that is not normal throughout the textile industry. If the latter interpretation is correct, however, it would be a perfectly adequate defence. As employment is defined as including any trade, business, profession, office or vocation (SSA 1975, Sch. 20), however, it is thought that the latter interpretation would be dismissed and that the regulation is concerned with what is normal in any particular sector of trade or industry.

Finally, it should be noted that any additional primary Class 1 contributions which become payable as a result of the application of reg. 21 are not recoverable from the earner concerned (DHSS Leaflet NP15, para. 154). This is because the underdeduction has not occurred by reason of an error made in good faith (SI 1979, No. 591, Sch. 1, reg. 13(2A)(b)).

8.05   The R.22 direction

By virtue of regulations made under SSA 1975, Sch. 1, para. 4(d) it is provided that

> '. . . the Secretary of State may, where he is satisfied as to the existence of any practice in respect of the payment of earnings whereby the incidence of earnings-related contributions is avoided or reduced by means of irregular or unequal payments, give directions for securing that such contributions are payable as if that practice were not followed' (SI 1979, No. 591, reg. 22).

A reg. 22 direction is, accordingly, of very wide application indeed, and (it should be noted) effectively renders the Secretary of State's powers under reg. 3(2) superfluous. Furthermore, while a judicious arrangement of earnings between salary and bonus may defeat a reg. 3(2) direction, it will not (if the Secretary of State chooses to be inflexible in the exercise of his powers under this regulation) defeat a reg. 22 direction. In the past, however, it has been DHSS practice not to make such a direction in cases where savings achieved in terms of contributions have not exceeded thirty-three per cent of the possible contribution liability, though, by that empirical and unconfirmable criterion, the arrangements illustrated in Examples 8(B) and 8(C) would both be vulnerable. Indicative of the little use to which this direction has, hitherto, been put is the fact that only just over two thousand reg. 22 directions were made in the five years to March 1980. It does seem, however, that its popularity has begun to increase among the DHSS inspectorate—presumably as a result of the increased public awareness of the ways in which a reg. 3(2) direction can be rendered inoperative—though DHSS activity in the whole anti-avoidance area is limited by its staff levels. The Department has recently confirmed that

> '. . . we shall be continuing with our general policy of applying directions in appropriate cases to secure individual liabilities which are commensurate with earnings. The operation of such a policy is, however, dependent on resources' (Letter. 7 September 1981).

It is important to be aware that the DHSS regard a reg. 22 direction as potentially applicable whenever the incidence of earnings-related contributions is reduced or avoided because of irregular or unequal payments, even if the reduction or avoidance of contributions is unintentional. It would, in any case, be extremely difficult to prove that contribution reduction was not a factor in the decision-making process that led to the practice in question being adopted.

The legislators' choice of the words 'were not followed' (rather than the possible 'had not been followed') in reg. 22 is recognised by the DHSS as robbing the regulation of any retrospective force it may otherwise have possessed (see DHSS Leaflet NI35, April 1981).

EMPLOYERS

8.06   Avoidance of secondary contributions

As has been pointed out, secondary Class 1 contributions, though providing some fifty per cent of national insurance fund income, do not and cannot benefit a secondary contributor in any way. Apart from the anti-avoidance regulations described, therefore, there is nothing to inhibit a secondary contributor should he wish to reduce or avoid a liability for secondary contributions. Some of the ways in which he may do this are described in the following paragraphs.

8.07   The engagement of self-employed labour

Secondary contributions are, of course, only payable where earnings are paid to employed earners in an employed earner's employment. As has been discussed in great detail in Chapter 2, such a situation will arise wherever there is, in reality, a master and servant relationship established by a mutual agreement or understanding that, in return for some specific remuneration in money or in kind or some other benefit or privilege, one party shall personally render services subject to the right of the other party to control or direct him in the work he does and the method and performance of his duties. A superficially similar but essentially different relationship is that of employer and independent contractor where, although one party is again engaged to render services for the other in return for specific remuneration, both parties are independent, there is no (or only very limited) right of control and the services rendered, although done for the employer's business, are accessory to it rather than integrated into it. A party rendering services under this latter kind of arrangement is a self-employed earner and remuneration paid to him does not constitute earnings for Class 1 purposes. From a contribution point of view, therefore, an employer will benefit from the engagement of persons under a contract for services rather than under a contract of service, though mere form will not override the substance of their relationship. It is worth noting that where the Secretary of State decides that a person has been wrongly categorised, the change of category is non-retrospective.

8.08   The engagement of part-time labour

It has been explained at **5.15** ante that the lower earnings limit for Class 1 purposes is not an exception limit but is the level at which a liability for both primary and secondary Class 1 contributions arises on all earnings paid up to the upper earnings limit. As the 1982–83 weekly lower earnings limit is £29.50 it can be seen that no contributions will be payable on earnings of £29.49 but that, if earnings are increased by one penny, both primary and secondary contributions will be payable on £29.50. The secondary contribution alone would then be £4.04! If it is practicable to do so, therefore, an employer may legitimately avoid a contribution liability by employing part-time staff at a level of remuneration just below the lower earnings limit.

EXAMPLE 8(D)

On 6 April 1982, Cedric opens a fish restaurant. He requires six waitresses to each of whom he would expect to pay £58 per week but is, instead, persuaded to employ twelve waitresses each of whom will work only three days per week for a weekly wage of £29. His secondary Class 1 contribution savings for 1982–83 will be £2,480.40 (ie £58 × 13.7% × 52 × 6) as £29 is below the lower earnings limit and will not attract any contributions whatsoever.

8.09   Beneficial remuneration

A study of Chapter 4 will reveal that not all remuneration is regarded as earnings for Class 1 purposes: in particular any paid in the form of benefits in kind. It will obviously be to any employer's advantage, therefore, to remunerate his employees in kind rather than cash wherever this can be arranged.

EXAMPLE 8(E)

Donald has a one-man business and employs Elsie as his cashier at a salary of £54 per week. Elsie is about to rent a flat at £25 per week. If Donald were to rent the flat instead of Elsie but were to allow her to occupy it rent-free he could reduce her salary to £29 per week and save £384.80 for 1982–83 in secondary contributions (ie £54 × 13.7% × 52). Furthermore, Elsie would save £245.44 in that year in primary contributions, though she would, of course, lose benefit rights from 1 January 1984.

8.10   Superannuation contributions

Further study of Chapter 4 will reveal that contributions made by an employee to a company pension scheme are not deductible in arriving at earnings for Class 1 contribution purposes, though they are so deductible for tax purposes. Considerable savings are possible, therefore, if a company scheme is changed from a contributory to a non-contributory scheme and salaries are reduced by the amounts formerly contributed by the employees.

EXAMPLE 8(F)

Eff Ltd employs thirty salaried staff all of whom are members of the company's contributory pension scheme. In 1982–83 their total remuneration before superannuation deductions will amount to £250,000 and their contributions to the pension scheme will be £12,500. None of them has gross earnings in excess of the upper earnings limit. If Eff Ltd were to make the pension scheme non-contributory and the employees were to agree to a corresponding reduction of their salaries by, in total, £12,500, Eff Ltd would save £1,150 (ie £12,500 × 9.2%) in 1982–83 and the employees would save, in total, £781.25 (ie £12,500 × 6.25%).

8.11   Interest

Where, before 27 March 1980, a director beneficially owned or was able to control, directly or indirectly, more than five per cent of the ordinary share capital of a company, interest paid to him on loans or advances made by him to the company was treated as a distribution for corporation tax purposes insofar as it exceeded seventeen per cent of the lower of the average total of the loans and the nominal amount of the company's issued share capital. In the case of companies with small amounts of issued share capital, therefore, it became the practice not to pay interest on directors' loans and this made good sense. It would seem, however, that this abstinence is still continuing, despite the fact that the provisions described were abolished in relation to interest paid in accounting periods ending after 26 March 1980 and that the payment of such interest provides a useful method of remunerating a director without either primary or secondary Class 1 contributions being attracted.

8.12   Pay intervals

It has already been explained at **8.03** ante that considerable savings may be achieved by breaking-down remuneration into two or more component parts (eg salary and bonus), each of which attaches to a pay interval of a different length (eg salary monthly and bonus annually). The shortest interval then becomes the earnings period which governs all earnings paid within it (including, for example, the annual bonus) and the higher earnings limit appropriate to the length of the earnings period operates so as to exclude from contribution liability all earnings in that period which exceed it. Such arrangements are vulnerable by reason of the various directions which the DHSS may make to counteract them, but provided the earnings attaching to the shortest pay interval involved are greater than any other component part of total remuneration and provided that the overall contribution saving does not exceed the empirical 33% of the possible liability on total remuneration, it is extremely unlikely that any arrangement will be challenged. This being so, it will obviously benefit an employer to break-down remuneration in the manner described whenever an opportunity to do so presents itself. Appendix 9 indicates the appropriate division between the two parts of earnings. Although such arrangements have become popular in connection with directors' remuneration, the principle may also be extended to commission and overtime payments earned by other employees.

EXAMPLE 8(G)

George employs four salesmen each of whom will earn a basic salary (paid monthly) of £7,800 in the year ended 5 April 1983. In addition, each salesman is paid commission which, on the basis of past performance, is likely to amount to £300 per month in each case. George's secondary Class 1 liability is, therefore, likely to be £6,247.20 (ie $((£7,800/12) + £300) \times 13.7\% \times 12 \times 4)$ for 1982–83, but this could be reduced to £4,606.88 (ie $4 \times £1,151.72$) with a saving of £1,640.32 if he were to pay commission only twice a year, viz:

	£
$(£7,800/12) \times 13.7\% \times 10$	890.50
$((£7,800/12 + (£300 \times 6))$ limited to UEL	
$£953.33 \times 13.7\% \times 2$	261.22
	1,151.72

In the light of what has been said at **8.04** ante, care must be taken that no such arrangement constitutes an abnormal pay practice.

8.13   Groups of companies

In situations where two or more companies operate as a group or in association with each other, it is not uncommon to find directors or employees employed and remunerated by more than one company in the group or association. Where the association between the relevant companies is such as to meet DHSS criteria (see **5.13** ante) and earnings from at least one of those companies is less than the lower earnings limit, no problem with secondary contributions arises as aggregation of earnings must take place. Where those criteria are not met, however, or where the earnings in each employment equal or exceed the lower earnings limit, no aggregation may take place and excessive and irrecoverable secondary contributions will be paid by the group as a whole if the total remuneration exceeds the annual upper earnings limit.

EXAMPLE 8(H)

Hubert is employed by I Ltd, J Ltd and K Ltd at a salary of £4,000, £5,000 and £6,000 respectively. I Ltd and J Ltd are in the ownership and control of K Ltd. In 1982–83 secondary Class 1 contributions of £2,055 (ie £15,000 × 13.7%) will be paid by the group as a whole whereas, if Hubert were to be paid by a single secondary contributor, the maximum liability would be only £1,567.27 (ie upper earnings limit £11,439.96 × 13.7%). Furthermore, that excess of £487.73 will, unless the re-arrangement is made, be irrecoverable.

If no re-arrangement is made, Hubert himself will, of course, also suffer payment of a greater contribution than he would suffer under a single secondary contributor but, in his case (as in the case of all primary contributors) the excess will ultimately be refunded.

The remedy in such a situation is to ensure that each director or employee is remunerated from only one of the companies for which he works and that a service charge of an appropriate amount is made to each of the other companies concerned so as to recover the amount which those companies would otherwise have paid in remuneration. Where both contracted-out and non-contracted-out employments are involved, the greatest saving in contributions will be achieved by remunerating the director or employee from the company in which his employment would be contracted-out.

Where companies are connected in some way but without meeting the 'association' criteria it may be possible to avoid contributions entirely by fragmenting an employee's remuneration into elements below the lower earnings limit and paying each of such elements through a different company. As such payments would be neither irregular nor unequal, a reg. 22 direction would not be supportable, though, unless the employee were in fact to divide his time equally between the various companies, the practice might be open to challenge on the grounds that it would represent an abnormal pay practice. In the event of the practice succeeding, the employee concerned would, of course, suffer a loss of benefit entitlement.

8.14   Non-executive directors

It is often the case that a company's professional advisors are appointed to the board of directors and are paid directors' fees. Where such fees exceed the lower earnings limit, both primary and secondary Class 1 liabilities will be attracted and, while the primary liability may be relieved in computing the contribution liability of the non-executive director concerned (see **5.34** ante), the secondary contributions are irrecoverable. It is sound practice, therefore, for a company to arrange with any non-executive director who is also in business as a self-employed earner that the directorship will carry no fees but that he will, instead, invoice the company annually for professional services equal in amount to the director's fees which would otherwise have been payable to him.

COMPANY DIRECTORS

8.15   The pre-1 September 1980 view

From 6 April 1975, the date on which the current social security scheme came into operation, all company directors have been regarded as employed earners for social security contribution purposes. As such they have been liable to pay primary Class 1 contributions on their remuneration and the paying company has been liable for secondary Class 1 contributions on that same remuneration. Although it has long been recognised that the status of a company director is essentially that of an office holder (see **2.08** ante), until 1 September 1980, no distinction had ever been drawn between those directors who were merely office holders and those who were, additionally, employed by their companies under contracts of service. The practical effect of this indiscriminatory approach was that a Class 1 liability arose whenever a payment on account of remuneration was made to any director, and the normal rules relating to earnings periods, earnings limits and contributions calculation were applied in exactly the same manner as they would have been applied to any other employed earner. It soon became clear, however, that the Class 1 rules which had been framed with the contractual and relatively inflexible earnings arrangements of the normal employed earner in mind, were being used to considerable advantage by company directors whose earnings arrangements were (particularly in small family companies) usually non-contractual and almost caoutchoucian in their flexibility. The procedures referred to have been fully described at **8.03** and **8.05** ante as have the directions whereby the Secretary of State sought to counteract them, but such measures were increasingly found to be of relatively small impact and effect as the contribution-avoiding practices at which they were aimed had generally been carefully tailored to render them impracticable or inappropriate. Possibly for these reasons, the Secretary of State sought an alternative weapon with which to combat the growing avoidance of contributions by company directors and, on 1 September 1980, he found it.

8.16 The current view

Since its introduction, the new weapon has been found, on close inspection, not to be new at all. It is, in fact, merely a strict application of an incontestable matter of general law already mentioned in **8.15** ante: namely, that company directors are office holders and, as such, are remunerated by way of fees voted by their companies in general meeting. Only if there is a contract of service between a director and his company will his remuneration include, or consist of, a salary—and then only to the extent to which his contract provides for it as of right. Where a company director is under a contract of service, the normal rules applicable to other employed earners continue to apply:

> 'Liability for contributions on regular payments of salary flowing from a contract of service between a director and his company arises at the time the payments are made. . . . The amount of the contribution depends upon the length of the earnings period . . . If there is more than one set of regular payments . . . the earnings period is usually the shorter or shortest of the regular intervals . . . Any additional payment, eg bonus, should be treated as part of the total pay in the earnings period in which it is paid' (DHSS Leaflet NI35, April 1981).

8.17 Fee-paid directors

The question of service contracts is discussed at **8.24** post, but sufficient has been said here to demonstrate that the procedures and contribution-planning opportunities for directors who are under such contracts remain quite unchanged. The directors with whom the 'new' rules are concerned are those who are merely office holders and are not under contract with their companies.

The DHSS challenge in relation to such directors concerns the intrinsic nature of periodic payments made to them. Though such payments may be described as salary, the DHSS view is that, in cases where a director's fees are voted for past periods, such payments are not earnings but merely periodic drawings in anticipation of those unvoted fees. In such circumstances

> '. . . liability arises only when the directors' fees are voted unconditionally by the company in general meeting'

and, if such voting takes place (as it normally will) on an annual basis,

> 'the interval of payment . . . will be an annual one and contributions should be assessed using an annual earnings period on all fees up to the annual upper earnings limit' (DHSS leaflet NI35, April 1981).

8.18   The *Garforth* case

In announcing its revised procedure on 1 September 1980, the DHSS intimated that its views on these matters had judicial support and it has been confirmed in subsequent correspondence that this support is derived from *Garforth (Inspector of Taxes) v Newsmith Stainless Ltd* ([1979] 1 WLR 409, [1979] STC 129). Referring to the principle stated above, the Department admits that

> 'This principle has not been tested by the Courts in relation to contributions but . . . was upheld in relation to the PAYE provisions in the case of *Garforth v Newsmith Stainless Ltd*. The Department is confident, therefore, that its views in this matter are correct' (Letter. 7 September 1981).

In the *Garforth* case it was held that the placement of money unreservedly at the disposal of directors is equivalent to payment. It follows, therefore, that the withdrawal of monies from a company before such placement has taken place is not payment and that the failure to withdraw monies after such placement does not alter the fact that payment has taken place.

8.19   Problems of the current view

Although the technical argument advanced by the Department and summarised above is doubtless sound, it is not without potentially disastrous repercussions in other areas. If payment of remuneration does not take place until fees are voted, drawings in advance of such fees are, in fact, loans which are being made by companies in direct contravention of the Companies Act 1980. As such they may be voided by the company and the director concerned (who has committed a criminal act!) may be made to account for any gains he has achieved by use of the monies drawn. Secondly, although the practice now adopted by the DHSS is inconsistent with that applied by the Inland Revenue (which, for PAYE purposes treats anticipatory drawings as earnings at the point when each drawing is made—see **4.03** ante) such drawings, if they are truly loans, give rise to a taxable benefit under Finance Act 1976, s. 66 once the average amount outstanding for the year is over £1,334 (the amount at which notional interest at 15% would exceed £200)!

8.20 Transitional problems

The new procedure should, where appropriate, have been fully implemented from 6 April 1981 with 1980–81 being treated as a transitional year. Where implementation has not yet taken place and contributions have been avoided by the breaking-down of total remuneration into salary and bonus in the manner formerly permissible, the unpaid contributions will be recoverable in the normal manner (see **6.07** ante) and penalties may be imposed. Where the transition has taken place and has resulted (as it may) in no contributions being paid for one whole tax year, Class 3 contributions may be paid to preserve pension rights. As Class 3 contributions cannot, however, fulfil the contribution conditions necessary for eligibility to sickness and unemployment benefit, the DHSS has undertaken to view each case on its individual merits where claims to short-term benefits are made but would fail because of the transition.

EXAMPLE 8(I)

Isaac is a director of Jay Ltd but is not under a contract of service. During 1980–81 he drew £700 per month as salary and paid contributions as appropriate. In October 1980 these drawings were recognised as anticipatory director's fees and no contributions were, thereafter, paid on them. On 31 March 1981 fees of £8,000 were voted to Isaac for the year ended 31 October 1980. On 30 April 1982 fees of £10,000 in respect of the year ended 31 October 1981 were similarly voted and on 28 February 1983 fees of £12,000 are to be voted in respect of the year ended 31 October 1982. Isaac's Class 1 contribution position will be as follows:

1980–81   Contributions would be paid on £8,000 using an earnings period of one year and contributions already paid on £4,200 (ie 6 × £700) would be deducted in arriving at the contributions paid in March 1981.

1981–82   As no fees were voted in this tax year, no contributions were payable, though Isaac might have paid Class 3 contributions to preserve pension rights had he wished to do so.

1982–83   It would appear that contributions should be paid on £22,000 limited to the annual upper earnings limit of £11,439.96 thus allowing fees of £10,560.04 to escape contribution liability. Note the comments at **8.21** post, however.

As no contributions have been paid in 1981–82 no short-term benefits will be available in the year commencing 2 January 1983 but since this deficiency arose by reason of the change in basis, the matter will be given special consideration by the DHSS if the need to claim any such benefits were to arise.

8.21   Avoidance by fee-date maneouvres

On the basis of present DHSS instructions, it would seem that, by the simple expedient of advancing or retarding the date of the general meeting at which directors' fees are voted, complete avoidance of contributions in alternate years is possible in the case of fee-paid directors. Such a practice could, however, be reversed by a reg. 22 direction as contributions would be being avoided by irregular payment of earnings. Furthermore, benefit entitlement would be completely lost for the related benefit years and pension rights could also be affected.

8.22   Invalidity of former directions

It should be noted that, because of the former view held by the DHSS, reg. 3(2) or reg. 22 directions may have been made concerning earnings periods in cases which are now seen to be 'office-holder only' cases. The DHSS has stated its attitude to such situations to be as follows:

> 'Turning to the question of directions made under Regulation 3(2) and 22 (formerly 19) of the Contribution Regulations, it is our view that, given our fresh understanding in this matter, these must be regarded as invalid in relation to directors who were formerly treated as having two or more intervals of payment but under the revised procedures only one. We are reviewing such cases and expect to be able to clarify the position in individual cases as appropriate. I should perhaps emphasise, however, that as these directions generally related to the application of an annual earnings period, which will normally be seen to be appropriate to these fee-paid directors, it is likely that no significant change in liability will be perceived in the majority of cases' (Letter. 7 September 1981).

8.23   Fees voted in advance

In the case of some fee-paid directors, fees are, in fact, voted in advance by the company in general meeting. In such cases, the earnings period will be determined by the terms of the resolution:

> 'Where a director's fees are decided by resolution in advance of payment, eg director "X" shall receive £500 on the 4th day of each month for the following 12 months, contribution liability will arise when the £500 is paid each month. It is expected that evidence of the existence of such a resolution would appear in the company records' (DHSS Leaflet NI35, April 1981).

In such instances, there would seem to be nothing to prevent a resolution also being made at the same time that director 'X' shall receive a bonus of (say) £4,000 in respect of the company's financial year last ended. The advantageous two-part type of pay arrangement referred to earlier might then be perpetuated, subject, of course, to such restraints as seem prudent in the light of the direction regulations.

8.24   Service contracts

As has been stated, the contribution position of any director who, although an office-holder, is also employed by his company under a contract of service is unaffected by the revised procedures. His contribution liability will continue to be calculated in the same manner as that of any other employed earner employed under a contract of service, and the same planning opportunities are open to him. Problems may now arise, however, in convincing the DHSS that such a director is under a contract of service. Prima facie, he is not and, accordingly, difficulties may arise unless

> '. . . the contract is written or a memorandum of an oral contract has been entered in the written records of the company' (DHSS letter. 7 September 1981).

It is, of course, true that, statutorily, there is no obligation to reduce an oral contract to writing or to record it in any way: its existence may be ascertained by reference to the behaviour of the parties involved. In the case of company directors, however, their behaviour vis à vis their companies and third parties will not be significantly different whether they are under a contract of service or not. The distinction is far more subtle than, for instance, that between a person under a contract of service and a person under a contract for services. It is not unreasonable, therefore, that the DHSS, in seeking to distinguish between mere office-holders and those who are contractually tied to their companies, should require concrete evidence of a contract where it is claimed that one exists. Indeed, where the contract itself has not been reduced to writing, such evidence ought, in any case, to be available in the form of the written statement of particulars of terms which the Contracts of Employment Act (CEA) 1972, s. 4 (as re-enacted in the Employment Protection (Consolidation) Act (EP(C)A) 1978, s. 11) requires an employer to give to each of his employees within the first thirteen weeks of the employee's period of employment. In addition to identifying the parties to the contract and specifying the date on which the employment began, the statement must disclose, inter alia, the scale or rate of remuneration (or the method whereby it is calculated) and the intervals at which remuneration is paid (Employment Protection Act 1975, Sch. 16, Pt. II, para. 4 and EP(C)A 1978, s. 1(2) and (3)). Furthermore, any changes in those contractual terms must be communicated to the employee in writing not more than one month after the change (CEA 1972, s. 5(1) and EP(C)A 1978, s. 4(1)). Merely by complying with these current requirements of employment protection law, therefore, sufficient documentary evidence to adequately meet all DHSS requirements would automatically be available in respect of any director who is truly in a contractual relationship with his company. Such evidence would also already be available in a great many instances if the current requirements of company law were being compiled with. By the Companies Act 1967, s. 26, every company is required to keep at an appropriate place (usually its registered office or principal place of business) copies of contracts of service (in the case of directors whose contracts are in writing) or written memoranda setting out the terms of contracts (in the case of directors whose contracts are not in writing) as well as copies or memoranda of variations. As these requirements apply wherever there are contracts which have a term of which the unexpired portion is twelve months or more or which can, during the ensuing twelve months, be terminated without payment of compensation by the company, it is again thought not to be unreasonable of the DHSS to expect to find copies of contracts or memoranda in most instances where it is claimed that a contract of service exists.

In the light of the foregoing, it is obviously advisable that any failure to comply with the requirements of employment protection law and company law in relation to contracts of service be rectified at the earliest opportunity.

In many small, family company situations, non-compliance is often attributable to the feeling that there is something ludicrous about a person in one capacity entering an actual agreement with himself in some other capacity. It is, however, an established matter of law that, even in the most extreme of such situations, the company continues to be an entity entirely separate from and independent of its individual shareholders. (See, for example, the leading case of *Salomon v Salomon & Co Ltd* [1897] AC 22.) Thus, in *Lee v Lee's Air-Farming Ltd* ([1961] AC 12, [1960] 3 All ER 420, PC), it was held that Lee, who, until killed in a flying accident, held 2,999 of the 3,000 issued shares of Lee's Air-Farming Ltd, had been working as a servant of the company under a contract of service negotiated by himself in the capacity of a pilot with himself as the governing director and principal shareholder of the company. Considering whether such an arrangement was possible, Lord Morris of Both-y-Gest declared:

> 'There was no . . . impossibility . . . a man acting in one capacity can give orders to himself in another capacity . . . The right to control existed even though it would be for the deceased, in his capacity of agent for the . . . company, to decide what orders to give' (*Lee v Lee's Air-Farming Ltd* [1961] AC 12, [1960] 3 All ER 420, PC).

OTHER EMPLOYEES

8.25   Status

Viewed solely in terms of contribution liability, there are distinct advantages in being a self-employed earner rather than an employed earner. The extent of contribution saving for a Class 1 standard rate contributor at any particular level of earnings in 1982–83 may be readily ascertained by reference to the following table:

Earnings between:		Saving:
£	£	
0.00 and	1,533.95	Nil
1,533.96 and	1,599.99	8.75% × Earnings
1,600.00 and	3,449.99	(8.75% × Earnings)—£198.75

3,450.00 and 11,000.00	$(8.75\% \times \text{Earnings})-$
	$(£198.75 + 6\%$
	$\times (\text{Earnings}-£3,450))$
11,001.01 and 11,439.96	$(8.75\% \times \text{Earnings})-£651.75$
11,439.97 upwards	$£349.25$

Even assuming that the factors in a particular employment situation are such as to enable a change of status from employed earner to self-employed earner to be justified (see Chapter 2), careful consideration ought to be given to the fact that entitlement to unemployment benefit will be lost as will the rights which an employee enjoys under current employment protection legislation.

8.26 Remuneration

The advantages of being remunerated, to some extent, in kind rather than in cash should be borne in mind whenever remuneration is under negotiation (see **8.09** ante), as should the contribution advantage which accrues when a contributory pension scheme becomes non-contributory (see **8.10** ante).

Anyone who is remunerated at a level below the lower earnings limit should (unless he wishes to pay contributions in order to build up a contribution record for benefit entitlement) refuse any increase which would bring him into the marginal band described at **5.15** ante, and should request some benefit in kind as an alternative.

Persons engaging in part-time employment should (with the same proviso) take, if at all possible, two or more unassociated jobs carrying remuneration at a level below the lower earnings limit rather than one job carrying remuneration at a level above it. By this means contribution liability may be avoided entirely.

Where an employment carries an entitlement to commission, overtime pay or any kind of periodic increment or bonus, consideration ought to be given to the possibility of requesting that this be paid at longer intervals than those at which basic earnings are paid. By this means contributions may, in many instances, be reduced (see **5.04** and **8.12** ante).

In circumstances where an earner's wife assists him in the performance of his duties (eg by acting as his secretary where his work overlaps into evenings and weekends or by acting as his chauffeuse where he is unable to drive), the possibility of that person's employer reducing the earner's remuneration by an amount slightly less than the current lower earnings limit and employing the earner's wife at a wage of that amount is worthy of consideration.

THE SELF-EMPLOYED

8.23 Employment of spouse

It is generally accepted by both the Inland Revenue and the DHSS that a self-employed person's spouse has an almost inevitable involvement in his business (eg answering the telephone, book-keeping, making appointments). This being so, remuneration at a level just below the lower earnings limit is usually justifiable (but see *Copeman v William Flood & Sons Ltd* [1941] 1 KB 202; 24 TC 53) and should be paid. In 1981–82, however, the wife's earned income relief for taxation purposes was less than the lower earnings limit for Class 1 contribution purposes and, accordingly, that relief was the key factor in setting the spouse's remuneration level. The rate of wife's earned income relief for 1982–83 will be fixed by the Finance Act 1982 and is, therefore, presently unknown, but if the figure exceeds £1,534, the lower earnings limit will again become the key factor.

8.28   Partnership with spouse

Where a sole trader's spouse holds a reduced rate certificate (see **3.20** ante) and profits exceed the Class 4 lower annual limit but are less than the Class 4 upper annual limit plus the lower annual limit, it will be of advantage from a contribution point of view for the trader to take his wife into partnership. This is because the Class 4 liability of husband and wife are calculated separately. The extent to which savings could be effected in 1982–83 by this means (assuming that the trader's wife is not already remunerated from the business and is to become an equal partner with her husband) may be ascertained by reference to the following table:

Profits between:	Savings:
£ £	
0 and 3,450	Nil
3,451 and 6,900	6% × (Profits—£3,450)
6,901 and 11,000	6% × £3,450
11,001 and 14,449	6% × (£14,450—Profits)
14,450 upwards	Nil

It will be noted from this table that the maximum possible saving is equivalent to the Class 4 percentage rate applied to the Class 4 lower annual limit. As this amount is only marginally in excess of the annual Class 2 contribution liability, it is clear that no worthwhile savings can result where a trader's spouse does not hold a reduced rate certificate.

If a trader's wife is already employed in his business and pays Class 1 contributions, savings may still be effected by taking her into partnership, even though she does not hold a reduced rate certificate. In such a case, however, detailed calculations will be necessary in order to ascertain the extent to which contribution liability might be reduced.

It is, of course, essential that all relevant factors other than contribution savings are also considered before any decision to take a wife into partnership is made. Furthermore, if a wife is taken into partnership, steps must be taken to ensure that the authenticity of the partnership is verifiable. This will involve, inter alia, her participation in business activities, her inclusion by name as a partner on business notepaper, on business bank accounts and on the VAT certificate of registration.

8.29   Incorporation

Where a self-employed earner finds it necessary to withdraw the whole of his profits by way of remuneration, no savings in contributions would result if his business were to be transferred to a limited company. Indeed, the contribution liability would be greater, though an entitlement to unemployment benefit would accrue as a result of paying Class 1 contributions rather than Class 2 and Class 4 contributions. Social security contributions are, however, a relatively minor consideration when a decision on incorporation is being made.

Appendices 1–10

Appendix 1: Contributions and benefit entitlement

CLASS (See 1.16)		TYPE OF CONTRIBUTION (For rates see Appendix 7)	STATUS OF CONTRIBUTORS (See Chapter 2 and Appendix 3)	DATE AT WHICH LIABILITY ARISES (See Chapter 6)	NATURE OF CONTRIBUTION (See App.2)
1	Primary	Earnings-related	Employed earners	When earnings (see App.5) are paid or credited to the employed earner.	Mandatory
	Secondary	Earnings-related	Employers or payers of employed earners	When earnings (see App.5) are paid or credited to an employed earner.	Mandatory
2		Flat rate	Self-employed earners	Weekly by stamps, Giro or banker's order.	Mandatory
3		Flat rate	Employed earners, self-employed earners and non-employed persons	Weekly by stamps, Giro or banker's order.	Voluntary to make good any deficiencies in a contribution record.
4		Earnings-related	Self-employed earners	With tax under Sch D assessment (normally at 1 January and 1 July.	Mandatory

Social Security Benefits are of two kinds – contributory and non-contributory. The extent to which contributory benefits are secured depends on both the class of contributions paid and the record of contributions which has been established. The following table gives an indication of the relationship between the classes of contribution shown above, the amounts of contribution required and the benefits available.

BENEFIT	CLASS OF CONTRIB-UTION REQUIRED	FIRST CONDITION (See 1.17)	SECOND CONDITION (See 1.17)
Unemployment benefit	1	Any tax year after 6.4.75: Primary Class 1 contributions paid on earnings = to at least 25 weeks at LEL, or 25 Class 2 contributions	Tax year prior to year of claim: Primary Class 1 contributions paid or credited on earnings = to at least 50 weeks at LEL, or 50 Class 2 contributions
Sickness benefit Maternity allowance Invalidity allowance Invalidity pension	1 or 2		
Widow's allowance Death grant	1, 2 or 3	As above	None
Child's special allowance	1, 2 or 3	As above but for "25" read "50"	None
Widowed mother's allowance Widow's pension Category A and B retirement pensions	1, 2 or 3	As above but for "25" read "52"	As above but for "50" read "52" and for "tax year prior to year of claim" read "for approx. 9 out of each 10 years of working life (ie between 16 and 65(60) or earlier death)"

NB Where any of the contribution conditions are not fully met or contributions are paid late (see 6.24), benefits may be reduced or lost entirely.

Appendix 2: Liability to social security contributions

EARNINGS-RELATED STATUS (See Chapter 2 and App.3)		RESIDENCE OR PRESENCE (See Chapter 3 and Appendix 4)	AGE (See Chapter 3)	LEVEL OF EARNINGS (See Chapters 4 and 5 and App. 5)	MARITAL STATUS (See Chapter 3)	RELATIONSHIP TO STATE PENSION SCHEME (See 5.17)	LIABILITY (See Chapters 5 and 6 and App.7)
Earner	Employed earner	Neither ordinarily resident nor resident nor present in nor merely temporarily absent from GB	–	–	–	–	None
		Ordinarily resident or resident or present in or merely temporarily absent from Great Britain	Under 16 or over 65(60) whether retired or not	–	–	–	None
			Over 16 (even if still at school) or under 65(60)	Under LEL	–	–	None
				LEL or over	Married woman or widow with RR election in force	–	Primary Class 1 at RR to UEL
					Others	Contracted-out	Primary Class 1 at NR to LEL then at COR to UEL
						Not con-tracted-out	Primary Class 1 at SR to UEL
	Self-employed earner	Neither ordinarily resident, nor resid-ent for 26 or more of 52 preceding weeks	–	–	–	–	None
		Ordinarily resident or resident for 26 or more of 52 preceding weeks	Under 16 or over 65(60) whether retired or not	–	–	–	None
			Over 16 (even if still at school) or under 65(60)	Under exception limit	–	–	None (but exception required)
				Over exception limit but under LAL	Married woman or widow with RR election in force	–	None
					Others	–	Class 2 contributions
				Over LAL	Married woman or widow with RR election in force	–	Class 4 contributions on earnings between LAL and UAL
					Others	–	Class 2 contributions and Class 4 on earnings between LAL and UAL

Appendix 2 (continued)

EARNINGS-RELATED STATUS	RESIDENCE OR PRESENCE	AGE	LEVEL OF EARNINGS	MARITAL STATUS	RELATIONSHIP TO STATE PENSION SCHEME	LIABILITY
Employer or payer of employed earner	Neither resident nor present nor having a place of business in Great Britain	–	–	–	–	None
	Resident or present or having a place of business in GB	Employed earner under 16	–	–	–	None
		Employed earner over 16 (even if still at school) or over 65 (60) whether retired or not	Employed earner's earnings below LEL	–	–	None
			Employed earner's earnings at LEL or over	Employer not affected by any election in force	Employed earner contracted-out	Secondary Class 1 at NR to LEL then at COR to UEL
					Employed earner not contracted-out	Secondary Class 1 at SR to UEL
Others	–	–	–	–	–	None

Appendix 3: Categories of earner for social security purposes

EMPLOYED EARNERS	SELF-EMPLOYED EARNERS
1.Persons gainfully employed in Great Britain under a contract of service (see 2.07) 2.Persons gainfully employed in Great Britain in an office (see 2.08) with emoluments chargeable to tax under Schedule E. 3.Ministers of religion whose earnings consist mainly of stipend or salary (see 7.07). 4.Examiners, moderators and invigilators etc who do fulfil the conditions in 3 across. 5.Wife (or husband) employed by husband (or wife) in connection with his or her trade, profession etc. (see 7.05). 6.Cleaners etc other than those in private houses (see 7.03). 7.Persons supplied through agencies if personal services are rendered, there is a continuing financial relationship with the agency, and the work is subject control and supervision. Eg. secretarial temps. NB Entertainers, actors, musicians, models, and outworkers employed in their own homes are excluded. (See 7.04). 8.Lecturers, teachers, instructors etc engaged by an educational establishment to teach in the presence of students (unless Open University) on 4 days or more over a period of 3 months, with payment by the establishment and not directly by the students (see 7.06).	1.Persons gainfully employed in Great Britain <u>other than</u> under a contract of service or in an office with emoluments chargeable to tax under Schedule E (see 2.09) 2.Ministers of religion supported mainly by gifts, offerings and fees (see 7.07). 3.Examiners, moderators and invigilators etc engaged by persons responsible for exams in connection with exams leading to some certificate or qualification etc, if the work is performed in under twelve months (see 7.09). 4.Persons supplied through agencies who neither fulfil the conditions in 7 across nor become employed by the person to whom supplied. 5.Lecturers, teachers, instructors etc who do not fulfil the conditions in 8 across. **NON-EMPLOYED EARNERS** 1.Relatives (including spouse) employed in private households where both parties live, provided the employment is not in connection with a trade or profession (see 7.11). 2.Returning officers etc (or persons they employ) in parliamentary or government elections or referenda (see 7.13). 3.Persons exceptionally self-employed (see 7.12). 4.Members of defence organisations and persons employed by visiting forces (see 7.14 and 7.15).

EMPLOYED OR SELF-EMPLOYED?	
The "Control Test" (see 2.11) 1.Is the person controlled by the person engaging him? 2.Has the person engaging him the <u>right</u> to control him? 3.Does (or could) such control extend not only to the method and performance of duties but also to dismissal? The "Integration Test" (see 2.12) 4.Does the person engaged provide his own equipment? 5.Does he engage and supervise his own work-force? 6.Does he run any financial risk in connection with the engagement? 7.Does he take responsibility for the funding and management of the work? 8.Does he stand to profit from efficient performance or to lose by inefficient performance of the work?	If the answer to questions 1 or 2 and 3 is Yes and the answers to all or most of the remaining questions is No, the person will be regarded as an employed earner under a <u>contract of service</u> (even if never expressed), regardless of any cloak of self-employment that has been assumed. If the answer to questions 1, 2 and 3 is No and the answer to some or all of the remaining questions is Yes, the person will be regarded as a self-employed earner with a <u>contract for services</u>.

Appendix 4: Residence and presence in relation to contribution liability

EARNINGS-RELATED STATUS (See Chapter 2 and Appendix 3)		MOVEMENT	LOCATION OF EMPLOY-MENT	LOCATION OF EMPLOYER	LIABILITY RULES (See Chapter 3)
Earner	Employed Earner	None: R or O.Resident in GB	Great Britain	Great Britain or else-where	Primary Class 1 from date employment begins.
		Arriving from abroad	Great Britain	Great Britain	Primary Class 1 from date employment begins.
				EEC	Primary Class 1 from 1st anniversary of date the employment begins. (NB Period may be extended)
				Elsewhere	Primary Class 1 from date the employment begins except for students, apprentices or temporary employees who are granted a 52 week deferment.
		Leaving Great Britain	Abroad	Great Britain	If the employed earner is ordinarily resident in Great Britain and is resident immediately before employment abroad begins, primary Class 1 payable for first 52 weeks (excluding periods of unpaid leave) of employment abroad then Class 3 on a voluntary basis. If not so resident and O.R., no liability. NB Paid leave following first 52 weeks attracts primary Class 1 liability for period of leave and further 52 weeks of employment abroad.
				Elsewhere	No liability.
	Self-employed Earner	None: R or O.Resident	Great Britain	–	Class 2 and Class 4 from date self-employment begins.
		Arriving from abroad	Great Britain	–	Class 2 once the self-employed earner has been resident for 26 out of the 52 weeks preceding the date self-employment begins. Class 4 liability follows income tax.
		Leaving Great Britain	Abroad	–	Class 4 follows income tax. No Class 2 liability, but such contributions may be paid voluntarily if (i) person was employed or self-employed before departure and (ii) had been resident in GB for 3 continuous years at any time and (iii) contrib-utions approx = to 52 primary Class 1 on LEL had been paid for each of 3 years prior to departure.
Employer or payer of an Employed Earner		–	–	Resident or present or having a place of business in G.Britain	Secondary Class 1 for employees working in GB from the date their employment begins, unless 52 week deferment granted to them in which case deferment applies to the employer also.
				Elsewhere or other-wise	No liability and primary Class 1 contributions are collected from employed earners in GB by a direct collection procedure where the employer is unwill-ing to operate a deduction scheme.

NB Special rules apply to mariners, airmen, divers and share fishermen (see Chapter 7).

Appendix 5: Earnings for social security contribution purposes

EMPLOYED EARNER (see Chapters 2 and 4)	SELF-EMPLOYED EARNER (see Chapters 2 and 4)
Gross earnings per tax deduction sheet (<u>excluding</u> pensions, earnings paid after pensionable age (unless they should have been made before), any amounts set aside from gross earnings at an earlier date but included at that time for contribution purposes; and <u>including</u> salaries, wages, fees (except fees paid to a minister of religion and not forming part of his salary or stipend), commissions, bonuses, shares of profits (except discretionary payments by trustees under a profit-sharing scheme, or appropriations of shares or proceeds thereof under such a scheme), overtime pay, any part of earnings not actually paid but set aside for later payment – eg at holidays, Christmas etc (except for holiday pay stamps bought from an independent holiday pay scheme etc), holiday pay (except receipts from certain independent holiday pay funds), sick pay (reduced by the extent to which any social security benefits due are not claimed or retained)).	Case I or II Schedule D profit (however remotely it relates to actual profit – eg because of opening or closing year provisions, averaging, etc) + Balancing charges + Stock-relief clawback – Capital allowances (both those given by deduction in the assessment and any given by discharge or repayment of tax – eg agricultural buildings allowances) – Stock relief – Business-related interest and other annual payments to extent not already deducted in arriving at profits (gross of amount actually paid in the tax year) – Loss relief allowed under s.168 and FA78, s.30 (even if claimed against other income), s.171 (brought forward), s.174 (carry back of terminal loss). NB Losses of one spouse may <u>not</u> be set-off against profits of the other for these purposes.
+ Superannuation contributions (deducted from gross pay by employer before entering pay on tax deduction sheets).	
+ Overseas earnings exempt from tax under FA77, s.31 and Sch.7	
+ Payments made after termination of employment (but not ex gratia, compensation, or redundancy payments or payments in lieu of notice, or certain awards by Industrial Tribunals).	
+ Maternity and other pay received under employment protection legislation.	NB Profits for small income exception purposes are <u>not</u> those computed as above but those shown or expected to be shown in the Profit and Loss Account prepared under normal accounting conventions and apportioned as necessary to coincide with the contribution year in question.
+ Liquidated benefits in kind (but not actual payments in kind, or personal gifts, or benefits accruing under share option or share incentive schemes, or meal vouchers, or removal expenses).	
+ Gratuities allocated by the employer (but not other gratuities, tips etc unless the employer is the paymaster of the TRONC scheme under which these are distributed).	
+ Home-to-business travelling expenses paid by the employer (but not such expenses paid to disabled persons in sheltered workshops etc, or the reimbursement of specific business travelling expenses).	

Appendix 6: Calculation of returnable contributions

```
┌─────────────────────────────────────────────────────────────────────────────────┐
│                              Tax year 19  -                                       │
│                                                                                   │
│ Contributions Paid:                                                               │
│                                                                                   │
│ Class 1 primary:                                                                  │
│                                                                                   │
│   At special forces rate         £    .   x SR/SFR    £   .  (a)                  │
│   At reduced rate                 £    .   x SR/RR     £   .  (b)                  │
│   At non-contracted-out standard rate                  £   .  (c)                  │
│   At contracted-out:                                                              │
│      normal rate                                       £   .  (d)                  │
│      contracted-out rate         £    .  (e) x SR/COR  £   .  (f)                  │
│                                                                                   │
│ Class 2                                                £   .  (g)                  │
│                                                                                   │
│ Class 4                                                £   .  (h)                  │
│                                                        £   .  (i)                  │
│ Annual maximum (w, if any Class 1 paid; x, if no Class 1)  £   .  (j)             │
│                                                                                   │
│ Overpayment (i-j)                                      £   .  (k)                  │
│                                                                                   │
│ Repay:                                                                 Repayment  │
│                                                                                   │
│ Class 4 (lesser of h and k)                           £   .          £   .        │
│                                                       £   .  (l)                   │
│ Class 1 special forces rate (lesser of a and l)       £   .   x SFR/SR £   .       │
│                                                       £   .  (m)                   │
│ Class 1 reduced rate (lesser of b and m)              £   .   x RR/SR  £   .       │
│                                                       £   .  (n)                   │
│ Class 2 (lesser of g and n)                           £   .          £   .        │
│                                                       £   .  (o)                   │
│ Class 1 non-contracted-out (lesser of c and o)        £   .          £   .        │
│                                                       £   .  (p)                   │
│ Class 1 contracted-out at normal rate (if e greater than y, lesser                │
│   of p and (d-z); if e equal to or less than y, lesser of p and d)  £   .     £  .│
│                                                       £   .  (q)                   │
│ Class 1 contracted-out at contracted-out rate (lesser of q and f)  £   .  x COR/SR £  .│
│                                                                                   │
│ Contributions returnable (if in excess of £0.50)                     £   .        │
│                                                                                   │
│                                                                                   │
│ Memo: Annual maxima:                                                              │
│                                                                                   │
│ Class 1 and 2: 53 x (UEL x SR) = £   .  (w)                                       │
│                                                                                   │
│ Class 2 and 4: Class 4 rate x (UAL - LAL) + (53 x Class 2) = £   .  (x)           │
│                                                                                   │
│ Class 1 contracted-out at COR: COR x (53 x (UEL -LEL)) = £   .  (y)               │
│                                                                                   │
│ Class 1 contracted-out at NR: 53 x (LEL x NR) = £   .  (z)                        │
│                                                                                   │
└─────────────────────────────────────────────────────────────────────────────────┘
```

Note: Overpayments are recoverable within 6 years of the year in which the contributions were paid and may be reclaimed on form CF28F (Class 1) or CF28E (Class 2 or 4).

Appendix 7: Social security rates, limits and contribution maxima: 1975–76 to 1982–83

	1975-76	1976-77	1977-78	1978-79	1979-80	1980-81	1981-82	1982-83
CLASS 1								
Non-contracted-out:								
Primary: SR	5.50%	5.75%	5.75%	6.50%	6.50%	6.75%	7.75%	8.75%
Secondary: SR*	8.50%	8.75%	10.75%	12/13.50%	13.50%	13.70%	13.70%	13.70%
Contracted-out:								
Primary: to LEL	–	–	–	6.50%	6.50%	6.75%	7.75%	8.75%
Primary: LEL to UEL	–	–	–	4.00%	4.00%	4.25%	5.25%	6.25%
Secondary: to LEL*	–	–	–	12/13.50%	13.50%	13.70%	13.70%	13.70%
Secondary: LEL to UEL*	–	–	–	7.5/9.00%	9.00%	9.20%	9.20%	9.20%
Reduced rate:								
Primary	2.00%	2.00%	2.00%	2.00%	2.00%	2.00%	2.75%	3.20%
Secondary: as above								
Lower earnings limits:								
Weekly	£11.00	£13.00	£15.00	£17.50	£19.50	£23.00	£27.00	£29.50
Monthly	£47.67	£56.33	£65.00	£75.83	£84.50	£99.67	£117.00	£127.83
Yearly	£572.00	£676.00	£780.00	£909.96	£1014.00	£1196.00	£1404.00	£1533.96
Upper earnings limits:								
Weekly	£69.00	£95.00	£105.00	£120.00	£135.00	£165.00	£200.00	£220.00
Monthly	£299.00	£411.67	£455.00	£520.00	£585.00	£715.00	£866.67	£953.33
Yearly	£3588.00	£4940.00	£5460.00	£6240.00	£7020.00	£8580.00	£10400.40	£11439.96
CLASS 2								
Male	£2.41 pw	£2.41 pw	£2.66 pw	£1.90 pw	£2.10 pw	£2.50 pw	£3.40 pw	£3.75 pw
Female	£2.10 pw	£2.20 pw	£2.55 pw	£1.90 pw	£2.10 pw	£2.50 pw	£3.40 pw	£3.75 pw
Exception Limit	£675 pa	£775 pa	£875 pa	£950 pa	£1050 pa	£1250 pa	£1475 pa	£1600 pa
CLASS 3	£1.90 pw	£2.10 pw	£2.45 pw	£1.80 pw	£2.00 pw	£2.40 pw	£3.30 pw	£3.65 pw
CLASS 4								
Rate	8.00%	8.00%	8.00%	5.00%	5.00%	5.00%	5.75%	6.00%
Lower annual limit	£1600	£1600	£1750	£2000	£2250	£2650	£3150	£3450
Upper annual limit	£3600	£4900	£5500	£6250	£7000	£8300	£10000	£11000
ANNUAL MAXIMA								
Class 1 only:								
NCO: SR	£200.87	£289.38	£320.12	£413.40	£465.07	£590.42	£821.50	£1020.25
CO: NR and COR	–	–	–	£277.72	£312.17	£401.74	£592.01	£767.97
NCO or CO: RR	£73.14	£100.70	£111.30	£127.20	£143.10	£174.90	£291.50	£373.12
Class 2 only:								
Male	£127.73	£127.73	£140.98	£100.70	£111.30	£132.50	£180.20	£198.75
Female	£111.30	£116.60	£135.15	£100.70	£111.30	£132.50	£180.20	£198.75
Class 4 only:	£160.00	£264.00	£300.00	£212.50	£237.50	£282.50	£393.87	£453.00
Both Class 1 and Class 2:								
If Class 1 NCO: SR	£200.87	£289.38	£320.12	£413.40	£464.81	£590.42	£821.50	£1020.25
If Class 1 CO: NR and COR	–	–	–	£277.72	£312.17	£401.74	£592.01	£767.97
If Class 1 NCO or CO: RR:								
Male	£127.73	£127.73	£140.98	£127.20	£143.10	£174.90	£291.50	£373.12
Female	£111.30	£116.60	£135.15	£127.20	£143.10	£174.90	£291.50	£373.12
Both Class 2 and Class 4:								
Male	£287.73	£391.73	£440.98	£313.20	£348.80	£415.00	£574.07	£651.75
Female	£271.30	£380.60	£435.15	£313.20	£348.80	£415.00	£574.07	£651.75

* Includes NI Surcharge of 3.5% from 2 October 1978 (2% from 6 April 1977 to 1 October 1978).

Appendix 8: DHSS explanatory leaflets

NI1   Married Women: your national insurance position
NI11   National insurance contributions for domestic workers
NI22   Stamping and returning contribution cards by people paying Class 2 and
         Class 3 (voluntary) contributions
NI24   Mariner's guide to NI contributions and benefits
NI25   National insurance guide for masters and employers of mariners
NI27A   NI contributions in 1982/83: People with small earnings from self-
         employment
NI35   National insurance for company directors (April 1981 issue)
NI38   National insurance guidance for people abroad
NI39   National insurance and contract of service
NI40   National insurance contributions for employees
NI41   National insurance guide for the self-employed
NI42   National insurance voluntary contributions
NI45   National insurance contributions for non-NHS nurses and midwives (includ-
         ing agency nurses)
NI47   National insurance guidance for share fishermen
NI48   National insurance unpaid and late paid contributions
NI50   National insurance guide for war pensioners
NI51   Widows: guidance about NI contributions and benefits
NI95   NI guide for divorced women
NI125   Training for further employment? How to protect your right to NI benefits
NI132   National insurance guidance for employers of people working abroad
NI192   National insurance contributions for people employed through agencies
NI208   National insurance contribution rates from 6 April 1982
NI216   Completing your employees' deduction documents
NI217   How to obtain your employees' NI numbers
NI222   NI guide for examiners and part-time lecturers, teachers and instructors
NI224   Employment Protection Acts: NI contributions on maternity pay and certain
         payments regarded as earnings
NI228   Paying national insurance by direct debit instead of stamping a card
NI232   The hotel and catering industry: national insurance contributions on tips and
         service charges
NP12   Social Security: school leavers and students: what you pay and what you get
NP15   Employer's guide to national insurance contributions
NP16   NI contributions for people working in the UK for embassies, consulates, or
         overseas employers
NP18   1982/83 Class 4 NI contributions
NP21   National insurance contributions for ministers of religion
NP23   Social Security Pensions Act 1975. Guide for employers: occupational pension
         schemes
NP28   More than one job? Your 1982/83 Class 1 NI contributions
SA4   Social security agreement between UK and Jersey and Guernsey
SA5   Social security agreement between UK and Australia
SA6   Social security agreement between UK and Switzerland
SA8   Social security agreement between UK and New Zealand
SA9   Social security agreement between UK and Sweden
SA11   Social security agreement between UK and Malta
SA12   Social security agreement between UK and Cyprus

SA14	Social security agreement between UK and Israel
SA16	Social security agreement between UK and Norway
SA17	Social security agreement between UK and Yugoslavia
SA19	Social security agreement between UK and Finland
SA20	Social security agreement between UK and Canada
SA22	Social security agreement between UK and Turkey
SA23	Social security agreement between UK and Bermuda
SA25	Social security agreement between UK and Austria
SA27	Social security agreement between UK and Jamaica
SA31	Social security agreement between UK and Portugal
SA34	Social security agreement between UK and Spain

All of the leaflets may be obtained from DHSS Leaflets, PO Box 21, Stanmore, Middlesex, though most are easily obtainable from local DHSS offices.

Appendix 9: Direction-avoiding divisions of remuneration

TERMS OF EMPLOYMENT	1981–82			1982–83		
	TOTAL REMUNERATION (TR) BETWEEN:	DIVIDE TR AS TO:		TOTAL REMUNERATION (TR) BETWEEN:	DIVIDE TR AS TO:	
		SALARY: (MINIMUM)	BONUS: (MAXIMUM)		SALARY: (MINIMUM)	BONUS: (MAXIMUM)
Non-contracted-out with weekly wage and annual bonus	£0 and £1,403	TR	Nil	£0 and £1,533	TR	Nil
	£1,404 and £10,399	68.31%TR – £204	Balance TR	£1,534 and £11,439	68.31%TR – £224	Balance TR
	£10,400 and £13,800	£6,900	Balance TR	£11,440 and £15,182	£7,591	Balance TR
	£13,801 and £20,799	50%TR	50%TR	£15,183 and £22,879	50%TR	50%TR
	£20,800 and above	£10,400	Balance TR	£22,880 and above	£11,440	Balance TR
Non-contracted-out with monthly salary and annual bonus	£0 and £1,403	TR	Nil	£0 and £1,533	TR	Nil
	£1,404 and £10,399	73.09%TR – £945	Balance TR	£1,534 and £11,439	73.08%TR – £1,040	Balance TR
	£10,400 and £13,312	£6,656	Balance TR	£11,440 and £14,644	£7,322	Balance TR
	£13,313 and £20,799	50%TR	50%TR	£14,645 and £22,879	50%TR	50%TR
	£20,800 and above	£10,400	Balance TR	£22,880 and above	£11,440	Balance TR
Contracted-out with weekly wage and annual bonus	£0 and £1,403	TR	Nil	£0 and £1,533	TR	Nil
	£1,404 and £10,399	68.31%TR – £433	Balance TR	£1,534 and £11,439	68.31%TR – £458	Balance TR
	£10,400 and £13,342	£6,671	Balance TR	£11,440 and £14,714	£7,357	Balance TR
	£13,343 and £20,799	50%TR	50%TR	£14,715 and £22,879	50%TR	50%TR
	£20,800 and above	£10,400	Balance TR	£22,880 and above	£11,440	Balance TR
Contracted-out with monthly salary and annual bonus	£0 and £1,403	TR	Nil	£0 and £1,533	TR	Nil
	£1,404 and £10,399	73.09%TR – £1,190	Balance TR	£1,534 and £11,439	73.08%TR – £1,261	Balance TR
	£10.400 and £12,822	£6,411	Balance TR	£11,440 and £14,204	£7,102	Balance TR
	£12,823 and £20,799	50%TR	50%TR	£14,205 and £22,879	50%TR	50%TR
	£20,800 and above	£10,400	Balance TR	£22,880 and above	£11,440	Balance TR

Appendix 10: Continued liability to Class 1 contributions in reciprocal agreement countries

DHSS LEAFLET	SI	NO.	COUNTRY	STATUS OF EMPLOYER	STATUS OF EMPLOYEE	EXPECTED TERM OF DUTY	TERM OF CONTINUING UK LIABILITY
SA22	1961	584	Turkey	Principal place of business in UK	Not ordinarily resident in, nor a national of, Turkey	Temporary	Full term
SA14	1957	1879	Israel	UK resident or head office in UK	Not ordinarily resident in Israel		
SA12	1969	1494	Cyprus	Place of business in UK			First 3 years
SA27	1972	1587	Jamaica				
SA6	1969	384	Switzerland				
SA25	1972	1586	Austria	Principal place of business in UK	None specified	Not exceeding 2 years	Full term up to 2 years
	1977	51					
	1981	605					
SA11	1956	1897	Malta	UK resident or head office in UK or place of business in UK to which employee usually attached	Not ordinarily resident in Malta	Temporary	Full term up to 1 year
	1958	772					
SA19	1960	212	Finland	UK resident or head office in UK	Not ordinarily resident in the overseas country concerned	None specified	
SA16	1958	423	Norway				
SA9	1957	856	Sweden				
SA17	1958	1263	Yugoslavia				
SA23	1969	1686	Bermuda		None specified		
SA31	1979	921	Portugal	Place of business in UK	Not replacing another person whose tour of duty is at an end	Not exceeding 1 year	
SA34	1975	415	Spain				
	1976	1916					
SA4	1978	1527	Jersey and Guernsey	UK ordinary resident or place of business in UK	Ordinarily resident in UK		
SA5	1958	422	Australia				
	1962	1869					
	1964	495					
	1975	812					
SA20	1959	2216	Canada		Normal rules described at 3.09 apply		
	1962	173					
	1973	763					
	1977	1873					
SA8	1970	150	New Zealand				
-	1969	1493	USA				

NB In most cases special rules apply to mariners, airmen, members of the armed forces, persons in government service or persons in diplomatic or consular posts and their staff.

Index

Age
Class 4 contribution, exception from liability
  on grounds of, 5.34
  exemption, 3.19
  lower age limit, 3.17
  pensionable, meaning, 3.18
  upper age limit, 3.18
  working life, 3.16

Agency
  person employed through, categorisation,
  7.04

Aircraft
  British, meaning, 7.18

Airman
  compliance rules, modification of, 7.20
  exclusion from categorisation, 7.16 *et seq.*
  meaning, 7.17
  modification of categorisation rules, 7.18
  non-domiciled, non-liability of, 7.19
  place of business, 7.18

Appeal
  categorisation decision, against, 2.14

Armed Forces
  categorisation, 7.50
  compliance rules, modification of, 7.56
  contributions—
    paid late, 7.53
    rate of, 7.52
  defence organisation, member of, exclusion
    from categorisation, 7.15
  earnings, 7.54
  earnings periods, 7.55
  establishments and organisations included,
    7.49
  payment to serving member of, as gross pay,
    4.21
  residence and presence, 7.51
  social security scheme, modifications of, 7.48
  visiting, person employed in or by, exclusion
    from categorisation, 7.14

Benefits
  child, family allowance superceded by, 1.05

Benefits—*continued*
  contributory, payment by National
    Insurance Fund, 1.15
  earnings-related, desire for, 1.05
  entitlement, contribution conditions for,
    1.16 *et seq.*
  gross pay, as, 4.15
  industrial injuries. *See* INDUSTRIAL INJURIES
    BENEFIT
  kind, in, 4.07, 8.09, 8.26
  late paid and unpaid contributions, reck-
    onability for, 6.24
  non-contributory. *See* NON-CONTRIBUTORY
    BENEFITS
  partial, entitlement to, 1.17
  supplementary. *See* SUPPLEMENTARY BENEFITS

Beveridge Report
  blueprint of present welfare state, as, 1.04
  proposals, 1.04

Business
  place of, meaning, 3.09

Capital allowances
  self-employed earner's earnings, 4.29

Categorisation
  agency, person employed through, 7.04
  appeal against decision, 2.14
  armed forces, member of, 7.50
  determination of doubtful cases, 2.14
  dispute referred to court on point of law, 2.14
  domestic cleaner, 7.03
  earners, 2.02 *et seq.*
  educational establishment, person employed
    in, 7.06
  examiner, 7.09
  exclusion from category, 2.16
  exclusions by regulation, 7.10 *et seq.*
  generally, 2.01
  inquiry, 2.14
  instructor, 7.06
  invigilator, 7.09
  lecturer, 7.06
  mariner, 7.25 *et seq.*
  minister of religion, 7.07